THE SOUTHWEST UNDER STRESS

THE SOUTHWEST

UNDER STRESS

National Resource Development Issues in a Regional Setting

Allen V. Kneese and F. Lee Brown

With contributions by
Frederick R. Anderson
Jeffrey D. Baxter
Bruce A. Bishop
David Brookshire
Albert M. Church
Mark O. Evans
Jerrold E. Levy
Alfred L. Parker
William D. Schulze
Walter O. Spofford, Jr.
Michael Williams

PUBLISHED FOR RESOURCES FOR THE FUTURE, INC.
By The Johns Hopkins University Press, Baltimore and London

Published for Resources for the Future
By The Johns Hopkins University Press, Baltimore. Maryland 21218

Library of Congress Cataloging in Publication Data

Kneese, Allen V.
    The Southwest under stress.

    "A 'capstone' report on the Southwest Region under Stress Project . . . 1973
through 1978"—Pref.
    Bibliography: p.
    Includes index.
    1. Environmental policy—Southwest, New. 2. Water resources development—
Southwest, New. 3. Energy policy—Southwest, New. 4. Poor—Southwest, New.
I. Brown, F. Lee (Franklin Lee)
II. Resources for the Future. III. Southwest Region under Stress Project. IV. Title.
HC107.A165K58   333.7'0979   81-47618

ISBN-0-8018-2707-8
ISBN 0-8018-2708-6 (pbk.)

RESOURCES FOR THE FUTURE, INC.
1755 Massachusetts Avenue, N.W., Washington, D.C. 20036

Resources for the Future is a nonprofit organization for research and education in the development, conservation, and use of natural resources and the improvement of the quality of the environment. It was established in 1952 with the cooperation of the Ford Foundation. Grants for research are accepted from government and private sources only if they meet the conditions of a policy established by the Board of Directors of Resources for the Future. The policy states that RFF shall be solely responsible for the conduct of the research and free to make the research results available to the public. Part of the work of Resources for the Future is carried out by its resident staff; part is supported by grants to universities and other nonprofit organizations. Unless otherwise stated, interpretations and conclusions in RFF publications are those of the authors; the organization takes responsibility for the selection of significant subjects for study, the competence of the researchers, and their freedom of inquiry.

This book is a product of RFF's Quality of the Environment Division, Clifford S. Russell, director. Allen V. Kneese is a senior fellow at RFF, and F. Lee Brown is associate professor of economics at the University of New Mexico.

The book was edited by Sally A. Skillings and designed by Elsa Williams. The index was prepared by Lorraine and Mark Anderson, and the figures were drawn by Art Services.

CONTENTS

PART III: AIR QUALITY AND OTHER ENVIRONMENTAL ISSUES

PART IV: WHO BENEFITS FROM ECONOMIC DEVELOPMENT?

TABLES

APPENDIX TABLES

FIGURES

NOTE ON THE ILLUSTRATIONS

The illustrations on the endpapers and part title pages of this book were gathered by John Wesley Powell from magazines and scientific publications for the first edition of the popular account of his journey down the Colorado. That account was published by Flood & Vincent in 1895. The Dover edition from which we have reprinted the illustrations was first published in 1961.

Endpapers: Grand Canyon at the foot of the Toroweap, looking east
Part I: Lagoon on the Kaibab
Part II: The Colorado River
Part III: Bird's-eye view of the land of the standing rocks
Part IV: A Navajo boy

PREFACE

This volume is a capstone report on the Southwest Region Under Stress Project, which was a cooperative research project among a group of researchers in the southwestern United States with the participation of scholars from other regions of the country. It lasted from 1973 through 1978. The project concerned policy issues surrounding the conflicts between economic growth and environment, and with matters of resources supply, in an arid mountainous region that is ecologically, economically, and culturally delicate. The structure was informal with the participants working within a common general framework permitting them to relate their work to a larger set of integrated or complementary studies. The initial funding was provided by Resources for the Future. In the course of its six-year history, the project acquired twelve sponsors, with the National Science Foundation becoming the largest single supporting institution. The other sponsors included: the Environmental Protection Agency, the Electric Power Research Institute, the Fish and Wildlife Service of the U.S. Department of Agriculture, the Four Corners Commission, the Los Alamos National Laboratory, the Office of Water Research and Technology in the U.S. Department of the Interior, the state of California, the state of New Mexico, and the Weatherhead Foundation.

The project benefited greatly from its close association with the large multiuniversity, multidisciplinary Lake Powell Research Project sponsored by the National Science Foundation. This was an intensive look at the effects of development in the neighborhood of Lake Powell.

There was considerable overlap of scholars between the two projects, and in their later stages they were for all practical purposes conducted jointly.

For most purposes of the research in the Southwest Region Under Stress Project, the region was defined to be the "four corners" states of Arizona, Colorado, New Mexico, and Utah. For some purposes, however, it was useful to treat this definition flexibly.

The region under consideration presents a pattern of contrasts, conflicts, and opportunities. On the one hand, the amenity features of the region—clean air, expansive vistas, sunshine, mountain wilderness, cultural diversity—are nationally valuable resources and a great attraction for people and industry. On the other, urban development and current and potential exploitation of natural resources, especially energy resources, threaten to further degrade and perhaps destroy many of these amenities.

The studies upon which this book is grounded have examined the various aspects of the development–environment conflict in the Southwest especially as it pertains to possible large-scale development of the energy resources of the region. The intent has been to help inform and guide public policy. Much of the information presented and many of the policy alternatives set out are aimed at state and local governments. The book is also intended to be an examination of national problems in their regional aspects. The authors are convinced that there is far too little attention given to the details of the functioning of national policy on the ground, so to speak. They are also convinced that examining national policy in its regional setting can provide much needed guidance for national policy making and implementation. Poverty alleviation, improvement in the lot of the Indians, water policy, environmental policy, natural resources development policy—these are all areas of special concern to the region. But the federal government has asserted a dominant role in many of these areas. We hope this book will aid understanding of how that role might best be exercised in cooperation with other levels of government.

Aside from the introductory and concluding material, the book is divided into two broad sections. The first, from chapter 3 through chapter 8, is mostly concerned with the effects of development on the resources and environment of the region and with policy issues in these areas. The second, which extends through chapter 10, is primarily devoted to an examination of the distribution of benefits from development especially in regard to the incidence of poverty in the region. Poverty is heavily centered in, but not limited to, the resource-rich Navajo Indian Reservation, and special attention is given to this largest (and among the poorest) of American Indian tribes.

We discuss each of the issues addressed in this book in general terms to provide a broad perspective. But to lend concreteness, we illustrate the ramifications surrounding it with a specific study of an important case or cases.

Because this book is based on the findings of a rather large cooperative research enterprise involving many individuals and institutions, we are indebted to numerous persons. Those most directly involved are listed on the title page as contributors, for they provided actual draft material for some portions of the book. Our debt extends much further than this, however. A list of publications resulting from the project is appended to the volume, and each of the authors listed there contributed in various degrees by providing information, ideas, and opportunities for discussion and consultation.

Finally, we wish to thank Marcella Dekker for assembling the bibliography, and for an outstanding job typing the manuscript, and Sally Skillings for helping us by using her considerable editorial skills to improve the presentation.

Allen V. Kneese
F. Lee Brown

May 1981

I BACKGROUND

1

THE SOUTHWEST
National Problems in a Regional Setting

INTRODUCTION

The four contiguous states of Arizona, Utah, Colorado, and New Mexico form a region defined by the commonality of a wide range of problems rather than by the existence of any cohesive regional policy for resolving them. Many of these problems are a matter of national concern. They reach beyond the regional setting in both implications for the national interest and for national policy making.

In this chapter and in later parts of the book the focus will rest primarily, but not exclusively, upon three of these problems—those which loom largest in the current regional and national perspective. These topics may be expected to continue as matters of controversy and dispute in the region's future. They are: (1) the regional water supply—its quantity, quality, and allocation; (2) the regional environment—the extent to which it should be preserved in the face of development and the preferred means to accomplish that preservation; and (3) the future of the Indian and other poverty-stricken peoples of the Southwest both culturally and economically.

As will be seen, each of these problems is regional in occurrence, yet each is so strongly affected by federal policy that it is inescapably a national problem. In turn, the regional resolution of water and environmental questions will significantly affect the material well-being of much of the rest of the nation. This is particularly true with regard to the country's use of energy, because the Southwest is a principal remaining domestic repository of fossil and nuclear fuels. In the longer prospect, the region has major potential for the capture of solar and geothermal energy, should those energy forms become significant future replacements for conventional fossil and nuclear fuels, as many expect. Historically the Southwest has exported intangible services of considerable value to the rest of the nation through the scenic quality of its mountains, deserts, canyons, rivers, and other natural formations. If the potential for these services is lost or reduced through inadvertence or inadequate planning, the loss will not be easily measured, but it will nevertheless be real and important.

In addition, the current and future status of the Indian people remains as a significant weight upon the American conscience. Although improvement has come to other disadvantaged groups in American society, the plight of the Indian peoples of the Southwest has remained largely unresolved. The precise path by which resolution could occur may be unpredictable, but the discrepancy between the status of the Indians and that of the surrounding cultures is sufficiently large that the question cannot long go unanswered.

WATER

Water is a constant theme in the history of the Southwest. No one thread illustrates this theme better than the conflicting claims for water from the Colorado River and particularly its San Juan tributary. The Colorado, as the largest single supply of water for the semiarid region, has long been the source of controversy, litigation, and political negotiation. Its critical importance to the development of the energy resources of the region was documented in a Department of the Interior[1] report on water for energy in the Upper Colorado River Basin, as well as in 1975 hearings of the Subcommittee on Energy Research and Water Resources of the Senate Committee on Interior and Insular Affairs.[2] At the same time, it is also clear that water must be a key consideration in the establishment of any long-term, permanent base for the region's economy beyond the temporary reliance on extractive industries. The combination of these two circumstances gives rise to concern that the region's water resources are inadequate for the demand that may be placed upon them. This concern is compounded when note is taken of the many institutional rigidities that surround water use in the Southwest. These range from the two Colorado River compacts, which have supposedly "once and for all" apportioned the flow of the Colorado River among the various states, to the water right transfer mechanisms characteristic of the region. Such rigidities force even the smallest application for transfer of water from one use to another to meet a series of complex and often expensive conditions before being legally permitted if, indeed, it is permitted at all. Finally, the ownership of the water itself is an unresolved question with particular reference to the rights of the native Indian peoples of the region. The Winters Doctrine claims of

---

[1] U.S. Department of the Interior, Water for Energy Management Team, *Water for Energy in the Upper Colorado River Basin* (Washington, D.C., July 1974).

[2] The authors have read selected written material submitted to the subcommittee either as oral testimony or as written testimony.

the Indians and the "reserved rights" doctrine of the federal government clash strongly with the existing water use patterns and practices of the states of the Southwest. (See chapter 3.)

In short, the scarcity of water in the Southwest has led to the evolution of a complex set of legal and political institutions governing the use of that water. There remain many important unresolved questions about the adequacy of these institutions and the scope of their separate jurisdictions. When projected demands for Southwest water are set down amid this institutional complexity, the basis for conflict is laid.

ENVIRONMENT

Clashes between environmental and development interests in the Southwest are increasing in frequency and severity. As the regional population grows and as regional energy production increases, airborne residuals creep outward from the expanding population centers and the multiplying energy facilities. Previously undisturbed landscapes are the sites for new cities, second-home developments, or energy production facilities. The choice between large-scale development and environmental preservation is a difficult one for the nation, particularly in the face of the heavy dependence on foreign energy sources. Yet almost no comprehensive planning is being done to help the region cope with the problem of fitting new production sources and the accompanying populations into the existing array of established production facilities and still maintain a high quality environment. Short of a comprehensive, planned, preventive solution for this increasingly difficult problem, resolution will come in the form of costly retrofitting, progressive requirements of ever more technologically costly (or even impossible) controls on new entrants, the costly forced siting of new entrants at increasing distances from the coal and water resources, or a progressive relaxation of environmental regulations accompanied by a deteriorating environment.

INDIANS

The third problem mentioned earlier concerns the future of the Indian tribes of the region. The ambiguous status of these native people somewhere between independent nations and wards of the federal government is increasingly tested. If the *causus belli* of the conflict between Indian and Anglo cultures in the nineteenth century was land and the resolution was through military force, the principal modern issue in the Southwest is the ownership of water, and the resolution is occurring in the courts and Congress. But perhaps the stakes are even larger than those of earlier times and accordingly, the commitment of human resources on all three sides (Indian, federal, and state) of the question grows inexorably larger.

Though the level of economic wealth is far from being the sole determinant of the future ability of the Indian peoples to choose their own destiny, it is inescapably a prime consideration. The most immediate key to improvement in the economic lot of the Indians must lie in control of their own natural resources and their ability to benefit from them, and of these resources the most important in the long run is water because—unlike coal, uranium, and other mineral and fossil resources—water is a renewable resource. Moreover, its scarcity and importance in municipal and industrial uses give it prospect for greatly enhanced value as a corollary to the general economic development of the region. But, as we will see, water ownership is still ill defined and is a very contentious issue.

We have stressed the matter of Indian economic development, and indeed, the tribes suffer under the most grievous poverty problem in the region. But low income is not limited to these people. Other groups, especially the rural Hispanics and many rural Mormons, also are income poor. As we will see in the next chapter, poverty, especially among the Indians, is concentrated in the very areas where energy resources are most abundant.

PROJECTIONS   Many projections are being made about the extent of energy or energy resource production that may be expected from the Southwest. They include projections for oil from shale, oil from coal, gas from coal, electricity from coal, development of the coal resource itself, and development of the uranium resource itself. Our own sets of such projections will be discussed in the next chapter. The question of which path among the many is actually to be followed will, of course, be answered by a combination of national and international policies and events as constrained by the regional circumstances outlined above. At one extreme the regional factors may exercise considerable force in shaping the path to be followed through a combination of legal actions that restrict the options available and a greatly increased cost burden imposed on energy development. At the opposite extreme the federal consensus may be sufficiently formed (as might occur in the case of a second oil embargo) as to virtually dictate the level and pattern of production that will emerge from the Southwest and largely override the regional constraints.

Whichever path that is followed, intermediate or extreme, it is clear to most observers that there will be considerable effect on the three problems discussed above. Since water has reached or is approaching full appropriation in all areas of the Southwest in advance of even the more modest forecasts of energy-related development, the water institutions of the region will be increasingly tested with the addition of demands for water for energy development. Because hard fought and expensive battles over environmental questions are already common to the region, the prospect of expanded energy production can only increase the conflict. And because there is increasing recognition nationally as well as regionally of the plight of the Southwestern Indians, and of poverty in general, the prospect of expanded energy production will provide an important opportunity to address this chronic problem and provide the Indian people with increased control over their own future.

There are other regional problems which do not have as large an effect upon national events nor require as extensive national policy consideration as those we have so far emphasized. Even so they are of major importance to the people dwelling in the Southwest. Included among these are financial and other problems associated with the explosive local population developments that inevitably accompany large-scale construction and extractive activities in remote areas. In the beginning, the new population centers exhibit the "boom-town syndrome" of rapid expansion of public service needs without the accompanying financial base to support these needs. As construction is completed and eventually as the natural resource is depleted, the equally difficult problems of contraction must be faced. While manifesting itself in particular locations, the prospect of a contracting economy is also a long-term problem for the Southwest region as a whole.

From petroleum, coal, and natural gas to copper, molybdenum, and iron, the extractive industries have long been a principal basis of the region's economy. This heavy reliance on nonrenewable resources, and therefore nonsustainable industries, has proved to be a chronic difficulty for state governors and legislators who attempt to provide for the long-term economic welfare of the area. With the expected spurt in regional energy production will go an expanding regional economy, but the potential benefit from expansion is tempered by the anticipation of likely decline or collapse. The search for economic replacements for a declining economic base is the single most important long-term problem facing the various regional populations. The long-run future of the region will be determined by how effectively it can use its renewable and permanent resources. These include pleasant climate, beautiful landscapes, clean air, alpine landscapes and ecosystems, and cultural diversity. Finding a development path that is compatible with and makes effective use of these delicate resources is the long-term economic problem for the region.

These and other more narrow regional problems are interwoven with the three nationally significant problems previously outlined, and

OTHER PROBLEMS

factors affecting the former have implications for the latter. Such interrelationships and their implications will be explored in later chapters.

The following chapter presents a profile of the region and establishes the context within which future regional development and policy making will take place. In addition, some alternative future development paths are explored with the aid of an economic and demographic projection model. This model, developed by the Southwest Region Under Stress Project (referred to hereafter as the Southwest Project) permits the simulation of effects of development on key variables for planning and policy making. Much of the discussion of later chapters relates back to alternative paths projected with the model. At the present time this model is still evolving and being refined to serve a number of continuing uses in the region. But we do not expect the results reported in the next chapter to change drastically.

2   A PROFILE OF THE SOUTHWEST REGION

In sharp contrast to most regions of the country the Southwest is most appropriately viewed as a large, natural landscape dotted sporadically with nodes of human activity. The principal cause of this pattern of development is the region's arid character that has historically constrained the base of human activity to the narrow boundaries of mountain valleys and lands contiguous to rivers. With the necessity of maintaining a secure source of water, most historical ventures away from these sources within the region have occurred in connection with highly valuable enterprises such as minerals extraction or transportation centers. A second factor has been the conscious public decision to reserve much of the natural landscape of the Southwest in national and state parks, monuments, forests, and wilderness areas. The motive force has in some instances been commercial (forests for timber and grasslands for grazing), while in others it is directly attributable to scenic preservation intentions alone (national parks). Even more land lies in at least a semiprimitive state including much owned or under the jurisdiction of the Department of Defense, the Bureau of Land Management, the Bureau of Indian Affairs, and other federal agencies. The federal government owns approximately 44 percent of Arizona, 36 percent of Colorado, 33 percent of New Mexico, and an extraordinary 66 percent of Utah.

At present, then, much of the Southwest remains in a semi-primitive condition, only intermittently disturbed by urban and industrial-type human activity. This condition ranges from the forested slopes and craggy peaks of the 12,000- to 14,000-foot mountains that exist in each state to the flat, arid plains and plateaus that may lie abruptly adjacent to the mountains. The future status of these natural areas amid the spreading impact of both direct and indirect

GENERALITIES

effects of human activity is part of the environmental preservation problem introduced in chapter 1.

As for the centers of activity themselves, they range in size and complexity from the manufacturing and distributional metropolises of Denver and Phoenix to the most remote villages of Spanish heritage and the most traditional of Navajo hogans. Economically, many of the small-to-intermediate communities are principally single-industry (and sometimes single-company) towns organized around mining and minerals processing, energy production, recreation, governmental services, ranching, agriculture, or transportation, all of which are important in at least one area of the region. The major cities, as well as the states, expend considerable effort at strengthening the manufacturing that has traditionally been the path to economic improvement, but only Phoenix and Denver have realized notable success.

The four states exhibit different levels of personal income, as indicated in table 2-1, with the most significant distinction being the

Table 2-1.   Personal Income 1973 (Preliminary)

	Dollars per capita	Rank	Percentage of U.S.
United States	4,918		
Arizona	4,504	31	92
Colorado	5,046	14	103
New Mexico	3,764	47	77
Utah	4,005	40	81

Source: U.S. Department of Commerce, *Statistical Abstract of the United States 1974* (Washington, D.C., 1974).

break between the income levels of Arizona and Colorado, which approximate the national average, and those of Utah and New Mexico, which lie well below the national figure. Parts of Utah, New Mexico, and northeastern Arizona form a resource-rich, income-poor, subregion. We will refer to this area, for convenience and necessarily with some implied overstatement, as the Southwest Poverty Diagonal, and we will take a closer look at the economic and demographic characteristics of this subregion later in this volume.

Figure 2-1 reveals another significant feature of the Poverty Diagonal, that is, the concentration of national parks, national monuments, and national forests in the area. It is a major focus of regional and national recreation activities. Figure 2-2 shows the distribution of coal, oil shale, and uranium resources. While these resources are widely distributed in the Southwest region, an especially heavy concentration of coal and uranium resources is found in the Poverty Diagonal area. The broad elements of the environment–development

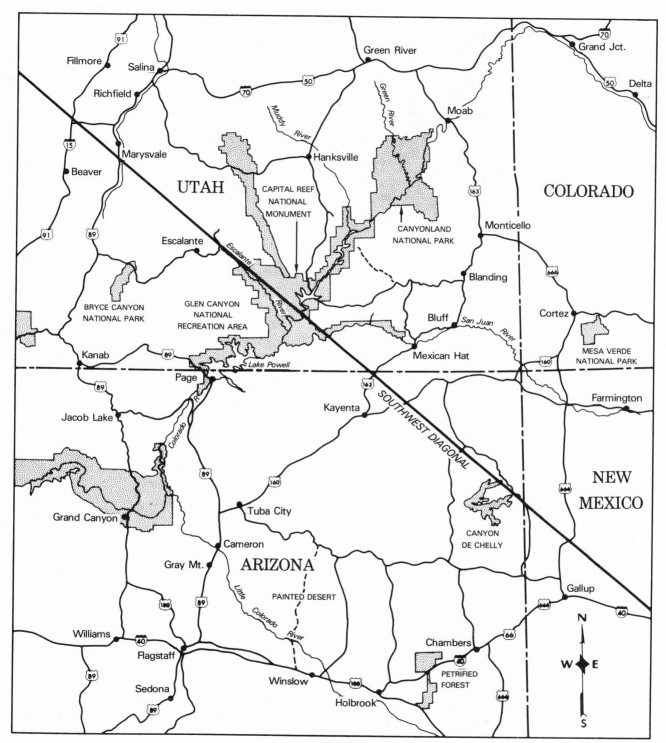

Figure 2-1. The Southwest Poverty Diagonal

9

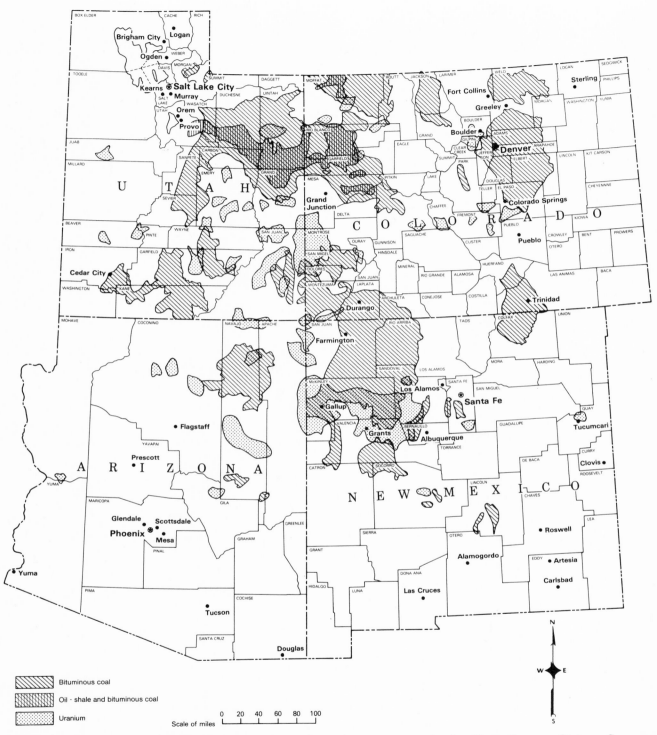

Figure 2-2. Known bituminous coal, oil shale, and uranium resources in the Four Corners States. *Sources:* Uranium resource areas from National Uranium Resource Evaluation, "Preliminary Report." Known occurrences of oil shale and of bituminous coal from Steven Bamre, Division of Economic and Business Research, University of Arizona, Tucson

10

conflict in the area are vividly illustrated by these two figures.

The federal government is a large factor in the Southwest region's economy, as it is in regional policy determination processes generally. There is no good quantitative measure of the federal importance to the region's economic health because most publicly available figures take no account of employment in privately operated but federally supported research laboratories and manufacturing tied to defense contracts, among other omissions.[1] Yet, the commonly voiced concern among many regional leaders about an overdependence upon the federal dollar is a good indicator of the size of the federal involvement. A feature of this heavy dependence on government expenditures is the lack of a substantial industrial infrastructure. This is a point of great importance for our analysis of the effect of energy investments on regional and subregional economies at various scales.

Despite the relative lack of industrial development, the population of the region has steadily increased at a rate well above the national rate itself (23.5 percent in the period from 1960 to 1970 as contrasted with a national figure of 13.3 percent for the same period). This growth has been unevenly distributed throughout the region and through different time periods. Table 2-2 gives the population totals for each of the four states and their average annual growth rates from 1960 to 1970. Even with the recent growth, the population density still remains well below that of the nation as a whole.

Table 2-2.   Regional Population, 1960 and 1970

Area	1960 (thousands)	1970 (thousands)	Average annual percentage change	1970 (persons per square mile)
U.S.	179,975	203,810	1.3	56.4
Arizona	1,321	1,792	3.1	15.7
Colorado	1,769	2,223	2.3	21.3
New Mexico	954	1,023	0.7	8.4
Utah	900	1,066	1.7	12.6

Source: U.S. Department of Commerce, Statistical Abstract, 1975 (Washington, D.C., 1975).

The regional population does not share equally in even the below-average personal income characteristic of most of the region. This becomes starkly apparent when the economic status of the Indian subpopulation is looked at separately as in table 2-3.

[1] One indicator, however, is the proportion of federal civilian employees to all nonfarm employees. For 1970, the national ratio was approximately 3.7 percent while for the states of the Southwest the figures were: Arizona 4.3; Colorado 5.0; New Mexico 7.5; and Utah 9.1. (U.S. Department of Commerce, Bureau of the Census, Statistical Abstract of the United States, 1975 [Washington, D.C., GPO, 1975].)

Table 2-3. Economic and Population Statistics for Selected Southwest
Indian Reservations

Reservation	State	1970 population (thousands)	1970 median family income (dollars)	Percentage of 1970 U.S. median family income
Fort Apache	Arizona	5,903	4,343	45
Gila River	Arizona	4,573	3,417	36
Hopi	Arizona	4,404	3,454	36
Navajo-Hopi	Arizona Utah }	7,726	2,052	21
Navajo	Arizona New Mexico }	56,929[a]	3,084	32
Papago	Arizona	4,879	2,500	26
Laguna	New Mexico	2,579	6,115	64
San Carlos	Arizona	4,525	4,006	42
Zuni	New Mexico	4,736	5,291	55
U.S. general population			9,590	

Source: Compiled by the Bureau of Business and Economic Research, University
of New Mexico, Albuquerque, from the 1970 census of population.

[a] This is a much disputed figure. The Bureau of Indian Affairs enumerates
126,000 Navajos.

This economic disparity between differing cultures extends to
the Spanish-surnamed people prevalent in Arizona and New Mexico,
and to many of the rural Mormons of southern Utah, so that on the
basis of economic conditions as well as traditional life-styles, societal
conflict in a large part of the Southwest is a three- or four-cornered
affair. Politically, however, the Spanish-speaking population have
found some expression in the two states where they constitute a
substantial part of the population. For example, both Arizona and
New Mexico have had governors of Hispanic origin. The Indian
populations have not achieved similar representation beyond the level
of the state legislatures owing in part to their small numbers within
the whole of each state's population.

Ideologically, a wide cross section of views can be found within
the region on most issues, although in conventional terminology,
voters in Utah and Arizona as a whole generally are found on the
more conservative end and Colorado voters on the more liberal end
of the spectrum. New Mexicans fall between these two voting groups
though most observers would place them as a voting population
closer to Arizona and Utah.

On the important conflict between economic improvement and
environmental preservation, Colorado and New Mexico have evi-
denced a stronger inclination toward environmental maintenance
than have Utah and Arizona, as reflected in their generally stronger
air quality standards. This is also apparent from recent state positions
on various development schemes such as the Kaiparowits power plant
in Utah and the Winter Olympics in Colorado. In both of these cases,

the proposed events did not take place. In Utah, however, both state and local interests strongly advocated the development, which was eventually shelved by its industry proponents citing governmental delay and increased costs arising from environmental considerations. In Colorado, the development proposal was defeated by popular referendum.

These conclusions are generally borne out by the results of an opinion survey, some of which are given in table 2-4. The citizens of New Mexico and Colorado gave higher spending priorities to pollution control and parks and recreation than did citizens of the other states. What stands out most clearly, however, is the much lower priority given to environmental issues by the still heavily development-oriented citizens of Utah than by those of other states.

Table 2-4. Opinions of Persons in the Southwest Region About Environmental and Resource Problems, 1975–76

(percentage)

Question	Weight	Arizona	New Mexico	Colorado	Utah
Spending priorities					
Pollution control:	Less	20	18	14	22
	Same	43	48	39	47
	More	37	34	47	31
	Total	100	100	100	100
		(824)	(1,043)	(1,053)	(637)
Parks and recreation:	Less	21	15	15	18
	Same	58	57	61	63
	More	21	28	24	19
	Total	100	100	100	100
		(835)	(1,013)	(1,065)	(642)
Seriousness of environmental problems					
Water pollution:	Very serious	21	19	26	13
	Serious	36	37	43	41
	Not sure	17	13	13	14
	Not very serious	22	26	16	29
	No problem	4	4	2	3
	Total	100	100	100	100
		(847)	(1,029)	(1,066)	(645)
Water shortages:	Very serious	27	25	25	14
	Serious	42	37	42	37
	Not sure	17	16	15	17
	Not very serious	12	16	16	26
	No problem	3	6	2	6
	Total	100	100	100	100
		(844)	(1,024)	(1,072)	(650)

Note: The numbers in parentheses are respondent counts. Numbers do not total 100 because of rounding.

Source: These are results from a survey conducted in 1975 and 1976 as part of the Southwest Region Under Stress Project under the direction of Helen Ingram. See Helen M. Ingram, Nancy K. Laney, and John R. McCain, *A Policy Approach to Political Representation: Lessons from the Four Corners States* (Baltimore, Johns Hopkins University Press for Resources for the Future, 1980) passim.

A CLOSER LOOK
AT THE POVERTY
DIAGONAL

To lend concreteness to our view of the resource-rich, income-poor Poverty Diagonal, we examined economic, demographic, and related data for fifteen counties in Arizona, Colorado, New Mexico, and Utah that we define as being in the Poverty Diagonal. (Supporting data for this section are in appendix 2-A.) This does not imply that they do not differ substantially among themselves in level of development and income. They consist of the following:

Arizona	*Colorado*	*New Mexico*	*Utah*
Apache	Dolores	McKinley	Garfield
Navajo	La Plata	San Juan	Kane
	Montezuma	Valencia	San Juan
	Montrose		Wayne
	San Juan		
	San Miguel		

The diagonal represents 15.6 percent of the land area in the four states, yet the population of the area is equal to only 5 percent of the total population of the states.

As already noted, however, the Four Corners States, and particularly the diagonal, are areas of rapid population growth. The population change in the United States from 1970 to 1976 was 5.32 percent, whereas in the diagonal the population increased by 26 percent and that of the Southwest region as a whole by 20 percent during this same time. Moreover, the population increase in the diagonal was heavily concentrated in those counties where energy development has already taken place or is in immediate prospect.

Given a very large concentration of federal and Indian land in the diagonal, it follows that the portion of the land under private ownership is well below national averages. Nationally, 59 percent of the land is privately owned, whereas only 37 percent of the Southwest region is so owned,[2] and within the fifteen counties in the diagonal, only 19 percent of the land is in private ownership.

One of the most striking characteristics of the diagonal is the low level of per capita personal income. According to 1975 data, Colorado was the only one of the four states to have a per capita personal income a little above the national figure. This is not the case in the Colorado counties in the diagonal where per capita personal income was $4,272 or only 73.23 percent of the national average. Income in the non-Colorado diagonal counties is considerably lower, and even this is extremely unequally distributed as can be seen from the fact that the median *family* income of the Navajo has been only about $3,000.

[2] It should be noted in passing that a high level of public ownership is typical of all of the states in the intermountain West.

Unemployment is also a serious problem in the diagonal. For 1977 the national average unemployment rate was 7.0 percent while the rate in the diagonal was 8.6 percent. This can be compared with the unemployment rate for the four states of 6.1 percent. Therefore the aggregated state average was significantly lower than that of the national average, while the average unemployment rate in the diagonal was much higher than the national average. Again, unemployment is unequally distributed. The concept is hard to apply to the Navajo and other Indians, but one can say that very few of them have access to gainful employment and that mostly they are on welfare.

In addition, the diagonal also displays a low level of educational attainment in comparison with the four states and the nation as a whole. As the appendix 2-A tables show, in 1970 the median educational level for the United States was 12.1 years, which was either met or exceeded by all four states. The state medians ranged from 12.2 years in New Mexico to 12.5 years in Utah. This high educational level is not reflected in the diagonal. For example, Arizona had a median educational level for those twenty-five years and older in 1970 of 12.3 years. Yet within the diagonal part of that state, the median ranged from 8.7 years in Apache County to 10.7 years in Navajo County. There are also reasons to believe that the quality of education in much of the diagonal is exceptionally poor.

Finally, and interrelated with the above characteristics, the diagonal has a substantially higher than average percentage of Indian and Spanish-surnamed population. Within the diagonal 36.6 percent of the population is Indian and 18.8 percent of the population has either Spanish surnames or heritage. This can be contrasted with the aggregated four states in which only 3.1 percent of the population is Indian and 9.2 percent has Spanish surnames or heritage. A further contrast is with national figures where 0.39 percent of the population is Indian and 4.56 percent of the population has Spanish surnames or heritage.

In contrasting the diagonal counties with the Four Corners States, it becomes obvious that the counties differ in many respects from the states as a whole. The population of the diagonal tends to be young, relatively poorly educated, and have low incomes. The diagonal tends to be sparsely populated, even by the standards of the Southwest region, with a substantial portion of the population being Indian or people with Spanish surnames or heritage. Much of the diagonal also contains landscapes of rare beauty as indicated by the presence of national parks and wilderness areas, and there are present a number of important archaeological sites. It is in the diagonal area that most future large energy resource developments are likely to take place.

In our analysis in the succeeding chapters of how these developments affect poor people in the region, we focus particularly upon the

Indians, for three reasons: (1) they are by far the poorest subgroup in the region; (2) they own a substantial share of the energy resources that may be developed in the region; and (3) they have a unique legal status both in the sense that they are wards of the federal government and that their status has some attributes of national sovereignty.

ENERGY RESOURCES AND DEVELOPMENT IN THE SOUTHWEST

Into this regional setting come the strong extraregional forces associated with energy development, since, as noted in the previous chapter, the Southwest is the repository of most of the nation's readily accessible uranium reserves and a significant portion of its coal reserves. Data on these reserves are shown in tables 2-5 and 2-6 respectively. Almost all of the uranium reserves are in the West with about 60 percent in the Southwest. For coal the distribution is not quite so skewed, since about 45 percent of the nation's underground *reserve base* and about 75 percent of the nation's strippable reserve base lies in the western part of the country. Much of this, however, lie in the Northern Great Plains region rather than the Southwest, with the latter containing approximately 10 percent of the total western reserve base. Two factors increase the importance of the Southwest coal beyond that which the relatively low 10 percent figure would seem to indicate.

First, the Southwest coal lies intermediate between the two large population centers of Southern California and Texas. It is proximate to both, and increasing amounts of coal or energy from coal are leaving the Southwest destined for these two areas.

Second, the reserve base concept represents a conservative estimate of the actual physical resource in place. Since many of the Southwest coal fields have yet to be carefully explored, delineated, and measured, much potential resource remains outside the reserve base concept but would be included under the broader term of identified resources. Much of the coal in the region is low sulfur, as is also indicated in table 2-6.

Whether it be electrical generation, coal gasification, oil from shale, or uranium mining and milling, the principal determinants of demand for extraction and conversion of these resources are external to the region. In this context, the principal policy questions associated with their use arise from the regional constraints—principally water and environment—upon the feasibility of fulfilling these extraregional demands and from the concern that regional populations, particularly the poverty-stricken Indians, share equitably in the economic return accruing from their development.

Table 2-5.   Uranium Ore Reserves by State, 1975
(at $10 per pound)

State	Ore (short tons)	Grade (% U_3O_8)	Short tons U_3O_8	Percentage
New Mexico	74,800,000	.22	168,000	53
Wyoming	62,200,000	.16	102,000	32
Colorado	2,900,000	.28	8,000	3
Utah	2,800,000	.21	6,000	2
Others	24,900,000	.12	31,000	10

Source: Taken from *1975 Uranium Statistics* which are compiled by Kerr-McGee Nuclear Corporation from a variety of sources including the January 1, 1975, Atomic Energy Commission publication, "Statistical Data of the Uranium Industry," table 4. The $10 case is representative even though much higher uranium prices have recently been quoted.

Table 2-6.   Reserve Base of Coal in the Southwest, by Method of Extraction and Sulfur Content
(million tons)

State	Method	1% sulfur or less	More than 1% sulfur	Unknown	Total	Percentage of western U.S. reserve base
Colorado	Deep	6,751	687	6,561	13,999	6.0
Colorado	Strip	724	146	0	870	.4
New Mexico	Deep	1,897	215	24	2,136	.9
New Mexico	Strip	1,681	577	0	2,258	1.0
Utah	Deep	1,916	1,405	460	3,781	1.6
Utah	Strip	52	192	13	262	.1
Arizona	Strip	173	177	0	350	.2
Total		13,194	3,399	7,063	23,656	10.2

Source: Compiled from U.S. Bureau of Mines data bank information.

The use of Southwest energy resources to produce energy to meet extraregional demands predates the oil embargo of 1973 and the greatly increased prices for energy that have prevailed subsequent to that event.[3] With the advent of the new era of high energy prices and a national objective of reducing foreign dependence, national planners and forecasters have quite naturally increased the attention paid to the coal, oil shale, and uranium reserves of the Southwest. The result has been a number of forecasts for Southwest energy development from national sources that have projected very large-scale energy-

REGIONAL SCENARIOS

[3] Both the Four Corners Power Plant, which uses coal from San Juan County, New Mexico, and the Mohave Power Plant, which uses coal and water from Black Mesa on the Navajo Reservation in Arizona, serve southern California's electricity demand and predate the events of 1973. Other energy facilities are in the planning or development stage.

related activity within the Southwest over the next twenty-five to fifty years. These "top-down" forecasts for the region may usefully be thought of as forecasts that seek to quantify national directions and policies and find feasible ways of achieving them. They have the principal advantages of a broad view of the national and international situation and an ability to make comparative judgments among producer regions about the relative advantages of each in responding to the changing energy circumstances.

The alternative, of course, is a "bottom up" forecast by regional institutions such as utilities and planning offices, which make their forecasts on the basis of evidence from within the region itself. The advantage of this approach is the greater familiarity with the idiosyncracies and specific conditions of the region that is generally possessed by the individual making these forecasts. Research done for the Southwest Project and the Lake Powell Research Project used a combination of these approaches to project quantitatively economic and population implications of energy development for the Southwest region and some subregions.[4]

As already mentioned, the level and pace of development that may occur is enormously uncertain. To provide meaningful analysis within this constraint, an alternative futures framework was used. First, owing to a lack of certainty about national and international events, alternative national scenarios were considered. Second, it was recognized that within the constraints imposed by federal policy, Southwestern mineral extraction and energy production would also be affected internally by political, administrative, and social action at the regional, state, county, and city levels. Since a region's response to a national trend cannot be known with certainty, the second component of each scenario related to alternative regional responses to each national course of events. A sketch of the form of the model used is found in appendix 2-B.

To take account of national tendencies, we used a study by Ronald Ridker and William Watson of Resources for the Future. They made long-run (to the year 2025) national projections based on alternative assumptions concerning population growth, labor force participation rates, productivity, unemployment, international developments, resource and environmental policy, agricultural export

---

[4] The research was performed by Jeffrey Baxter and Mark Evans of the University of New Mexico Economics Department. See: Jeffrey D. Baxter and Mark Evans, "Potential Impacts of Energy Development on Population Growth and the Economy of the Four Corners States," in Walter O. Spofford, Jr., Alfred D. Parker, and Allen V. Kneese, eds., *Energy Development in the Southwest: Problems of Water, Fish, and Wildlife in the Upper Colorado River Basin,* Volume I, Research Paper R-18 (Washington, D.C., Resources for the Future, 1980) pp. 201–300.

policy, style of living changes, and technology.[5] Table 2-7 summarizes the scenarios that were considered by Resources for the Future and gives an indication of the flexibility and potential of their quantitative framework. To account for alternative national and international events, the final demands for several of the RFF projections were used as national control totals for the regional projections.

The linkage between the regional economic submodel and an associated one which predicts population is twofold—the regional allocation of several final demand sectors is population dependent, and the demographic model has a provision accounting for economically induced migration. The diagram below summarizes the link between the two submodels.

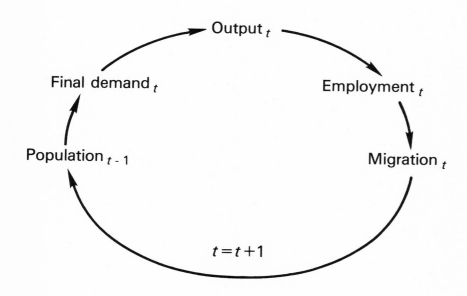

Six energy-related activities were altered in each scenario—coal mining, oil shale mining, uranium mining, shale processing, electricity generation, and coal gasification.

[5] Their model is an adaptation of the Clopper Almon INFORUM-EPA SEAS model. See: Ronald G. Ridker and William D. Watson, *To Choose A Future: Resource and Environmental Consequences of Alternative Growth Paths* (Baltimore, Johns Hopkins University Press for Resources for the Future, 1980).

Table 2-7.   National Scenarios

	Scenarios	Characteristics
I	EXTRAPOLATED CASE	This scenario represents what is believed to be most likely to occur given current trends; in other words, all dimensions extrapolated on the basis of best judgment. This case will be run for high and low population and economic growth.
II	MOST DIFFICULT CASE	In this case we attempt to maximize U.S. self-sufficiency; maximize environmental quality; maintain high population and economic growth, and current trends in technology; and maintain current styles of living.
III	INTERDEPENDENT WORLD	This scenario lifts the import restrictions of scenario II, while maintaining all its other dimensions.
IV–A	ACCELERATE RESOURCE SUPPLY TECHNOLOGIES	This scenario is the same as scenario II, except that technologies for finding, extracting, and developing resources are accelerated.
IV–B	ACCELERATE INTERMEDIATE EFFICIENCY	This scenario is identical to scenario II, except that technologies for improving the efficiency of conversion, utilization of resources, or both are accelerated.
IV–C	MINIMIZE FINAL DEMANDS ON RESOURCES	This scenario is identical to scenario II, except that we consider technological changes meant to more efficiently meet final demands. (This is meant to be distinct from exogenous changes in styles of living, which we will eventually put in as scenario VIII, but which is not considered here because it does not help us to classify technological changes.)
V	EASE ENVIRONMENTAL STANDARDS	This scenario allows compromises with environmental quality, while maximizing U.S. self-sufficiency, maintaining high economic growth, current trends in technology, and the like. It is therefore otherwise identical to scenario II.
VI	SLOWER ECONOMIC AND POPULATION GROWTH	This scenario is identical to scenario II except for slower economic and population growth.
VII	INTERDEPENDENT, HIGH-TECHNOLOGY CASE	This scenario accelerates all levels of technology while removing import restrictions. Maximum environmental quality and high economic growth are maintained. In other words, it is a combination of scenarios III and IV.

Source: The Renewable Resources Division, Resources for the Future, Inc., Washington, D.C.

SOUTHWEST PROJECT
SCENARIOS

Four scenarios were considered. Scenario A is a very conservative projection of future energy developments in the Four Corners States, while scenario D assumes levels of energy development consistent only with a national mobilization on the scale of the Manhattan

Project. Scenarios B and C assume levels of Southwestern energy development intermediate to these two extremes. Because the bases for the scenarios are rather involved, they are presented in appendix 2-C to this chapter. The descriptions presented there are in two parts. First, assumptions made at the national level in generating control totals for each scenario are described. Then the assumptions made in regionally allocating energy related activities are explained.

A flavor of the scenarios can be obtained by noting that under scenario A electric generating capacity in the Southwest increases at a relatively modest pace from a capacity of 15,400 megawatts in 1970 to 28,500 megawatts in 2000. This is the equivalent of five or six large new plants. Under scenario D, the increase is from 15,400 to 108,200, the equivalent of about forty large plants. Scenario A sees no coal gasification plants in the region by the year 2000 while scenario D has forty. As mentioned, scenario D is an extreme which is quite unrealistic except under brute force conditions accompanying a severe national crisis. Unfortunately such a situation cannot be entirely ruled out.

Intermediate cases see a successful effort to reduce dependence on foreign energy sources, among other means through subsidized development of domestic sources. Scenario B assumes a nuclear moratorium while scenario D does not.

ECONOMIC AND DEMOGRAPHIC EFFECTS

A large, multiregional model of the type used in this study has both advantages and disadvantages. The large quantity of numerical information generated by such a model can lead to doubts concerning the accuracy of individual numerical values considered in isolation. On the other hand, a primary advantage of the model rests in its ability to depict interindustry and interregional relationships. Consequently, in evaluating scenario results, most emphasis should be placed on relative—not absolute—magnitudes.

In assessing specific scenarios, the sensitivity of the model to several sets of assumptions should be kept in mind. First, assumptions concerning the differential between rates of change in output and productivity differ among industries. Since the future characteristics of a region (for example, population, size and composition of the labor force) are largely determined by the region's relative share of static (output growth rates are smaller than productivity growth rates) and dynamic industries (output growth is larger, so that labor demand grows), national assumptions concerning these relative growth rates strongly affect the forecast. Second, demographic assumptions (birthrates, mortality rates, labor force participation rates, and migration relationships) affect the relative size and growth of each region's population, which in turn influences the regional breakdown of several final demand categories. The present version of the model, while being keyed to general national growth trends, does not reflect the strong "sunbelt shift" of recent years and therefore the rates of population growth generated are probably too low. Consequently, comparison across scenarios has more meaning than comparison over time.

Listed in table 2-8 are state populations for the Four Corners States by scenario for selected years. An identical format is used in table 2-9 to summarize projected per capita incomes of the four Southwestern states. As an aid to examining relative numerical values, average annual growth rates between 1975 and 2000 are also presented. As expected, projected per capita income and population grow over time for all scenarios, reflecting general economic growth.

Projected estimates of population and income naturally become larger as one moves from lower to higher energy development scenarios. The tables strikingly depict the magnitude of these effects. For example, table 2-9 indicates that an energy future in the Southwest similar to that described in scenario D can result in gains by the year 2000 in state per capita income of from $1,000 (New Mexico) to $3,000 (Utah), as compared with the future described by scenario A. A similar comparison holds for projected population increases. Although these figures are substantial, it must be recalled that scenario D contemplates a huge development, which would almost certainly be disastrous for the region in other respects. The calculations indicate that despite the open nature of the region's economies, if heavy industry investment is enormously large and sustained, the effect on income and population growth rates can be substantial. This does not mean, however, that the existing population of the Poverty Diagonal will necessarily be affected positively in proportion. We return to a detailed analysis of this matter in part IV of this book.

Because unemployment rates were held within prescribed bounds, differences in population levels can be used as a proxy for economic activity. The relatively large populations shown in table 2-8 for scenarios C and D imply levels of economic activity that can be expected to place massive demands on Southwestern water, clean air, and scenic recreational sites. These effects are examined in some detail in subsequent chapters. In conjunction with these demands, the economic and demographic forces set in motion by large-scale energy expansion could lead to considerable stress on social institutions—a matter also examined later.

The effect of energy development on the composition of industry is also striking. In all states, mining, utilities, and construction sectors become relatively larger (both in terms of gross output and employment) as one moves from scenario A through scenario D. Agricultural sectors were the only ones that consistently tended to decline

Table 2-8.   Population of the Southwest, 1900–2000, by Scenario
(absolute numbers are persons)

Scenario	Year	Arizona	Colorado	New Mexico	Utah
A	1980	2,335,000	2,442,000	1,182,000	1,230,000
	2000	3,354,000	2,880,000	1,480,000	1,734,000
	Percentage increase	43.6	17.9	25.2	41.0
B	1980	2,334,000	2,452,000	1,193,000	1,252,000
	2000	3,560,000	3,089,000	1,635,000	2,114,000
	Percentage increase	53.5	26.0	37.0	68.8
C	1980	2,367,000	2,468,000	1,199,000	1,263,000
	2000	3,734,000	3,336,000	1,932,000	2,473,000
	Percentage increase	57.8	35.2	61.1	95.8
D	1980	2,367,000	2,473,000	1,198,000	1,265,000
	2000	3,838,000	4,202,000	2,006,000	3,415,000
	Percentage increase	62.1	69.9	67.4	70.0

Source: Jeffrey D. Baxter and Mark Evans, unpublished report for the Southwest Project (Albuquerque, N.M., 1977).

Table 2-9.   Per Capita Income in the Southwest, 1975–2000
(absolute numbers in 1971 dollars)

Scenario	Year	Arizona	Colorado	New Mexico	Utah
A	1980	5,000	5,400	4,200	4,300
	1990	4,300	6,400	4,700	4,900
	2000	7,000	8,200	5,900	6,500
	growth rate (percentage)	2.3	2.4	2.0	2.3
B	1980	5,300	5,800	4,400	4,700
	1990	6,100	7,100	5,300	5,500
	2000	8,000	9,500	6,600	7,700
	growth rate (percentage)	2.8	3.0	2.5	3.0
C	1980	5,300	5,800	4,400	4,700
	1990	6,100	7,200	5,400	5,700
	2000	8,300	9,900	7,100	8,400
	growth rate (percentage)	2.9	3.2	2.8	3.3
D	1980	5,300	5,800	4,400	4,700
	1990	6,200	8,100	5,400	7,000
	2000	8,600	10,600	7,100	9,900
	growth rate (percentage)	3.1	3.5	2.8	4.0
For reference	1975	4,000	4,500	3,600	3,700

Source: Jeffrey D. Baxter and Mark Evans, "Potential Impacts of Energy Development on Population, Growth and the Economy of the Four Corners States," chapter 4 in Walter O. Spofford, Jr., Alfred L. Parker, and Allen V. Kneese, eds., *The Impact of Energy Development on the Water , Fish and Wildlife in the Upper Colorado River Basin* (Washington, D.C., Resources for the Future, 1980).

in importance as sources of employment to the Southwestern economies, even though gross output generally increased.

Comparisons between scenario B and scenario D are of interest.
The former can perhaps be taken as illustrative of what might happen
in the region if there is some public policy pressure to develop energy
resources but not at the frantic pace contemplated in scenario D.
In that case, B would have perhaps a dozen large new generating
plants in the region whereas D would have forty or fifty. In contrast
to B's seven, D foresees forty gasification plants; and while B has
five oil shale plants, D has more than seventy. In view of the
enormous difference in levels of development, it is interesting to note
that the effect on per capita income growth is generally small except in
Utah.

As a final general comment, it should be emphasized that computed effects from energy scenarios will not appear as dramatic when
looking at state totals as they actually are. These effects will be felt by
localized areas much smaller than an entire state. We discuss these
more specifically in later chapters when we disaggregate some of the
projections and look at specific developments in particular counties.

In closing, we should note that the economic-demographic model
is being further developed and maintained at the Bureau of Business
and Economic Research at the University of New Mexico. It has seen
service in studies for the state of New Mexico, the Four Corners
Regional Commission, and the U.S. Department of Energy, among
others.

APPENDIXES TO CHAPTER 2

APPENDIX 2-A. GENERAL DATA ABOUT THE SOUTHWEST REGION AND THE POVERTY DIAGONAL

Table 2-A-1. General Data About the Southwest Region and the Poverty Diagonal, by State and County

State and county	1976 Population (provisional) (1)	1976 Population per square mile (2)	1976 Population per square mile of private and Indian land (3)	Population percent urban 1970 (4)	Population percent change 1960–70 (5)	Population percent change 1970–76 (6)
Arizona	2,270,000	20.0	45	76.6	36.0	27.9
Apache	43,800	3.9	5	—	6.1	35.6
Navajo	61,200	6.2	7	26.9	25.6	28.7
Colorado	2,583,000	24.9	40	78.5	25.8	16.9
Dolores	1,700	1.7	4	—	—25.3	5.5
La Plata	23,400	13.9	33	53.8	— 0.1	27.8
Montezuma	14,300	6.8	11	46.6	— 7.6	10.4
Montrose	21,300	9.52	34	35.4	.4	15.8
San Juan	900	2.3	26	—	— 2.1	4.5
San Miguel	2,500	1.9	4	—	—33.8	28.6
New Mexico	1,168,000	9.42	18	69.8	6.8	14.9
McKinley	56,000	9.6	13	42.9	16.1	29.5
San Juan	67,700	12.3	19	48.2	— 1.5	29.0
Valencia	48,400	8.6	12	33.5	3.7	19.3
Utah	1,228,000	15.0	57	80.4	18.9	15.9
Garfield	3,300	.6	16	—	—11.74	— 2.1
Kane	3,400	.9	15	—	— 9.2	27.3
San Juan	12,200	1.6	5	—	6.3	42.2
Wayne	1,700	.7	11	—	—14.2	16.4
U.S.	214,659,000	60.7	99	73.5	13.5	5.32

continued

Table 2-A-1. (continued)

State and county	Net migration percent 1960-70 (7)	Net migration percent 1970-76 (8)	Land ownership (9)				
			Percent federal	Percent Indian	Percent state	Percent private and other	Percent private other and Indian
Arizona	17.4	20.1	44	27	12	18	44
Apache	−41.6	15.3	9	64	10	18	81
Navajo	−11.5	13.9	10	66	5	19	85
Colorado	12.3	10.7	35	1	4	60	62
Dolores	−38.7	1.6	58	—	1	42	42
La Plata	−10.8	16.7	38	19	1	42	61
Montezuma	−20.6	3.6	37	32	1	30	62
Monrose	−10.4	12.1	68	—	4	28	28
San Juan	−28.2	−5.8	91	—	1	9	9
San Miguel	−44.6	22.4	54	—	2	44	44
New Mexico	−13.6	6.6	34	9	12	44	54
McKinley	−20.0	14.5	16	62	5	17	79
San Juan	−26.4	16.9	29	60	5	6	66
Valencia	−16.6	10.5	19	23	7	50	74
Utah	−1.2	3.3	67	4	7	22	26
Garfield	−22.2	−3.7	89	—	7	4	4
Kane	−8.2	26.8	86	—	8	6	6
San Juan	−28.9	11.3	62	24	6	8	33
Wayne	−24.1	10.7	84	—	9	6	6
U.S.	1.7	1.3	34	2	5	59	61

State and county	Per capita personal income 1975 (10)		Percent of population income below poverty level 1969 (11)	Unemployment rate 1977 (percent of labor force) (12)	Age composition 1970 (13)			
	1975	Percent of national average 1975			Percent under 5 years	Percent 18 years and over	Percent 65 years and over	Median age
Arizona	5,316	90.05	15.3	5.8	9.0	63.4	9.1	26.4
Apache	2,986	50.58	52.7	14.2	13.4	48.8	4.7	17.5
Navajo	3,612	61.20	39.2	11.2	13.1	51.6	5.7	18.9
Colorado	5,998	101.60	12.3	6.2	8.4	64.8	8.5	26.3
Dolores	4,641	78.62	9.6	8.3	8.6	63.0	10.0	26.6
La Plata	4,296	73.64	18.5	7.4	7.4	64.5	9.9	26.4
Montezuma	3,912	66.27	19.2	8.1	9.1	59.8	9.0	27.3
Montrose	4,521	77.49	19.3	7.2	8.2	61.2	10.1	28.9
San Juan	3,744	64.18	8.5	5.5	8.2	66.5	6.4	27.9
San Miguel	4,116	69.73	13.4	14.7	9.3	60.4	8.6	26.2
New Mexico	4,768	80.77	22.8	7.8	9.5	59.8	7.0	23.8
McKinley	3,675	62.26	40.1	6.7	12.9	51.0	4.4	18.5
San Juan	4,205	71.23	26.5	7.5	10.9	53.7	4.9	20.6
Valencia	3,846	65.15	20.9	7.5	11.0	55.1	5.6	21.7
Utah	4,938	83.65	11.4	5.3	10.6	59.8	7.3	23.0
Garfield	3,785	64.12	16.3	7.9	8.2	59.2	9.8	26.4
Kane	3,527	59.75	12.4	6.5	10.1	60.3	9.8	27.3
San Juan	2,805	47.52	38.3	8.1	13.9	50.1	4.5	18.0
Wayne	3,568	61.12	16.5	7.2	7.4	57.2	7.9	27.3
U.S.	5,834	—	13.7	7.0	8.4	65.6	9.9	28.3

Table 2-A-1.   (continued)

State and county	Education — 1970 persons 25 years and over (14)				Birth rate per 1,000 population 1968 (15)	Death rate per 1,000 population 1969 (16)
	Median	Percent less than 5 years	Percent 4 years high-school or more	Percent 4 years college or more		
Arizona	12.3	6.1	58.1	12.6	19.1	8.1
Apache	8.7	34.3	34.0	8.2	43.7	8.3
Navajo	10.7	17.7	41.5	6.9	29.2	7.0
Colorado	12.4	3.1	63.9	14.9	17.2	7.9
Dolores	10.8	1.1	39.6	2.2	31.5	10.1
La Plata	12.3	3.6	60.1	11.9	15.9	11.4
Montezuma	11.8	7.4	48.6	7.9	18.8	10.2
Montrose	12.1	3.8	53.5	8.8	16.5	9.3
San Juan	12.3	4.4	58.6	17.5	7.2	4.8
San Miguel	11.8	4.1	48.5	4.1	24.0	6.9
New Mexico	12.2	8.9	55.2	12.7	20.1	7.1
McKinley	10.1	26.2	39.7	8.2	32.3	7.5
San Juan	12.0	15.1	50.9	8.8	21.9	5.6
Valencia	11.3	10.4	44.8	6.9	21.3	6.7
Utah	12.5	2.0	67.3	14.0	22.4	6.5
Garfield	12.2	.3	59.0	8.7	14.9	9.1
Kane	12.5	1.5	66.9	13.4	19.6	10.3
San Juan	10.7	27.0	44.0	8.8	30.6	5.6
Wayne	12.1	1.2	54.3	8.9	15.9	7.3
U.S.	12.1	5.5	52.3	10.7	17.5	9.5

State and county	Population distribution by race 1970 (17)[a]				Spanish surname or heritage percent 1970 (18)[a]
	Percent White	Percent Negro	Percent Indian	Percent other	
Arizona	90.6	3.00	5.40	.95	18.78
Apache	23.94	1.29	74.29	.48	10.46
Navajo	49.09	1.92	48.25	.74	11.26
Colorado	95.70	3.00	.40	.90	2.23
Dolores	89.80	—	9.40	.80	—
La Plata	94.57	.14	4.77	.53	19.36
Montezuma	91.30	.11	8.14	.43	11.29
Montrose	97.75	.08	1.57	.60	12.00
San Juan	99.52	—	—	.48	—
San Miguel	93.18	.05	6.77		—
New Mexico	90.10	1.90	7.20	.80	13.07
McKinley	37.00	.90	61.30	.70	19.96
San Juan	63.90	.60	35.10	.40	13.14
Valencia	83.90	.50	15.00	.60	55.51
Utah	97.40	.60	1.10	.89	4.11
Garfield	99.21	—	.79	—	—
Kane	98.97	—	.95	.08	—
San Juan	50.24	.17	49.34	.25	—
Wayne	99.80	.07	.07	.07	—
U.S.	87.50	11.10	.39	1.03	4.56

continued

Notes to table 2-A-1

Note: Dashes = not applicable.

Sources:

(1) *Population*

    a. States and counties: U.S. Department of Commerce, Bureau of the Census, *Current Population Estimates,* Series p-26, no. 76-31, July 1977.

    b. United States: U.S. Department of Commerce, *Statistical Abstract of the United States 1977* (Washington, D.C.) table 10, p. 11.

(2) *Land area*

    a. States and counties: U.S. Department of Commerce, Bureau of the Census, *1970 Census of the Population: Characteristics of the Population, U.S. Summary* (Washington, D.C., 1971) table 9.

    b. United States: *Statistical Abstract of the United States 1977,* table 4, p. 8.

(3) *Land ownership*

    a. Arizona Valley National Bank of Arizona, *Arizona Statistical Review 1975* (Phoenix, Ariz., 1975) p. 40.

    b. Colorado:

        1. Interstate Gas Co. Division of Colorado Interstate Corp., *Colorado 1973 Yearbook* (Colorado Springs, Colo. 1974).

        2. Indian Land: U.S. Department of the Interior, Bureau of Indian Affairs, *Annual Report of Indian Land 1795–76* (Washington, D.C., GPO, 1977).

    c. New Mexico: Bureau of Business and Economic Research, *New Mexico Statistical Abstracts 1977* (Albuquerque, N.M., University of New Mexico, 1978) p. 70.

    d. Utah:

        1. Bureau of Economic and Business Research, *Statistical Abstract of Utah 1976, Bicentennial Ed.* (Salt Lake City, University of Utah, 1977) p. VII-27.

        2. Indian Land: Bureau of Indian Affairs, *Annual Report of Indian Land 1975–76.*

(4) Same as (2).

(5) Same as (2).

(6) Same as (1).

(7) U.S. Department of Commerce, Bureau of the Census, *County and City Data Book, 1972 (A Statistical Supplement)* (Washington, D.C., GPO, 1973).

    a. States and counties—table 2, item 6.

    b. United States—table 1, item 6.

(8) Same as (1).

(9) Same as (5).

Note: Percentages may not add up to 100 because of rounding.

(10) "County and Metropolitan Area Personal Income," *Survey of Current Business* (April 1977).

(11) U.S. Department of Commerce, U.S. Bureau of the Census, *1970 Census of the Population: Characteristics of the Population,* respective state summaries.

    a. Counties: table 124.

    b. States: table 58.

    c. United States: U.S. summary table 95.

(12) *Arizona:* Arizona Department of Economic Security (Phoenix, Ariz.).

    Colorado: Colorado Department of Employment and Training, table "Official Labor Force Estimates for Federal Programs" (Denver, Colo.).

    New Mexico: Employment Security Commission of New Mexico, table A (Albuquerque, N.M.).

    Utah: Utah Department of Employment Security, table "Utah Civilian Labor Force by Planning District and County 1976 and 77" (Salt Lake City, Utah).

    United States: U.S. Department of Commerce, "Selected Unemployment Rates," *Economic Indicators* (January 1978) p. 12.

(13) U.S. Department of Commerce, Bureau of the Census, *City and County Data Book* (Washington, D.C., GPO, 1977).

    a. Counties and states: table 2, items 12–15.

    b. United States: table 1, items 12–15.

(14) Ibid.
    a. Counties and states: table 2, items 24–27.
    b. United States: table 1, items 24–27.
(15) Ibid.
    a. Counties and states: table 2, item 21.
    b. United States: table 1, item 21.
(16) Ibid.
    a. Counties and states: table 2, item 22.
    b. United States: table 1, item 22.
(17) U.S. Department of Commerce, Bureau of the Census, *1970 Census of the Population: Characteristics of the Population*
    a. Counties and states: respective state summaries.
        1. Counties: table 34.
        2. States: table 17.
    b. United States: U.S. summary table 48.
(18) U.S. Department of Commerce, Bureau of the Census, *1970 Census of the Population: Characteristics of the Population*
    a. Counties and states: respective state summaries.
        1. Counties: table 130.
        2. States: table 48.
    b. United States: U.S. summary table 86.
[a] Signifies fewer than 400 persons in county with that background.

Table 2-A-2.   General Data About the Southwest Region and the Poverty Diagonal, by Subregion

State	1976 population (1)	1976 population of region as a percentage of the state (2)	Land area (square miles) (3)	Land area 4 Corners Region as a percentage of the state (4)	1976 population per square mile (5)
Arizona	2,270,000	—	113,417	—	20.00
Poverty Diagonal	105,000	4.6	21,081	18.59	4.98
Colorado	2,583,000	—	103,766	—	24.90
Poverty Diagonal	64,100	2.5	8,715	8.40	7.36
New Mexico	1,168,000	—	121,412	—	9.42
Poverty Diagonal	172,100	14.7	16,610	13.70	10.36
Utah	1,228,000	—	82,096	—	15.00
Poverty Diagonal	20,600	1.7	19,255	23.40	1.07
4 Corners States	7,249,000	—	420,691	—	17.23
Poverty Diagonal	361,800	5	65,611	15.60	5.51
U.S.	214,659,000		3,536,855		60.70

continued

Table 2-A-2. (continued)

State	1976 population per square mile of private and Indian land (6)	Population percent change 1960–70 (7)	Population percent change 1970–76 (8)	Net migration (percent) 1970–76 (9)	Age composition 1970 (10) Percent under 5 years	Age composition 1970 (10) Percent 18 years and over	Age composition 1970 (10) Percent 65 years and over
Arizona	45	36	27.9	20.1	9.0	63.4	9.1
Poverty Diagonal	6	17	31.0	14.4	13.3	50.8	5.2
Colorado	40	25.8	16.9	10.7	8.4	64.8	8.5
Poverty Diagonal	17	−4	17.0	4.55	8.2	62.4	9.6
New Mexico	18	6.8	14.9	6.6	19.5	59.8	6.9
Poverty Diagonal	14	5	26.0	14.3	11.6	53.6	4.9
Utah	57	18.9	15.9	3.3	10.6	59.8	7.3
Poverty Dianonal	7	−2	24.0	10.8	11.6	53.8	7.0
4 Corners States	36	24	20.0	11.47	9.1	62.9	8.2
Poverty Diagonal	10	6	26.0	12.27	11.4	54.5	6.0
U.S.	99	13.5	5.32	1.3	5.5	65.6	9.9

State	Land ownership (11) Percent federal	Land ownership (11) Percent Indian	Land ownership (11) Percent state	Land ownership (11) Percent private and other	Land ownership (11) Percent private, other, and Indian	1977 unemploy- ment rate (percent of labor force) (12)	Per capita personal income 1975 (13) 1975	Per capita personal income 1975 (13) Percent of national average 1975
Arizona	43	27	12	18	44	5.8	5,316	90.05
Poverty Diagonal	9	65	8	18	83	12.3	3,290	56.39
Colorado	35	1	4	60	62	6.2	5,998	101.60
Poverty Diagonal	54	11	2	34	44	7.8	4,272	73.23
New Mexico	34	9	12	44	54	7.8	4,768	80.77
Poverty Diagonal	22	48	6	25	73	7.3	3,958	67.84
Utah	67	4	7	22	26	5.3	4,938	83.65
Poverty Diagonal	77	10	7	6	16	7.7	3,137	53.77
4 Corners States	43	11	9	37	48	6.1	5,414	92.80
Poverty Diagonal	38	37	6	19	55	8.6	3,772	64.65
U.S.	34	2	5	59	61	7.0	5,834	

continued

Table 2-A-2. (continued)

State	Population distribution by race 1970 (14)				Spanish surname or heritage percent in 1970 (15)
	Percent White	Percent Negro	Percent Indian	Percent other	
Arizona	90.6	3.0	5.4	0.9	18.8
Poverty Diagonal	38.9	1.7	58.8	0.6	10.9
Colorado	95.7	3.0	.4	0.9	2.2
Poverty Diagonal	94.7	.1	4.6	0.5	13.4
New Mexico	90.1	1.9	7.2	0.8	13.1
Poverty Diagonal	61.3	.7	37.4	0.9	28.1
Utah	97.4	.6	1.1	0.9	4.1
Poverty Diagonal	71.0	.1	28.7	0.2	—
4 Corners States	93.6	2.41	3.1	0.9	9.2
Poverty Diagonal	62.0	.8	36.6	0.6	18.8
U.S.	87.5	11.1	.39	1.03	4.56

Note: Dashes = not applicable.

Sources:

(1) *Population*

    a. States and counties: U.S. Department of Commerce, Bureau of the Census, "Current Population Estimates," Series p-26, no. 76-31, July 1977.

    b. United States: U.S. Department of Commerce, *Statistical Abstract of the United States 1977* (Washington, D.C., 1977) table 10, p. 11.

(2) Ibid.

(3) *Land Area*

    a. States and counties: U.S. Department of Commerce, Bureau of the Census, *1970 Census of the Population: Characteristics of the Population, U.S. Summary* (Washington, D.C., GPO, 1971) table 9.

    b. United States: *Statistical Abstract of the United States, 1977* table 4, p. 8.

(4) Ibid.

(5) Ibid.

(6) *Land ownership*

    a. Arizona Valley National Bank of Arizona, *Arizona Statistical Review 1975* (Phoenix, Ariz., 1975) p. 40.

    b. Colorado:

        1. Interstate Gas Co. Division of Colorado Interstate Corp., *Colorado 1973 Yearbook* (Colorado Springs, 1974).

        2. Indian Land: U.S. Department of the Interior, Bureau of Indian Affairs, *Annual Report of Indian Land 1975–76* (Washington, D.C., GPO, 1977).

    c. New Mexico: Bureau of Business and Economic Research, *New Mexico Statistical Abstracts, 1977* (Albuquerque, N.M., University of New Mexico, 1978) p. 70.

    d. Utah:

        1. Bureau of Economic and Business Research, *Statistical Abstract of Utah 1976, Bicentennial Ed.* (Salt Lake City, Utah, University of Utah) p. VII-27.

        2. Indian Land: U.S. Department of the Interior, Bureau of Indian Affairs, *Annual Report of Indian Land 1975–76.*

(7) Same as (3).

(8) Same as (1).

(9) Same as (1).

continued

(10) U.S. Department of Commerce, Bureau of the Census, *1970 Census of the Population: Characteristics of the Population*
   a. Counties and states:
      1. Counties: table 35.
      2. States: table 20.
   b. United States: U.S. Department of Commerce, Bureau of the Census, *City and County Data Book* (Washington, D.C., 1972) table I, items 12–15.

(11) Same as (6).

(12) *Arizona:* Arizona Department of Economic Security (Phoenix, Ariz.).

   Colorado: Colorado Department of Employment and Training, table "Official Labor Force Estimates for Federal Programs" (Denver, Colo.).

   New Mexico: Employment Security Commission of New Mexico, table A (Albuquerque, N.M.).

   Utah: Utah Department of Employment Security, table "Utah Civilian Labor Force by Planning District and County 1976 and 77" (Salt Lake City, Utah).

(13) "County and Metropolitan Area Personal Income," *Survey of Current Business* (April 1977), and U.S. Department of Commerce, Bureau of the Census, "Current Population Estimates."

(14) U.S. Department of Commerce, Bureau of the Census, *1970 Census of the Population: Characteristics of the Population*
   a. Counties and states: respective state summaries.
      1. Counties: table 34.
      2. States: table 17.
   b. United States: U.S. summary, table 48.

(15) U.S. Department of Commerce, Bureau of the Census, *1970 Census of the Population: Characteristics of the Population*
   a. Counties and states: respective state summaries.
      1. Counties: table 130.
      2. States: table 48.
   b. United States: U.S. summary, table 86.

APPENDIX 2-B
SKETCH OF THE INTERREGIONAL INPUT–OUTPUT MODEL

The two prime considerations in selecting a projections methodology were:

1. The parameters and exogenous variables of the model should have the capability of being altered to reflect the implications of alternative regional responses to national policy decisions.

2. The model should have the capability of accounting for indirect economic and demographic consequences of the structural changes being considered.

   It was decided that a particular type of input–output model (called a Chenery-Moses interregional model) linked to a Cohort Survival demographic model would be most appropriate. The input–output simulation model consists of twelve regions (seven multicounty planning districts in New Mexico, Arizona, Colorado, Utah, and a "rest of the United States" as a residual) and forty economic sectors. The Chenery-Moses model contains two sets of parameters: direct requirements technical coefficients and trade coefficients. A technical coefficient, a_{ij}^{r} ($r = 1, \ldots, 12$; $i, j = 1, \ldots, 40$), represents the necessary expenditures on products from sector i per dollar of production in sector j, using region r's technology.

A trade coefficient, c_i^{rs} $(r, s = 1, \ldots 12; i = 1, \ldots, 40)$, denotes the share of regions' demand for products of sector i satisfied by importing from region r. The exogenous variable, y_i^r $(i = 1, \ldots, 40; r = 1, \ldots, 12)$, represents region r's final demand for products of industry i. These parameters and exogenous variables are used to project a vector x_i^r $(i = 1, \ldots, 40; r = 1, \ldots, 12)$, of gross outputs by sector and region. These projections of gross output account both for indirect effects in the traditional input–output sense and for import and export patterns among the model's regions. The complete model is found in Mark Evans' *Evaluating the Implications of Structural Change* (Ph.D. dissertation, University of New Mexico, 1977).

APPENDIX 2-C
THE SCENARIOS

Construction

Scenario A used national control totals from the "extrapolated case" mentioned in table 2-7 in the text. Bureau of the Census series E population projections were used to make this national projection. Use of this series assumed that the recent downturn in fertility rates is a temporary phenomenon, since the series E total fertility rate of 2.1 births per woman is above the current rate. It was also assumed that increases in female labor force participation rates and in the proportion of the population in working age groups (sixteen to sixty-four years) would offset the downward trends in retirement age, working hours, and male participation rates. The economy returned to a 4 percent unemployment rate by 1980, after which unemployment remained at this level. The rate of increase in productivity returned to its former, pre-recession level, but productivity itself shifted downward from its previous secular path in this national projection. International developments were taken into consideration by considering the relative prices of both oil and nonfuel minerals. It was assumed that solidarity within the Organization of Petroleum Exporting Countries (OPEC) would enable the maintenance of 1975 petroleum prices ($12 per barrel) in real terms for the next decade, at which time real prices would remain at this level because of demand pressure. In the case of nonfuel minerals, world reserves were considered to be sufficiently dispersed geographically to avoid increases in real price caused by market cartelization. Resource policy considerations also centered around petroleum and nonfuel minerals. Petroleum and natural gas prices rose to the world level by 1985. No substantial effort was made to increase domestic supplies or to dampen growth in demand. Hence, oil imports continued to fill the growing gap between domestic supply and demand. This same import assumption was followed in considering nonfuel mineral policies. The national "extrapolated case" allowed delays in implementing environmental standards for both automobiles and water pollution. Finally, it was conjectured that the U.S. government would not permit agricultural exports to seriously affect domestic price.

Scenarios C and D used national control totals from the "most difficult case." As mentioned in table 2-7 in the text, this set of projections placed maximum pressure on the U.S. resource base and at the same time minimized environmental side effects. Hence, a higher Bureau of the Census projection series (series D), which represents a 2.5-births-per-woman total fertility rate, was used. Higher productivity rates were also assumed, as output per worker was extrapolated from the secular trend. Resource policy in the "most difficult case" assumed that a serious attempt would be made to reduce U.S. dependence upon foreign supplies. Under this set of assumptions, the federal government intervened to stockpile petroleum and to ensure the development of domestic substitutes with subsidy programs. Increased stockpiling was also a significant ingredient of nonfuel minerals policy. Environmental regulations were stringently enforced in the "most difficult case." Not only were current cleanup timetables met, but further, more demanding requirements were assumed to be met by the year 2000. It was also assumed that foreign countries might experience setbacks in planned agricultural production, and that U.S. exports would be significant enough to exert upward price pressure on domestic consumers. Finally, the "most difficult case" was identical to the "extrapolated case" with regard to assumptions concerning labor force participation rates, unemployment rates, and international developments.

Scenario B used "nuclear moratorium" (not shown in table 2-7) national control totals. This scenario was similar in all ways to the "most difficult case," except that no new nuclear power plants (except those already planned) were allowed to come on line. Also, older plants were not replaced as they depreciated.

The above discussion focused upon the national considerations made in constructing a set of alternative futures for the Southwest. However, alternative regional responses to a national course of events are sometimes possible. A description of each scenario's regional assumptions concerning energy-related activities will now be presented.

Electrical generating capacity assumptions for scenario D were made by utilizing Southwest Power Pool of the Western Systems Coordinating Council (WSCC) forecasts incorporated in a reply (dated April 1976) to Federal Power Commission Docket RO362. This forecast contained a chronological ordering of site-specific projections of new generating capacity from 1976 to 1985. Also contained in this document were non-site-specific projections of peak load from 1986 to 1995. From 1996 to 2000, a 5 percent growth in capacity was assumed. To allocate regionally new capacity brought on line after 1985, additions to capacity were sequentially ordered according to water and coal availability, and transportation and environmental considerations. This forecast of generating capacity represented a 7.8 percent annual rate of increase, much higher than most experts expect. To derive projections of capacity for the other three scenarios, lower growth rates of approximately 2.5, 3.75, and 6.75 percent were used. In allocating these generating capacities among the model's regions, the same sequential ordering of site-specific plants was used. Table 2-C-1 summarizes the electrical generating assumptions of the four scenarios.

Table 2-C-1.   Electrical Generating Capacity, 1975–2000
(megawatts)

State	1975	1980	1985	1990	1995	2000
			Scenario A			
Arizona	6,700	7,700	8,200	9,100	10,000	12,100
Colorado	3,700	4,400	5,200	6,300	7,100	8,000
New Mexico	3,900	4,200	4,300	4,800	5,300	5,400
Utah	1,100	1,100	1,900	2,100	2,800	3,000
SW total	15,400	17,400	19,700	22,300	25,200	28,500
U.S. total	505,000	682,000	860,000	992,000	1,131,000	1,275,000
			Scenario B			
Arizona	6,700	7,600	9,100	11,100	12,800	14,700
Colorado	3,700	4,700	5,300	7,200	8,500	8,700
New Mexico	3,990	4,100	5,000	5,200	5,200	5,400
Utah	1,100	1,500	2,100	2,800	5,900	10,700
SW total	15,400	17,900	21,500	26,300	32,400	39,500
U.S. total	505,000	793,000	999,000	1,205,000	1,426,000	1,660,000
			Scenario C			
Arizona	6,700	9,600	13,000	15,400	21,000	26,800
Colorado	3,700	6,300	8,600	10,700	12,600	19,600
New Mexico	3,900	4,800	5,400	6,400	9,400	15,300
Utah	1,100	2,300	6,100	13,100	18,100	21,000
SW total	15,400	23,000	33,100	45,600	61,100	82,700
U.S. total	505,000	793,000	999,000	1,205,000	1,426,000	1,660,000
			Scenario D			
Arizona	6,700	9,600	13,000	18,000	28,100	39,000
Colorado	3,700	6,300	8,600	10,600	17,700	24,700
New Mexico	3,900	4,800	5,400	8,400	14,600	17,400
Utah	1,100	2,300	6,100	15,000	15,100	27,100
SW total	15,400	23,000	33,100	52,000	75,500	108,200
U.S. total	505,000	893,000	999,000	1,205,000	1,426,000	1,660,000

The report of the task force for Project Independence was the principal document consulted to develop the alternative coal mining assumptions presented in table 2-C-2. The coal task force was formed to provide estimates for the Project Independence blueprint of potential production capabilities of the coal industry. The task force provided two sets of potential production estimates to 1990. The first assumed a continuation of all current policies that could affect levels of coal production, while the second assumed selected changes in policies or practices that would permit a greater expansion of potential production. Scenario A coal mining projections were derived from information presented in the task force's lower set of estimates, while scenarios B, C, and D made use of their higher estimates. Reserve estimates were used to extend the task force projections to the year 2000.

In specifying coal gasification for each scenario, the set of national control totals used dictated the total number of gasification plants by year. Since other parts of the United States contain abundant coal reserves, it

*Project Independence
Task Force Report—Coal*

Table 2-C-2.   Coal Mined, 1975–2000
(thousands of tons)

State	1975	1980	1985	1990	1995	2000
			Scenario A			
Arizona	3,500	4,600	5,600	6,700	7,500	7,900
Colorado	6,700	8,600	10,500	12,500	14,000	14,800
New Mexico	9,800	12,700	15,700	18,600	20,800	22,100
Utah	5,100	6,200	72,002	8,500	9,500	10,000
SW total	25,100	32,100	39,000	46,300	51,800	54,800
U.S. total	610,000	736,000	839,000	821,000	878,000	1,025,000
			Scenarios B, C, and D			
Arizona	3,900	6,900	11,100	14,500	15,900	17,500
Colorado	7,600	13,100	21,400	29,200	35,600	42,000
New Mexico	10,700	19,300	31,000	40,200	44,300	44,300
Utah	5,300	8,800	13,000	20,100	28,800	37,400
SW total	27,500	48,100	76,500	104,000	124,600	141,200
U.S. total (B)	643,000	874,300	1,059,000	1,352,000	1,894,000	2,707,000
U.S. total (C, D)	643,000	874,300	1,059,000	1,102,000	1,227,000	1,380,000

was possible to specify widely varying levels of coal gasification within the Southwest by assuming that the remaining plants were located elsewhere. Scenario D assumed the highest number of coal gas plants within the Southwest—forty. A location-specific sequential ordering of the forty plants was acquired from coal, water, transportation, and environmental considerations. This ordering was used in determining the location of plants for all the coal gasification assumptions enumerated in table 2-C-3.

The allocation of oil shale plant national control totals required a somewhat different conceptualization than coal gas allocations. Since oil shale deposits occur primarily in the Four Corners area, it was not possible to project varying levels of activity by assuming the residual was shifted to other areas of the United States. The national control totals provided by RFF assumed either zero or eighty-four oil shale plants in the year 2000, with no coal liquefaction plants assumed on line by year 2000 in any of the scenarios. To obtain the varying levels of oil shale plants depicted in table 2-C-4, scenarios B and C assumed that some of the eighty-four oil shale plants were actually coal liquefaction plants located outside the Four Corners area. As in the other energy activities (including uranium, which is discussed below), reserves, water, transportation, and environmental considerations were made in localizing the plants.

Since a substantial percentage of uranium reserves is located in the Four Corners States, uranium and shale were treated similarly. Reserve estimates were used in determining what portion of the national production total would occur within the Southwest. Within the four states, sequential ordering of standard-sized 2,000-ton-per-year mining and milling plants was derived. Production estimates, by scenario, were obtained by trending existing production patterns within the Southwest to the patterns prevailing under the sequential ordering. Table 2-C-5 summarizes these assumptions.

Table 2-C-3. Coal Gasification Plants of 250×10^6 Cubic Foot per Day Capacity, 1975–2000

States	1975	1980	1985	1990	1995	2000
Scenario A						
U.S. total	0	0	0	0	0	0
Scenario B						
New Mexico	0	0	1	2	5	6
Utah	0	0	0	0	0	1
SW total	0	0	1	2	5	7
U.S. total	0	0	28	56	84	112
Scenario C						
Arizona	0	0	0	0	1	1
Colorado	0	0	0	0	1	1
New Mexico	0	0	5	7	8	8
Utah	0	0	0	1	4	6
SW total	0	0	5	8	14	16
U.S. total	0	0	28	56	84	112
Scenario D						
Arizona	0	0	0	1	1	1
Colorado	0	0	0	1	6	16
New Mexico	0	0	5	7	8	11
Utah	0	0	0	2	7	12
SW total	0	0	5	11	22	40
U.S. total	0	0	28	56	84	112

Table 2-C-4. Oil Shale Plants of 50,000 Barrel per Day Capacity, 1975–2000

States	1975	1980	1985	1990	1995	2000
Scenario A						
U.S. total	0	0	0	0	0	0
Scenario B						
Colorado	0	0	0	1	3	4
Utah	0	0	0	0	1	1
SW total	0	0	0	1	4	5
U.S. total	0	0	0	1	5	6
Scenario C						
Colorado	0	0	0	4	8	14
Utah	0	0	0	0	2	6
SW total	0	0	0	4	10	20
U.S. total	0	0	0	5	12	23
Scenario D						
Colorado	0	0	19	33	39	46
Utah	0	0	7	13	20	27
SW total	0	0	26	46	59	73
U.S. total	0	0	26	46	64	84

Table 2-C-5.   Mining and Milling of Oxides of Uranium, 1975–2000 (tons per year)

States	1975	1980	1985	1990	1995	2000
Scenario A						
Arizona	0	0	0	2,000	2,000	2,000
Colorado	1,000	500	1,000	4,000	6,000	6,000
New Mexico	5,500	6,000	8,500	16,000	18,000	18,000
Utah	1,000	500	500	4,000	4,000	4,000
SW total	7,500	7,000	10,000	26,000	30,000	30,000
U.S. total	12,600	12,000	16,800	41,800	54,500	54,300
Scenario B						
Arizona	0	0	0	2,000	0	0
Colorado	1,000	500	2,000	4,000	4,000	2,000
New Mexico	5,500	6,500	10,000	14,000	14,000	8,000
Utah	1,000	500	0	4,000	4,000	0
SW total	7,500	7,500	12,000	24,000	22,000	10,000
U.S. total	12,600	13,000	19,200	39,700	36,300	17,000
Scenarios C, D						
Arizona	0	0	0	2,000	2,000	2,000
Colorado	1,000	500	2,000	6,000	8,000	8,000
New Mexico	5,500	6,500	10,000	22,000	36,000	44,000
Utah	1,000	500	0	4,000	4,000	6,000
SW total	7,500	7,500	12,000	34,000	50,000	60,000
U.S. total	12,600	13,000	19,200	53,900	83,700	107,200

II WATER IN THE SOUTHWEST

3 WATER SUPPLY AND USE

Perhaps the central fact about the Southwest region is its aridity. Throughout the history of settlement of this area, whether by more recent immigrants or natives, human beings have tried to adapt to this condition. Sometimes the adaptation has been successful and led to a prosperous life; other times it has led to misery and eventual failure.

As we related in chapter 2, large-scale development of the natural resources superimposed on the existing tendency for people and industries to move to the Sunbelt will make major additional demands on the limited water supplies. This is true for all credible scenarios. Certainly, many fear that water scarcity will put a tight constraint on further development of the region's energy and other natural resources. In this and the following three chapters, we examine the question of how the development scenarios of the previous chapter can be influenced by the fact of water scarcity, what kinds of demands may be made on the region's water allocation institutions, and the central policy issues that emerge from additional water demands.

The discussion focuses on the Upper Colorado River Basin and emphasizes the development of energy resources (for a map showing the boundaries of the basin see figure 3-1). The Upper Colorado Basin is not only the source of the largest renewable water supply in the region but, as the discussion in chapter 2 shows, it is also the repository of almost all the remaining unexploited energy resources of the region. Thus, it is where the heavy demands for water for resources development will be concentrated.

In addition to demands within the basin, the water resources of the Colorado are presently, and will in the future continue to be, heavily called upon to meet out-of-basin demands by diverting water between basins. Such diversions are now made to the eastern slope of the Rocky Mountains in Colorado, to the Rio Grande Basin in

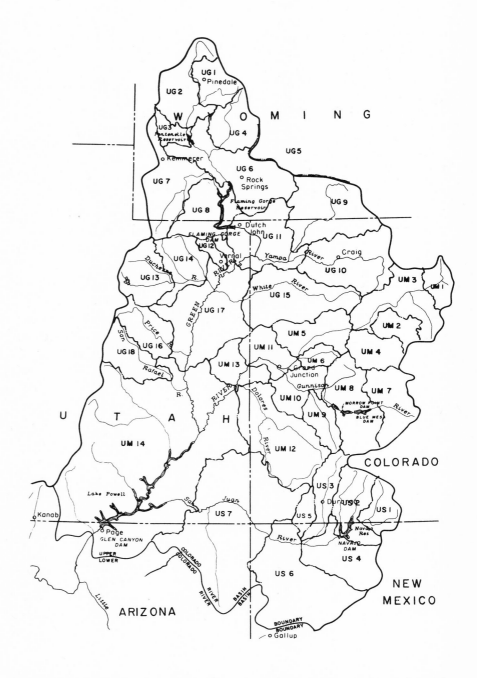

Figure 3-1. Upper Colorado River hydrologic subbasins. *Source:* Walter O. Spofford, Jr., Alfred L. Parker, and Allen V. Kneese, eds., *Energy Development in the Southwest: Problems of Water, Fish and Wildlife in the Upper Colorado River Basin,* Volume I (Washington, D.C., Resources for the Future, 1980) p. 20

New Mexico, and to southern California. Two other major diversion projects, the Central Utah Project and the Central Arizona Project, are under development although their future is presently somewhat in doubt.

The natural physical setting of the Colorado River Basin is best characterized by the word "diversity." The description of John Wesley Powell, as he explored the Colorado River and its canyons, eloquently depicts the intimate relation of the river and the lands from which its flows arise:

THE UPPER
COLORADO
RIVER BASIN

All winter long snow falls on its mountain-crested rim, filling the gorges, half burying the forests, and covering the crags and peaks with a mantle woven by the winds from the waves of the sea. When the summer sun comes this snow melts and tumbles down the mountain sides in millions of cascades. A million cascade brooks unite to form a thousand torrent creeks; a thousand torrent creeks unite to form half a hundred rivers beset with cataracts; half a hundred roaring rivers unite to form the Colorado.

Consider the action of one of these streams. Its source is in the mountains, where the snows fall; its course, through the arid plains. Now, if at the river's flood storms were falling on the plains, its channel would be cut but little faster than the adjacent country would be washed, and the general level would thus be preserved; but under the conditions here mentioned, the river continually deepens its beds; so all the streams cut deeper and still deeper, until their banks are towering cliffs of solid rock.

For more than a thousand miles along its course the Colorado has cut itself such a canyon.[1]

This marvelous interaction of water and land, which has etched out the basin over geologic time, represents a truly unique resource system among the river basins of the country.

While the natural contrasts of verdant slopes, trout streams, deep canyons, and desert ranges remain, human beings have wrought great change in this arid, but spectacularly beautiful river basin. The wild, uncontrolled river that John Wesley Powell ran in 1869 is now highly developed and totally regulated. The waters of the Colorado now serve 15 million people and many uses in supplying water for cities, irrigated agriculture, energy production, industry, mining, and in supporting wildlife, recreation, and areas of great aesthetic value to the nation.

For all these varied activities, demands are made upon the river as both a source of water and a carrier of residuals and by-products of human-made as well as natural processes. Consequently, as energy

[1] John Wesley Powell, *The Exploration of the Colorado River and Its Canyons* (1895; reprinted, New York, Dover Publications, 1961) p. 29.

development and other pressures increase water use and pollution over time, the future ability of the Colorado to sustain these additional uses, its beauty, and its unique fish and wildlife will be dependent on the quantities and qualities of water available for these uses.

PHYSICAL CHARACTERISTICS

Physiography

The 1,440-mile-long Colorado River Basin, containing one-twelfth of the land area of the forty-eight states, has the most varied physical setting of any American river. High mountainous elevations (exceeding 14,000 feet) are ultimately succeeded by high plateaus and low desert valleys. Geological structures and formations include deep, intricately carved river canyons, high mountain slopes, large saline shale structures, and long verdant irrigated river valleys. Fir forests are succeeded by arid rangelands. The boundaries of the Upper Colorado River Basin consist of uplifted earth masses heavily dissected by erosion, glaciation, and weathering. In the interior of the basin are plateaus, mesas, and basins all considerably affected by erosion. As estimated by the sediment load, erosion above Grand Canyon is about 6.5 inches per 1,000 years. This erosion is attributed mainly to the Cretaceous marine shales which were essentially continuous across the Colorado Plateau when it was uplifted. These erodible shale beds are still a major source of river sediment.

Water Resources

The Upper Colorado River Basin divides naturally into three major drainage systems (figure 3-1): the Upper Main Stem, the Green, and the San Juan. The entire Green River drainage comprises the Green subregion. The San Juan subregion is the drainage area of the Upper Basin between the junction of the Green River with the Colorado River and Lee Ferry, Arizona. A broad range of climate and streamflow conditions exist within the Upper Colorado River region. The input of water to the hydrologic system, in the form of precipitation, varies from over 50 inches in the high-elevation headwaters to fewer than 6 inches in desert areas. Most of the streamflow is provided by snowmelt from the mountainous areas, which produces high rates of runoff during the snowmelt period each year. Historic per-unit area discharge rates decrease rapidly as the tributary streams flow from their headwaters at high altitudes into the less humid areas and finally into desert areas (see table 3-1). The river produces the lowest outflow per unit area (60 acre-feet per square mile) of any river basin in the United States.

Large variations in annual discharge also occur from year to year because of variations in precipitation, and over periods of years because of long-term climatic trends. The average annual discharge of the Colorado River at Lee Ferry was 12,426,000 acre-feet for the

Table 3-1.   Drainage Area and Historic Unit Discharge of the Upper
Colorado Basin

Gauging station	Drainage area (square miles)	Streamflow record prior to 1965 (years)	Unit discharge (cubic ft. per second per sq. mi.)
Colorado R. near Grand Lake, Colo.	103	46	0.922
Colorado R. at Glenwood Springs, Colo.	4,560	66	.596
Colorado R. near Cameo, Colo.	8,050	32	.484
Colorado R. near Cisco, Utah	24,100	54	.327
Colorado R. at Compact Pt. Lee Ferry, Ariz.	109,580[a]	52	.155

Source: Utah Water Research Laboratory, *Colorado River Regional Assessment Study,* Report to the National Commission on Water Quality (Logan, Utah, Utah State University, October 1975).

[a] Drainage area as measured in connection with this study; other area figures are from U.S. Geological Survey water supply papers.

fifty-two year period from 1914 to 1965, with extremes of 21,894,000 acre-feet in 1917 and 4,396,000 in 1934. For the seventeen-year period from 1914 to 1930, the average discharge was 15,919,000 acre-feet per year, while for the twenty-six-year dry cycle, from 1931 to 1956, the average discharge was 11,183,000 acre-feet per year. These are residual flows reflecting upstream depletions approximating 1,800,000 acre-feet in 1914 and increasing to about 2,800,000 acre-feet in 1962. The average annual virgin flow at Lee Ferry, as unaffected by the activities of man, is estimated at 14.872 million acre-feet over the fifty-two year period from 1914 to 1965. This contribution would average about 2.5 inches in depth over the entire Upper Basin. Later in the chapter we show that there is substantial disagreement about how much water remains in the basin for further exploitation.

Water is presently exported from the region through approximately forty transmountain canals and tunnels, mostly located at the headwaters of small tributaries. Several of these diversions have operated for many years, and in 1965 the diversions totaled 651,000 acre-feet. As of 1967, there were 117 storage reservoirs in the region having usable capacities of greater than 1,000 acre-feet and a total usable capacity of more than 29 million acre-feet.

Water Quality

To identify water quality problems one compares water quality data with state and federal standards to develop a profile of types of problems throughout the basin. When the water quality parameters that violate these standards are analyzed, a general list of problems results. Such a list is typified by the one compiled by the Utah Water Research Laboratory in 1975 for the Colorado River Basin:

    salinity
    pollution from municipal discharges
    eutrophication in reservoirs
    sedimentation in reservoirs
    heavy metals
    high temperatures from energy production
    high temperatures from reservoir releases
    pollution from industrial discharges
    petroleum spills
    risks to rare and endangered species
    significant recreational impacts
    general environmental impacts

When viewed from the standpoint of the sources of the problem and the incidence of effects, the problems are primarily local (although they may occur in several places in the basin), or both local and regionwide where the problem is of a pervasive nature.

Serious local water quality problems include acid mine drainage and heavy metal pollution in the tributaries of the west slope of the Rockies, reservoir eutrophication and sedimentation problems, low dissolved oxygen (DO) below treatment facilities, and pathogens. Such conditions may interfere with rare and endangered floral and faunal species and recreational pursuits.

But at present, from the standpoint of the entire basin, the overwhelming water quality problem of the Colorado River is the salinity or total dissolved solids (TDS) content of the water. It is also the problem that is most affected by the natural background conditions of the basin. Comparisons of salt-loading and salinity concentrations at various points on the river system have been estimated in a number of different studies.[2] These studies have employed techniques to identify and separate the sources of salinity. While varying in their estimates, they suggest that approximately two-thirds of the salt burden and 50 percent of the concentration in the river at Lake Mead originate from natural point and diffuse sources.[3] Natural factors in the Colorado system that can cause salt loading and concentrating

---

[2] See, for example, Colorado River Board of California, *Need for Controlling Salinity of the Colorado River* (Los Angeles, Calif., June 1970); M.L. Hyatt, J.P. Riley, M.L. McKee, and E.K. Israelsen, *Computer Simulation of the Hydrologic-Salinity Flow System Within the Upper Colorado River Basin*, PRWG54-1 (Logan, Utah, Utah Water Research Laboratory, Utah State University, 1970).

[3] Point sources are those where there is a clearly definable channel by which pollutants enter a stream; diffuse sources are those where the input is spread out and difficult to identify exactly.

effects include: the arid nature of the climate; the geology of the basin with its vast areas of erodible, salt-yielding shales; the great tracts of range and forest lands which consume water and then concentrate the residual salt in less water as it moves by subsurface flow to the river; and evapotranspiration losses from marshy areas and phreato-phytes (deeply rooted plants) along the river system.

Like natural factors, human activities contribute salts and then concentrate them through evapotranspiration losses from irrigated agriculture and reservoir surfaces, and through those stemming from municipal and industrial uses. In addition, the exportation of high quality water from the basin and its diversion for energy development (involving evaporation of cooling water in disposal ponds) have the effect of increasing downstream salinity. Because these practices reduce water supply in the river, they all contribute to salinity in the river as it flows downstream.

ECOSYSTEM CHARACTERISTICS

The usual method of defining an ecosystem is to analyze those physical characteristics of the system that are necessary to support natural aquatic and terrestrial communities of species in the system. To begin with, the diversity and uniqueness of species demonstrate that the Colorado River system is a complex and ecologically isolated system. It has, in fact, the largest list of rare and endangered species of any area in the United States.

The definition of biological subbasins is based primarily on the distributions of fish, which are, in turn, a function of the physical characteristics affecting fish life. To a great extent, stream elevations can be used to describe the distributions of fish because of the relation-ship between elevation and temperature. Although fish species operate within a range of temperatures, in some cases quite wide, temperature is still a major variable controlling the distribution of species.

Factors other than temperature, however, do have a significant effect on ecotype. Silt loads, stream gradient, and food chains have major effects on fish communities and these, of course, are reflected in ecotype classifications of the kind shown in figure 3-2 for streams. If significant natural or humanly induced concentrations of materials occur that directly affect adult fish in their life cycles, food chains, and habits, then the fish will not be found in that particular ecotype of a species. Thus, the distributions of fish shown in figure 3-2 would be characteristic of a stream community if "natural conditions" prevailed; that is, there was no loading of deleterious materials by human beings.

Most of the higher elevation streams are trout habitat. This results from appropriate temperature, clear water, good food chain development, and high gradients that produce turbulence and high oxygen content. Lower down in the river system there is a transition between trout waters and mainstream stretches. Whitefish, which need high quality water and have relatively strict habitat requirements, characterize this type of water in the Upper Basin.

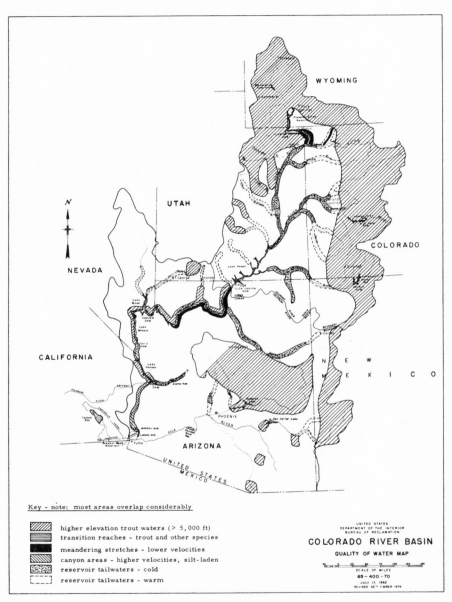

Figure 3-2. Generalized ecotypes based on expected distribution of specific fishes in the Colorado River Basin (reservoirs not included). *Source:* Utah Water Research Laboratory, *Colorado River Regional Assessment Study,* Report to the National Commission on Water Quality (Logan, Ut., Utah State University, October 1975)

This transitional zone is followed by meandering stream reaches which generally are found in agriculturally developed areas, have higher silt loads, and in which are found various minnows, catfish, and carp. Carp is an introduced species that has become established as an important part of the Colorado fish community. In point of fact, as discussed later in the chapter, introduced species have taken over many stream stretches previously occupied by native species. The canyon reaches have the highest silt load, and fish in these reaches are generally dependent on food materials washed in from tributary streams.

The terrestrial component of the Colorado River Basin is largely open range, desert, and some forests, as indicated by figure 3-3, which displays the major vegetation types occurring in the basin. The 37,400,000 acres of Upper Basin rangelands have four specific vegetal communities, namely (1) grass, (2) northern desert shrub, (3) southern desert shrub, and (4) salt desert shrub. These lands have many uses, including grazing, recreation, wildlife production, and watershed areas.

Anyone who takes a careful look at the Colorado River recognizes that this is a stream expected to bear burdens far beyond its capacity to sustain them. The river is overappropriated, that is, there are more paper rights to water in the river than water, even when instream[4] uses are totally neglected. Many of these rights, however, have not been exercised historically so that there has been a net flow of water from the Upper Basin states to the Lower Basin states in excess of the commitment made under the interstate compact of 1922, which apportions the river's water between the Upper Basin and Lower Basin states. The point of division between these two regions is Lee Ferry, Arizona, near Glen Canyon Dam.

The compact negotiators intended that the Upper Basin would deliver half of what was thought to be the average flow of the Colorado to the Lower Basin. The language of the compact states that the Upper Basin shall not prevent the flow of 75 million acre-feet to the Lower Basin in any ten-year period. This figure, of course, represents an average annual delivery of 7.5 million acre-feet even though there is no fixed annual commitment under the compact. In addition, the Mexican Water Treaty of 1944 guarantees Mexico an annual quantity of 1.5 million acre-feet of water. As the secretary of the interior is

WATER SUPPLY IN THE UPPER COLORADO

[4] Instream uses are those, such as fish habitat and navigation, that are dependent upon the water being left in the watercourse in contrast to those uses like irrigation that require the water to be diverted from it.

interpreting and applying this treaty, it effectively imposes an additional .75 million acre-feet annually on the Upper Basin. The Lower Basin is also mining groundwater at a very substantial pace, at least 2.5 million acre-feet annually. The net effect is that the Lower Basin plus Mexico are already consuming water, including groundwater, at a

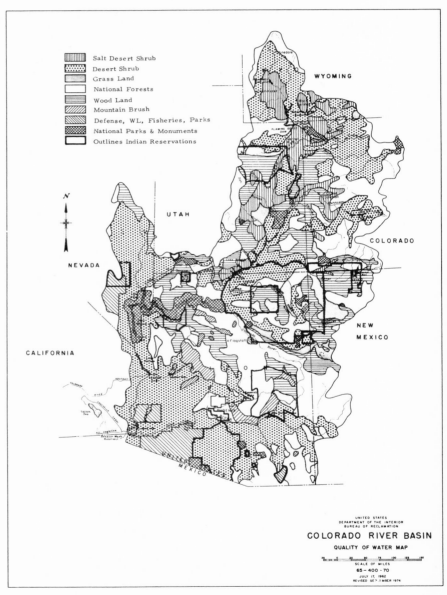

Figure 3-3. Terrestrial ecosystems and land use in the Colorado River Basin. *Source:* Utah Water Research Laboratory, *Colorado River Regional Assessment Study,* Report to the National Commission on Water Quality (Logan, Ut., Utah State University, October 1975)

rate exceeding many estimates of the dependable flow of the upper river.[5] Since groundwater mining cannot be sustained indefinitely, the Lower Basin's consumptive (mostly evaporation and transpiration) demands may be expected to increase at the same time that (1) the Upper Basin, continuing past trends, puts its entitlement of water to increasing municipal, industrial, and irrigation uses and (2) accumulating evidence indicates that the annual flow of the Upper Colorado is significantly less than the amount upon which the 1922 compact was based. Superimposed on this situation are the increased demands for energy and other resource development-related water use in the Upper Basin at the same time that there is increased concern for water quality and for instream uses. The potential for conflict is readily apparent.

Even though there are some sources of quantitative estimates of water supply in the basin, in general the literature on the Colorado River water situation reveals a bewildering array of estimates of available supply for the upper river. In fact, the water supply estimates exhibit a world of considerable uncertainty, conjecture, and differences in assumptions. The Department of the Interior estimates that at least 5.8 million acre-feet should be available for consumptive use annually in the Upper Basin and that depletion in 1974 was 3,707,000 acre-feet.[6] This figure was derived by assuming that 8.25 million acre-feet of water will be released to the Lower Basin through the existing flow regulation and power generation system. Although precise statements of the assumptions underlying this figure are not given in the report, the general discussion does indicate that (1) bank storage[7] in the system can be used for a portion of the water delivered; (2) the basic flow figure (from which the 5.8 million acre-feet is derived) is sustainable significantly less than 100 percent of the time, thereby necessitating shortages in some years for some users; and (3) the assumption is made that the average annual natural flow is 15 million acre-feet per year.

But, in contrast with other estimates of supply, the Department of the Interior figures look rather optimistic. Based on an analysis performed by the U.S. Geological Survey, Wollman and Bonem, in a Resources for the Future study, estimated that the dependable supply

[5] Nathaniel Wollman and Gilbert W. Bonem, *The Outlook for Water: Quality, Quantity, and National Growth* (Johns Hopkins University Press for Resources for the Future, 1971); G. Weatherford and G. Jacoby, "Impact of Energy Development on the Law of the Colorado River," *Natural Resources Journal* vol. 15, no. 1 (January 1975) pp. 171–213.

[6] U.S. Department of the Interior, Water for Energy Management Team, *Water for Energy in the Upper Colorado River Basin* (Washington, D.C., July 1974).

[7] Bank storage refers to water that penetrates into the sides of a reservoir and then when the reservoir is drawn down, returns to it.

of the *entire* Colorado River system (dependable supply meaning one that can be sustained 98 percent of the time) is about 12.7 million acre-feet per year.[8] Note that this number is not necessarily inconsistent with the Department of the Interior estimate because it is based on a virtually certain delivery, thereby greatly limiting the possibility of shortfalls to irrigation or other users. If one assumes that the Upper Basin will have to deliver 8.25 million acre-feet on the average to the Lower Basin to meet compact and treaty commitments, this would leave a supply of approximately 4.5 million acre-feet for the Upper Basin.[9] (Once again, the Upper Basin is not called upon to deliver 7.5 million acre-feet to the Lower Basin every year, but it is required to deliver an average of 75 million acre-feet per year over a period of ten years.)

Dendrochronological estimates (estimates based on tree ring studies) by the Lake Powell Research Project produced a supply figure of 5.25 million acre-feet. This is somewhat higher than the Wollman-Bonem figure but significantly lower than the Department of the Interior estimate.

FUTURE WATER
USE AND ENERGY
DEVELOPMENT

As pointed out in chapter 2, in the years since the oil embargo of late 1973, increasing attention within the United States has been focused upon the Southwestern states of New Mexico, Arizona, Colorado, and Utah as a principal locus of remaining domestic fuels. Because most of the present and contemplated energy production technologies are large water-consuming processes, an immediate corollary of a strong national development of the Southwest's energy resources is a greatly increased demand for use of the region's water resources. Essentially, this means those of the Upper Colorado.

Summary projections of energy-related water consumption figures in the Colorado have appeared in various places. The earliest, authoritative study is the July 1974 *Water for Energy in the Upper Colorado River Basin* prepared within the U.S. Department of the Interior. The supply estimates of this report were outlined in the previous section. We combined these with estimates of consumptive use shown in table 3-2. The Interior report was filled with so much

---

[8] Wollman and Bonem, *The Outlook for Water.* This substantially different flow estimate is lent some support by a Water Resources Council report to Project Independence. Table 8 of that report lists two figures for the Colorado River. The latter, totaling 14.8 million acre-feet (maf), is apparently taken from the Department of the Interior report discussed above, while the first reported total, 13.1 maf for the entire basin, is based upon the 1968 National Assessment and a U.S. Geological Survey report and assumes 98 percent certain flow. The 13.1 figure is based on similar assumptions to those of Wollman and Bonem and is in substantial agreement with them.

[9] Weatherford and Jacoby, "Impact of Energy Development."

detail and so many caveats that summarizing it risks oversimplification. Yet based upon a specific projection of oil shale, fossil fuel electric, and coal gasification plants to be built within the basin together with projections of increased nonenergy water uses, the Department of the Interior study team stated that, "Under this set of projections there could be significant shortages occurring in all States (of the Upper Basin) except Wyoming by year 2000."[10] If the lower figures for supply estimated by Wollman and Bonem and the Lake Powell Project are accepted, the shortages would of course be considerably greater.

Table 3-2. Existing and Projected Water Losses and Supply Flow Under the Department of Interior's Assumptions, Upper Colorado Basin

(thousand acre-feet per year)

Water loss from	1974	2000
Agriculture	2,153	2,913
Other nonenergy uses	1,628	2,378 (min)
		2,673 (max)
Steam electric	38	514
Other energy uses	0	398
Total losses	3,819	6,203 (min)
		6,498 (max)
For reference		
Supply flow	5,800	5,800

Notes: Table entries for the year 1974 are extracted from table 1 of U.S. Department of the Interior, Water for Energy Management Team, *Water for Energy in the Upper Colorado River Basin* (Washington, D.C., July 1974). However, total depletions consist of more than what is shown in the table. Our total depletion is 112 acre-feet more than that reported and is estimated present annual consumption water requirements for public lands. Water requirements for energy for the year 2000 are derived from what is used in 1974 plus development projected for the year on page 42 of the report. Consumptive use of water for 2000 is calculated by summing 1974 use with projected use and is extracted from tables on page 44 of the report. Total projected consumptive use for the year 2000 also includes water for public land administered by the Bureau of Land Management, which is 17 acre-feet higher than what was calculated for the year 1974.

Source: Quoted in "Water Demands for Energy Development," Allen V. Kneese and F. Lee Brown, *Natural Resources Lawyer* Vol. VIII, No. 2 (1975).

All projections as far as the year 2000 can, of course, be little more than educated guesswork. The authors of the Interior Department report recognized this and took a relatively conservative approach to the development of future energy facilities, relying where possible on existing plans and probable expansions of existing facilities.

---

[10] U.S. Department of the Interior, *Water for Energy,* p. 62.

Recent studies have reached more reassuring conclusions about the adequacy of water supplies. The August 1976 '75 *Water Assessment* of the U.S. Water Resources Council states, "The projected future modified flow at the outflow point of the region when compared with the delivery requirements to the Lower Colorado Region implies surplus water still available after year 2000 for Upper Basin use."[11] The draft report "The Water for Energy Question in the West: State Perspectives" is even more sanguine, stating, "Generally, the results of this inquiry suggest that water considerations are not perceived as being a serious limiting factor to energy development."[12] In addition, a recent U.S. Bureau of Reclamation memorandum[13] detailing projected water supply and depletion for the Upper Colorado Region estimates a 207,000 acre-feet surplus[14] in the year 2000. Since the bureau was a major participant in the 1974 Interior Department study, this projected surplus may reasonably be interpreted as a reduction in the earlier projection and, as such, reflects once again the lowered expectations for energy development in the basin.

As this evaluation of projections indicates, expectations for energy development in the Upper Colorado are volatile commodities. Although there is now a temporary glut of world oil, that condition will not hold for many years into the future. With a new embargo or even threat of one, these expectations could easily be wrenched once again upward. Or if some optimistic portrayals of a future demise of the oil cartel were realized, expectations could easily be reduced further, at least for the next couple of decades. There are few questions within the region or the nation that involve more contingencies than the future path of energy development. Accordingly, the subsequent discussion in this chapter will be cast in terms of possible scenarios of energy development within the Upper Basin. However, it should be noted that as of this writing, the nation was contemplating policies which could lead to the large and rapid development of Southwestern resources.

[11] U.S. Water Resources Council, '75 *Water Assessment Upper Colorado Region, Technical Memorandum No. 2, State/Regional Future* (Washington, D.C., August 1976) p. 46.

[12] W. Darrell Gertsch, "The Water for Energy Question in the West: State Perspectives," draft (Los Alamos, N.M., Los Alamos Scientific Laboratory, December 1976) p. 95

[13] Memorandum to the regional director of the U.S. Bureau of Reclamation in Boulder City, Nevada, from the regional director in Salt Lake City, Utah, August 20, 1976.

[14] This surplus figure is based on the current Bureau of Reclamation estimate of 5.8 million acre-feet of reliable annual flow. The "surplus" quickly disappears if the more conservative 5.25 million acre-foot figure reported in Weatherford and Jacoby is used.

Table 3-3 is a summary of projected additions of electrical generation, syngas, and syncrude capacity by the year 2000 under four energy development scenarios, in addition to the projection developed in the 1974 Department of Interior study. Because detailed versions of these Southwest Project scenarios were described in chapter 2, for purposes of this discussion there is no need to present any more detail than is provided in table 3-3.

QUANTIFIED
SCENARIOS

Table 3-3. Additions to Energy Production Facilities in the Upper Colorado River Basin by the Year 2000

Production form	Scenario A	Scenario B	Scenario C	Scenario D	1974 Dept. of Interior projection
Electrical generation (megawatts of capacity)	5,200	15,060	31,060	35,560	25,670[a]
Coal gasification (10^6 ft³,/day of capacity)	0	1,750	4,000	10,000	2,902
Oil shale (1,000 bbl./day capacity)	0	250	1,000	3,650	1,515

Note: The base year against which the additions are measured is 1975.

[a] Total of planned and projected facilities only.

Table 3-3 presents the cumulative totals for four separate time series for the construction of electrical generating capacity to 2000. The highest two series rely heavily upon the 1976 forecasts made by the electrical utilities in responding to Docket R-362 of the Federal Power Commission.[15] In the highest series, scenario D, the assumption is made that approximately 50 percent of the additional capacity projected by the Western Systems Coordinating Council beyond 1985 is constructed in the Southwest.[16] The figure is quite high, as is likely the case with the total capacity projections themselves. This series

Electricity

[15] U.S. Federal Power Commission, *FPC News* vol. 9 (July 16, 1976).

[16] For additions to capacity in earlier years, the site-specific projections of the utilities were used with some modification to take account of more recent information. More detailed breakdown of each of these series can be found in James W. Sawyer, F. Lee Brown, and David Abbey, "Energy Development Scenarios for the Four Corners States and the Upper Colorado River Basin," in Walter O. Spofford, Jr., Alfred D. Parker, and Allen V. Kneese, eds., *Energy Development in the Southwest: Problems of Water, Fish, and Wildlife in the Upper Colorado River Basin,* Volume 1, Research Paper R-18 (Washington, D.C., Resources for the Future, 1980) pp. 201–300. The actual numbers presented for electricity here are the sum of (1) the Upper Basin portion of the numbers in the Sawyer, Brown, and Abbey chapter and (2) the "in process" (scenario B), "planned" (scenario C), and "projected" (scenario D) totals for Wyoming in the 1974 Department of Interior *Water for Energy* study, table 11. Wyoming was not included in the first-named source.

thus provides a useful upper bound to possible additions to electrical generating capacity within the region. It represents a strong shift toward use of Upper Basin coal as the principal source of fuel for West Coast electricity.

Scenario C is much like the highest series except that a 33 percent factor is used as the share of projected generating capacity to be built in the region.

Scenario B lowers the overall growth rate in capacity from the approximate 5 percent figure that underlies the series of scenarios C and D to a 3 percent annual growth rate. The 33 percent factor for apportioning the total capacity additions is maintained. Finally, scenario A may be interpreted as the minimum capacity expansion necessary to support the growth in population and electrical usage that arises from within the region itself with no expansion in export. This series furnishes a reasonable lower bound for capacity additions. Although one conventional nuclear facility is under construction in Arizona, the proximity of substantial coal reserves lends strong advantage to coal-fired facilities in the Southwest region. Hence the figures for additions to generating capacity are interpreted in this paper as being entirely coal-fired.

Synthetic Fuels   Projections of facilities for producing syngas from coal and syncrude from oil shale can only be termed highly speculative. Realistic lower bounds for each of these forms through the year 2000 are essentially *no plants*, and it is that assumption that appears in scenario B. Scenario B presumes a low level of development of both syngas and syncrude facilities. The seven syngas units are those that already have been proposed for northwestern New Mexico by WESCO and El Paso Natural Gas. The figure of five oil shale plants in scenario B is quite arbitrary and represents a level of expansion only minimally beyond an experimental program.

The capacity figures of scenario C represent a sizable national initiative to develop synfuels capability within the region. The individual numbers are arbitrary, although in the case of syngas, some use has been made of other projections in establishing likely ranges.

The numbers for syngas and syncrude in scenario D can only be described as representing a "crash" program to achieve energy independence in a conservation-resistant society. The scale of development is massive. The specific number of plants is essentially arbitrary.

No particular importance should be attached to any one of these numbers. None of them is intended as a "most probable" projection; they merely represent a reasonable range of values for probable as well as improbable (but possible) energy futures for the region. With the numbers of table 3-3 as background, we turn to the associated question of water consumption.

The speculative nature of the scenarios also applies to the question of water consumption. The level of water consumption in an electrical generating station, coal gasification plant, or oil shale unit is dependent on a number of factors including the technology used in the energy facility (which in turn depends on the cost of water and other inputs), the quality of coal or shale consumed, and the percentage of capacity at which the facility is usually operated.[17]

Water Implications

Because a full-scale analysis of all the factors affecting water use was not possible, it was necessary to choose a somewhat arbitrary set of numbers to start with. For purposes of the discussion here, the following water consumption factors are used: 8,560 acre-feet per year for a 1,000-megawatt electrical generating station operating at 50-percent capacity using entirely wet cooling technology; 7,560 acre-feet per year for a 250-million-cubic-foot-per-day coal gasification plant operating at 90-percent capacity; 6,615 acre-feet per year for a 50,000-barrel-per-day oil shale plant operating at 90-percent capacity; and 2,650 per year for a 1,000-megawatt electrical generating station operating at 50-percent capacity with a substantial utilization of hybrid cooling systems.[18] Application of these water consumption coefficients to the levels of additional facilities appearing in the scenarios in table 3-4 will produce the schedule of additional water consumption in the Upper Colorado River Basin in the year 2000 that appears in table 3-4. It is readily noticeable in the table that significant reduction in water consumption may be achieved by the use of hybrid cooling towers in electrical generation.

It should be noted that the water consumption scenarios (of approximately 900,000 acre-feet per year) projected in the 1974 Department of Interior study as arising from the additional development of energy facilities within the Upper Colorado Basin are only part of the additional consumptive use of water projected for the basin. In that report, the study team combined the approximately 900,000 acre-feet of additional water for energy use with agricultural and other projected additions to consumptive use of water in the Upper Basin

[17] Winston Harrington, David Abbey, and James W. Sawyer, Jr., *The Electric Power and Synthetic Fuels Industries in the Southwest: Production and Environmental Control Technologies* (Washington, D.C., National Science Foundation, August 1977) (available from the National Technical Information Service, PB273–847).

[18] The 1974 study in particular used different factors for some energy uses from those used here. No attempt is made in this discussion to elaborate on the basis for the difference.

Table 3-4.   Additional Water Consumption in the Year 2000
              Associated with Energy Scenarios for the Upper Colorado
              River Basin, and Alternative Estimates of Supply Flow

(acre-feet per year)

Scenario	Energy only, wet tower	Total, wet tower[a]	Energy only, hybrid tower	Total, hybrid tower[a]
A	44,500	5,344,500	13,800	5,313,800
B	214,900	5,514,900	125,900	5,425,900
C	519,100	5,819,100	335,600	5,635,600
D	1,089,700	6,389,700	879,500	6,179,500
Department of Interior study	913,000	6,203,000	—	—

For reference

Estimates by	Supply flow	1970 uses	Estimated use
Department of the Interior	5,800,000	Nonenergy	3,781,000
Lake Powell Research Project	5,250,000	Energy	38,000
Wollman and Bonem (calculation based on estimate of total for whole basin minus compact and treaty obligations to the Lower Basin and Mexico)	4,500,000	Total	3,819,000

Note: Dashes = not applicable.

Source: Based on information in table 3-3 and other information presented in the text and in the results of scenario calculations.

[a] Calculated by adding Department of the Interior low projection of nonenergy uses (rounded), see table 3-3, to entry in the previous column.

and compared those totals with the estimated available surface water supply in the basin. They then reached the conclusion reported earlier, namely, that the waters of the Upper Basin would be put to virtually full consumptive use by the year 2000, with the probable level of energy development. In the Southwest Project energy scenario projections (in table 3-3), this result would be approached by scenario C, and scenario D would produce an enormous shortfall even given the high Department of the Interior estimate of supply flow. But perhaps the most striking aspect of the results reported in table 3-4 is that for the lower estimates of supply *every* scenario, even the lowest ones, shows a shortfall.

As stated earlier, no brief should be held for any particular set of numbers for a specific year in the region's future. There are simply too many uncertainties underlying such forecasts to attach a high degree of confidence to any set of numbers. What should be clear, however, from this discussion is that irrespective of whether the year will be 2000, 2005, 2010, or later, the Upper Colorado River Basin states are fast approaching a situation in which the surface waters to which they are entitled under the Colorado River Compact will be fully appropriated and consumed if growth in use continues. Awareness of that fact should underlie all planning for the region's future.

Before saying more in the following chapters about water management in this new context, it should be pointed out that the gross comparisons of consumptive use and some of the estimates of renewable supply that we have just made (and that have been done in many government analyses) do not reveal certain important considerations. The supply estimates should only be taken as extreme upper bounds on what may be available. For at least two reasons the stresses and strains on the region's water management institutions will be more severe than the above comparisons suggest: (1) although water can be moved around and stored, monetary and ecological costs can be prohibitive. Therefore, analyses that truly reveal the situation must be location specific, and very few of these have been done; (2) the analysis neglects instream uses. Clearly water left in the stream can be valuable for aesthetic reasons, water quality maintenance, and wildlife habitat. The latter problem is mitigated considerably in the Upper Basin by the requirement under the compact that on the average 7.5 million acre-feet must be permitted to flow downstream annually. Consequently most upstream water courses cannot be depleted completely. But in specific cases the problem does exist.

We illustrate the importance of the analysis of specific cases in the Upper Basin with a case study. The Yampa River, a tributary of the Green River, is located mostly in northern Colorado. It is celebrated for its beauty and is a prime sports fishery. It also contains abundant resources of coal and is being considered for possible energy development.

To assess the effect of energy and fuel production on the Yampa River flows at Maybell, Colorado (USGS gauging station 2510), the following scenarios were assumed for 1990.

YAMPA RIVER CASE STUDY

A. A 2,000-Mw thermal electric power plant using 6.7 million tons of coal per year; the remainder of the 24 million tons per year of coal mined shipped out of the basin by unit train.

B. A 2,000-Mw thermal electric power plant; 250-million-standard-cubic-foot-per-day (SCFD) coal gasification plant using 6.94 million tons of coal per year; the remainder of the 24 million tons per year of coal mined is shipped out of the basin by unit train.

Details of these two energy development scenarios are presented in table 3-5. For assessing the water consumed in these two scenarios a "base case" plant and a "complete" plant are considered for both the power plant and the coal gasification plant. The "base case" represents a situation in which no restrictions are placed on waste discharges to the environment; the "complete plant," a situation where zero waste water discharges are imposed. As shown in table 3-5, the

Table 3-5. Consumptive Use of Water in the Yampa River Basin Under Energy Development Assumptions

Energy Development Assumptions
    Development projection: 1990
    Surface mining of coal: 24 million tons/year
    Thermal electric power plant: 2,000 megawatts
    Coal gasification plant: 250 million standard cubic feet/day

    Coal input:
        Power plant: 6.70 million tons/year
        Gasification plant: 6.94 million tons/year
        Excess coal: 10.36 million tons/year
        (shipped by unit train out of the Yampa River Basin)

Water Consumption Scenarios (cubic feet per second)

	Scenarios[a]					
	A1	A2	B1	B2	B3	B4
Power plant[b]—base case[c]	54.8		54.8	54.8		
complete plant[d]		49.4			49.4	49.4
Gasification plant—base case[c]			36.5		36.5	
complete plant[d]				27.9		27.9
Mining and land reclamation	10.0	10.0	10.0	10.0	10.0	10.0
Total water consumption	64.8	59.4	101.3	92.7	95.9	87.3

Source: Nicholas C. Matalas and Richard Smith, "Yampa River Case Study," paper presented at the Resources for the Future Forum on the Impact of Energy Development on the Waters, Fish and Wildlife in the Upper Colorado River Basin, in Albuquerque, New Mexico, October 1976.

[a] Scenario A—power plant only; scenario B—power plant plus gasification plant.
[b] Mechanical draft-cooling towers.
[c] No restrictions on waste dischargers.
[d] Zero waste discharges (except for condensate).

two energy development scenarios, and the "base" and "complete" plant options for both the thermal power plant and the gasification plant, result in six combinations of water consumption scenarios. For these six combinations, the water consumption rates for the year 1990 range from a low of 59.4 cubic feet per second (cfs) (43 thousand acre-feet per year) to a high of 101.3 cfs (73.3 thousand acre-feet per year).

The effect of this consumptive use of water on the flow of the Yampa River at Maybell is depicted in table 3-6. For comparison, energy scenario B with "complete" plants for both the thermal power and coal gasification facilities was assumed (scenario B4 in table 3-5). This consumptive use of water is compared with the mean annual flow, the mean monthly flows, and various measures of the low flows in the Yampa River at Maybell. It is clear from table 3-6 that energy development could not occur in the Yampa River Basin without either surface or groundwater storage or supplemental supplies from another subbasin. There simply is not enough water there for energy and fuel production purposes during the low flow periods. Moreover, tradeoffs with other uses of these waters might have to be made during large parts of the year, especially the seven-month period from August through February. It also appears from this rough analysis of the stream flows in the Yampa that the fisheries there might be in serious jeopardy if energy development occurs, or that hydraulic works might have to be undertaken that many think would greatly alter the character of the basin in an adverse fashion.

The only way to understand the full implications of energy development is to look at the details of specific situations. Unfortunately, such analyses are seldom a part of studies aimed at assessing the energy potential of the region. Such studies should have high priority.

Table 3-6. Comparison of Streamflows and Consumptive Use of Water for Energy Development in the Yampa River Basin (USCS gauging station 2510 at Maybell, Colorado)

(cubic feet per second)

Streamflows	Streamflow at USGS station 2510	Water consumption in the Yampa caused by energy development[a]	Net flow at Maybell, Colo.
Mean annual	1,560	87	1,473
Mean monthly			
October	343	87	256
November	345	87	258
December	298	87	211
January	272	87	185
February	320	87	233
March	671	87	584
April	2,620	87	2,533
May	6,280	87	6,193
June	5,540	87	5,453
July	1,360	87	1,273
August	380	87	293
September	241	87	154
Low flows (10 year):			
1-day	41	87	b
3-day	41	87	b
7-day	45	87	b
30-day	62	87	b
365-day	1,060	87	973

[a] Water consumption scenario B4, table 3-5
[b] Storage will be required for the low flow periods.

POTENTIAL EFFECTS
ON THE MARINE
ECOSYSTEM

The possible effects of energy development on the rare and endangered species in this unique ecosystem deserve particular attention. The present drainage of the basin resulted from two separate river systems forcing a connection by cutting through the present Grand Canyon several million years ago in Pliocene times. Except for species in the mainstream, there has always been a sharp separation between upper and lower basin fishes (above and below the Grand Canyon). Consequently, the Colorado River Basin probably lacked direct connections with any other major drainage for millions of years. This resulted in long isolation of the fish fauna. Except for species inhabiting headwater streams, such as trout, sculpins, speckled dace, and mountain suckers (which can be transferred between drainage basins by stream capture), the majority of the native species of the Colorado Basin are endemic; that is, they have been so long isolated from their nearest relatives that they have evolved into species now restricted to the basin. The great antiquity of the native fauna is revealed by chub and squawfish fossils of mid-Pliocene age found in Arizona. The Colorado Basin fishes exhibit the highest degree of endemism of any fish from major drainages in North America. The minnow and sucker families comprise about 70 percent of the freshwater fish species native to the Colorado Basin.

Of the more than thirty-five species of freshwater fishes native to the Colorado River Basin, twelve are native to the Upper Basin. It should be pointed out that a comprehensive, basic ichthyological survey of the upper and lower basins has yet to be made.

Prior to the advent of human activities, the Colorado River system was characterized by tremendous fluctuations in flow and turbidity. Miller cites flows recorded in the Colorado River at Yuma, Arizona, ranging from 18 cubic feet per second in 1934 to 250,000 in 1916.[19] Because the drainage basin lacked large natural lakes, the native fishes did not evolve specializations for lake environments. In addition, there were no barriers to prevent free movement along the main channels and into major tributaries, and thus it is likely migratory movements were a regular part of the life history of the mainstream species. The major tributaries draining the mountains and foothills formed meandering streams with quiet backwater areas which were probably important reproductive and nursery areas for the native fishes.

For millions of years the unique environment of the Colorado River with its great diversity and torrential flows through canyon areas, directed the evolutionary pathways followed by the native fishes and

---

[19] R.R. Miller, *Man and the Changing Fish Fauna of the American Southwest* (Ann Arbor, Mich., Michigan Academy of Science, Arts, and Letters, 1961) pp. 365–404.

molded the bizarre morphologies of the razorback sucker, the hump-back, and bonytail chubs and produced the largest of all North American minnows, the giant squawfish.

Before major dams were built on the mainstream, the larger tributaries were drastically altered because of irrigation dewatering, vegetation removal, and concomitant erosion and channelization. Beginning at the turn of the century, in the Lower Basin a dramatic shift from native species to introduced species better adapted to the changing conditions has occurred. This process was helped by the construction of mainstream dams, which formed large lakes, regulated flow regimes, precipitated out the silt load, and released cold, clear water, thus creating new environments for which the native mainstream fishes were ill adapted. The four specialized species in the main-stream—squawfish, humpback chub, bonytail chub, and razorback sucker—have suffered enormous declines from their former abundance. Although the razorback sucker has maintained limited popula-tions sporadically throughout its former range, the squawfish, bonytail, and humpback chubs are on the verge of extinction. The native cut-throat trout of the upper basin are also considered to be threatened, with this beautiful fish being virtually extinct as a pure population. Although also suffering from habitat loss, the major factor in the de-cline of the native trout has been the introduction of nonnative trouts that have replaced or hybridized with the native subspecies.

With the trend of decline of endangered and threatened species such as the squawfish well documented, the apparent conclusion is that the curve of abundance is likely to reach the zero point of extinc-tion in the next 20 to 25 years, *even if all further development in the basin is brought to a halt*. Although the environmental changes and the fate of the native fishes makes a sad tale, the fact remains that the new reservoirs support multimillion dollar recreational fisheries—based entirely on nonnative fishes—and a fishery that was never possible under pristine conditions with the native fishes. Thus a large unplanned tradeoff has occurred in the character of the river ecology and in the associated recreational and aesthetic opportunities.

The situation is such that one noted specialist on the subject has come to believe that the most hopeful, if not the only, option for avoiding extinction of species such as the squawfish is for future development projects to incorporate endangered species mitigation and enhancement plans. This would be analogous to salmon restora-tion projects on Pacific Coast rivers.[20] Without successful mitigation

[20] Robert J. Behnke, "The Impacts of Habitat Alterations on the Endangered and Threatened Fishes of the Upper Colorado River Basin," in Walter O. Spofford, Jr., Alfred D. Parker, and Allen V. Kneese, eds., *Energy Development in the Southwest: Problems of Water, Fish and Wildlife in the Upper Colorado River Basin*, Volume II, 204–212.

projects it appears that the days of the endangered fish species of the Colorado are numbered. This appears to be true whether or not further resource development takes place.

IMPLICATIONS FOR WATER MANAGEMENT WITHIN THE REGION

The prospect of a condition throughout the Southwest in which all water is fully appropriated has been avoided for many years because many of the region's leaders have relied on speculative schemes to augment the region's water resources. In particular, the Texas Water Plan, which proposed enormous diversions of waters of the Mississippi River to the high plains of Texas and New Mexico, is an example of a scheme that has received large-scale public interest but has consistently fallen short of final approval. Even grander notions to divert water from the northern areas of the continent into the semiarid areas of the Southwest have been proposed at one time or another. Locally, within the region there have, of course, been many examples of interbasin transfers in which augmentation of one basin's surface water flows has been achieved by reducing the available water in a contiguous basin. Although elaborate benefit–cost studies have commonly accompanied the approval of these interbasin diversions, in the final analysis their approval has always been a political matter rather than an economic one.[21]

Although some additions to the usable water supplies of the region may be developed either through streamflow augmentation or exploration and development of deep groundwater, the conflict in the second half of the 1970s between President Carter and some elements of Congress about water projects may be symptomatic of the coming of the end of any large-scale schemes for further diversions of water into the region or even any sizable shifts of water from one basin to another within the region. Thus, for practical purposes it would seem that the region must accept the limited nature of its water supplies and should move strongly to adapt itself to that condition.

In accepting the limited nature of the region's water supplies, however, acceptance of the apparent but untrue corollary that limited water places an absolute limit on development within the region must be avoided. Any rigid, immutable barriers within the region created by limited water are more a construction of human beings than they are a matter of physical reality. In particular, it is the human institutions that prevent in the state of Arizona and elsewhere the transfer of water from agricultural uses into other, more highly valued, uses. Also it is social insistence on artificially low prices for municipal water

---

[21] Helen M. Ingram, *A Policy Approach to Political Representation: Lessons from the Four Corners States* (Baltimore, Johns Hopkins University Press for Resources for the Future, 1980).

that creates the apparent rigid barriers to residential or other development in many of the urban areas of the region.[22] Instead of promoting rigid constraints on water use patterns within the region, political effort should be directed toward increasing the flexibility and allowance for modification of current water use practices on the part of all water users within the region. Generally speaking, there is considerable opportunity for such modification if the region's institutions would simply permit and encourage it. As an example, in planning new electrical generation facilities in the San Juan portion of the Colorado River that lies in New Mexico, utilities have available several options regarding the use of cooling water even though the New Mexico state engineer has projected a fully appropriated condition for the San Juan Basin without the addition of any new generating facilities.[23] First, technological adjustment could be made in the cooling process with dramatic savings in cooling water required as was indicated in table 3-4 earlier. Second, existing privately held water rights in the basin could be purchased. With approval of the appropriate authorities, this water could then be transferred into industrial use from its current predominant use in agriculture. Third, cooling water may be drawn from deep groundwater stocks as opposed to the reliance that has been placed on surface water supplies up to the present. These and other options illustrate the range of possibilities available if and when flexible conditions surround water use within the region.

One general institution that contributes to this flexibility is the existence, where permitted, of an economic market for water rights. Such a market, if it works properly, provides a signal to all water users in the form of the price that a water right may command in the marketplace. This price simultaneously measures the availability of water and the competing demands for its use. With the information provided by the price signal, current and prospective water users can make more informed and intelligent decisions regarding the water use options that are available to them. In addition, as the price of the water rights increases, there is a strong incentive to conserve water.

Thus, full appropriation is not a solid wall blocking development. Rather, it presents a test of the region's institutions' ability to function effectively, efficiently, equitably, and in a timely manner in the face of true water scarcity, and in such a way that all values are given due consideration. It is to these issues that we turn in the next chapter.

---

[22] The urban areas of Tucson, Denver, and Santa Fe are experiencing painful battles over water prices and the extension of water service to new customers.

[23] From the testimony of Stephen E. Reynolds, New Mexico State Engineer, "Statement on the Operation of the San Juan-Chama Project and the Related Impacts in the San Juan River Basin," in hearings before the Subcommittee on Energy Research and Water Resources of the Senate Committee on Interior and Insular Affairs, June 12, 1975.

4 CONFLICTING CLAIMS TO SOUTHWESTERN WATER
The Equity and Management Issues

As noted at the end of chapter 3, the steadily increasing human activity in the Colorado River Basin and throughout the Southwest has placed growing stress on the water institutions of the region. The situation is exacerbated by some special characteristics of the Colorado and other rivers in the region such as highly variable annual stream-flow. Accordingly, public water policy has been increasingly subject to challenge in the modern era, and these challenges promise to become even more stringent in the future.

Water has always been a critical public concern in the arid West. In prehistoric times, ancestors of the modern Indian tribes were torn between their desire for safety and the need for an assured supply of water, since these goals could only occasionally be fulfilled in the same place. Great value was attached to any location that would satisfy both needs. The task of water-gathering continued as a central concern with the addition of Spanish and Anglo populations to the region in recent centuries. From the Spanish culture came community irrigation systems coupled with societal norms governing their maintenance and use. Modified descendants of these systems still exist in the form of *acequias* or community irrigation ditches, which are common to those areas of the Colorado and Rio Grande river basins in which Spanish populations settled. The influx of Anglo populations, and their preoccupations with mining and ranching activities, led to the development of the prior appropriation system of water rights, a legal doctrine strikingly different from the riparian doctrine which prevails in the eastern United States in which closer proximity to water produces a higher claim to it. Prior appropriation or "first in time, first in right," developed as a solution to the conflicts among placer miners in the mountains of California. Mining activity, which was commonly

THE LEGACY OF SCARCITY

67

located in the mountainous upper reaches of the region's streams, required the storage and diversion of the river flow to points some distance away from the stream itself. Prior appropriation was adopted as a means of solidifying the water rights of the earliest mining claimants who might be some distance from their water source. Because this system also was compatible with farmers' needs, mining and farming interests succeeded in codifying the prior appropriation doctrine into the laws of the western territories and states. In general, under this system, a right to the use of water is obtained by putting water to "beneficial use." The earlier a user establishes claim to the water, the more senior the right, that is, the higher the priority of the right in time of drought.

The controversies and problems that surround the use of water in the arid West today can only be understood by first recognizing the separate water traditions, practices, and needs that each of the three major regional cultures has historically evolved. In some cases, the modern issues reflect direct conflicts between the descendants of these separate cultures who seek to enhance or preserve the legacies they have inherited. With respect to other issues, there are strong traditions, such as the desire to preserve water for agricultural uses, that are common to all three cultures and that are raised in opposition to new, external forces acting upon the region. In either instance, policy analysis of a water issue in the West must begin with a description and assessment of the products of centuries of scarcity—the region's laws, institutions, economic interests, and societal desires—that are related to water use in the West. Water scarcity has bred a sophistication and complexity in laws and institutions and a tenacity and toughness of purpose which are unsurpassed by any other area of activity in the region and which demand consideration far beyond the usual weight assigned regional interests in national policy formation.

In the decade of the 1970s, the water controversies and public policy issues underwent a subtle, but significant, change. They attracted national attention and have been, accordingly, escalated into a national problem. For most of this century, regional leaders courted national opinion on water issues almost exclusively for the purpose of acquiring the necessary dollars to finance water development projects within the region.[1] Arguments and compromises were principally concerned with the allocation of federal dollars rather than with the underlying water issues themselves. In the 1970s, however, events combined to change this situation. What formerly seemed

---

[1] For a case study see Helen Ingram, *Patterns of Politics in Water Resource Development: A Case Study of New Mexico's Role in the Colorado River Basin Bill* (Albuquerque, N.M., University of New Mexico, 1969).

important only in a parochial, regional context has become important nationally as well. The most dramatic event precipitating this change was the oil embargo of 1973, which focused national attention on the Southwest as the location of large domestic deposits of energy fuels, including uranium, coal, and oil shale. Since virtually all processing of these fuels into usable energy forms requires large quantities of water, the attention of national policy makers was drawn to the water resources of the region.

The decade of the 1970s also saw the steady strengthening of Indian assertions of rights to water, land, and other natural resources. These assertions are being made with increasing sophistication, and at a time when the general public is increasingly cognizant of the extreme poverty in which many Indian tribes live. The various Indian claims to water are generally lumped together, as a matter of convenience, under the term "Winters Doctrine rights."[2] Since, as a matter of treaty and statute, Indian affairs lie almost exclusively within federal jurisdiction, resolution of Winters questions requires federal action and is thereby a national question. Additional importance is attached to the Indian claims by virtue of the proximity of the Indian reservations to the energy resource deposits in the West. Substantial portions of the known reserves of these resources lie within Indian lands. Of even greater significance, however, is the fact that development of the energy resources in virtually any subregion of the Southwest will require use of water resources that are subject to Indian claim. The combination of a federal responsibility for Indian welfare, a national energy policy promoting energy production, increasing assertion of Indian interests by Indians, and a greater general public awareness of Indian problems produces a mixture which will certainly require national action.

There are other factors pushing the region's water problems into the national arena. The question of federal reserved rights parallels the Indian Winters doctrine claims and in most respects encompasses them. Simply stated, the doctrine of federal reserved rights means that whenever the United States sets aside its own public domain land for specific purposes, there is implied, even if not expressed, a concomitant intent to reserve that amount of water required to fulfill the purpose for which the land was set aside.

The importance of reserved rights is underlined by the substantial federal presence in the West, in national parks and monuments, national forests and wildernesses, federal laboratories and military

[2] This term stems from the landmark Supreme Court decision in *Winters* v. *United States*, 27 U.S. 564 (1980), which is discussed extensively in a later section of this chapter.

reservations, and other federal installations. It was inevitable that as activity within these installations grew, their demand for water, which was left implicit and unquantified when the installations originally were established, would become explicit and definite. Yet, in many of the region's watersheds, these new needs arose after the water within the basin had already been fully appropriated by other users. The notion of implicit reservation of federal rights is in clear conflict with the prior appropriation system of water law already in place within the region. Additionally, the imposition of federal water quality standards on the rivers of the region will provide the fuel for extended environmental battles. Though not so hotly contested as the current battles over air quality in the region, the prospective impact of quality standards on consumptive use of water also contains the ingredients for conflict. Another aspect of the water quality issue that is of particular relevance to the Colorado River concerns the U.S. treaty obligation to Mexico. Specifically, the high salt levels present in the Colorado River water delivered to Mexico have proved damaging to the agricultural industry in that country, and consequently, they have been a matter of international dispute. The United States has recognized its responsibility for the quality of the water delivered to Mexico and has agreed to build a purification facility on the Colorado River near the international border.

Early budgetary decisions in the Carter presidency deleted a number of water development projects and cut most deeply in the arid West. Those actions and the current general emphasis on reduced federal expenditure may signal the end of public investment practices heretofore held to be sacrosanct within the region. No longer can it be said that the water controversies of the West are almost exclusively a financial or a regional problem. Not only will the resolution of these problems require federal action, but their outcome will have national importance.

FOUR FUNDAMENTAL ISSUES

Events with important consequences for water use occur almost daily in the Southwest. A utility may decide to obtain water for cooling a new power plant from groundwater as a better alternative to the purchase of existing rights to surface water or to the construction of a dry cooling tower. A federal agency may begin drilling a series of new wells to determine the depth, quality, and extent of underground water sources. A federal judge may deny a motion in an Indian water rights case, thereby further sharpening the legal issues involved.

The variety of unanswered questions, problems, and conflicts surrounding water in the West may be collected and sorted into four categories which we shall label (1) the equity issue, (2) the management issue, (3) the environmental quality issue, and (4) the water development issue. Each is discussed in turn.

The existing claimants for water in the Southwest can be put into three broad groups with sharply differentiated interests: the various Indian tribes of the region, the federal government, and the large number of established water users in the region, which includes farmers, mining companies, manufacturers, and municipalities. Stated in the simplest terms, the claims of the Indian tribes rest upon (1) their status as the first occupants of what is now the western region of the United States, (2) the historical policy of the federal government in establishing reservations for Indians which, as interpreted by federal courts, implied the allocation of water for use by Indians on the reservations, and (3) the obligations of the federal government as trustee for the Indian tribes in promoting their economic development. Although Indians already control substantial water rights,[3] the increasing value of water rights and the steadily rising aspirations of the Indian tribes themselves have led to a dramatic escalation in the claims of the tribes for water, well beyond the quantity of rights they currently control.

The claims of the federal government to Southwestern water rest generally on constitutional grounds and in particular on the navigation and commerce clauses of the Constitution. The impetus for assertion of federal claims, apart from the federal government's role as trustee for the Indians, does not arise predominantly from the quantities of water needed for federal installations, which are relatively small within the entire pattern of water use in the region. Instead, the federal concern is linked to the government's need to ensure adequate water supplies to meet federal objectives, in particular the development of western energy resources. Of course, there are many aspects to federal objectives and responsibilities. Specifically, the national government has extensive responsibilities as manager of water storage facilities, hydroelectric generators, recreational lakes, irrigation delivery systems, wildlife refuges, international monitoring systems, and other operations that require maintenance of a certain streamflow or that create water loss as a by-product (as in evaporation from lake surfaces). Meeting these evolving responsibilities and more recent policy objectives often leads to direct conflicts with existing users of water. In some instances, regional leaders have adopted public stances in opposition to the

The Equity Issue

---

[3] In particular, the court-appointed watermaster in *Arizona* v. *California,* 373 U.S. 546, 600-1 (1963) quantified rights to large amounts of water for several Indian tribes in the Colorado River Basin.

movement of water into new uses, and in many instances, the conflict is sharpened by state laws that make it difficult to acquire water for new purposes in an economical and timely fashion.

The claim of established holders of rights to the use of water, as previously indicated, rests on the legal doctrine of prior appropriation, which is embodied in the existing law in all states of the region. This doctrine, moreover, has been explicitly recognized by the federal government on several occasions and tacitly accepted by it on others.[4] Because the surface waters and much of the groundwater of virtually all subbasins within the region have reached or are nearing full appropriation, it is clear that all of the claims and potential claims to water cannot be realized. Thus, the equity issue is starkly apparent. Which claimants are entitled to the water of the region, and to what extent?

The Management Issue   There are, of course, many possible ways in which the political, legal, and economic conditions surrounding water in the region may ultimately lead to an apportioning of the region's water resources among the competing claimants. Whatever the resolution of the equity issue, it is clear that it must come relatively soon in most areas. For most basins, a condition of fully appropriated surface waters either is at hand or is a not-too-distant future prospect. The groundwater situation resembles that of the surface supplies in some areas except that hydrological information on groundwater is much less accurate and complete. Some of the region's groundwater aquifers are being steadily drawn down, particularly in association with irrigation. The most notable examples occur in southeastern Arizona around Tucson and in eastern New Mexico and Colorado in the Ogalalla formation that lies under those states (and west Texas) and extends into the Midwest. However, there are known aquifers throughout much of the region which have not been mined significantly, and some evidence indicates the presence of deep aquifers under many energy resource locations in the region. With the increased depth, of course, the cost of lifting the water for surface use increases also. Since pumping costs have risen with the increase in energy prices, much of the groundwater physically available has become economically less attainable. In short, despite the uncertainty created by the unresolved equity issue, which discourages exploitation of some water resources, the region is approaching a condition in which the renewable supplies of water are fully utilized and the untapped stocks of groundwater have become very expensive to obtain.

In the absence of new additions to the water supply of the region, new uses can be accommodated only by retiring old uses or by turning

---

[4] See, for example, the Reclamation Act of 1902, 43 U.S.C. et cit. g, June 17, 1902, as Chapter 1092, 32 Stat. p. 388.

to other, more costly, sources. Any shift away from old uses will be socially painful if it is accepted at all. Already rumblings of discontent have been heard from interest groups and public officials, focusing particularly on the growing shift of water from agriculture to energy uses. These expressions of concern are legitimate, since any significant reallocation of societal activity commonly is disruptive and costly to many individuals within the society. Moreover, the rural agrarian way of life has many strong adherents in the Southwest, as elsewhere, and for these people, the value of maintaining an agricultural way of life cannot be captured by a formula which purports to show that a greater net economic value is gained from diverting water to nonagricultural uses. This point of view is reinforced by recognition of the ultimately transient nature of energy activity within the region. The argument is made that each of the principal energy resources of the region—oil, natural gas, coal, uranium, and oil shale—is nonrenewable and therefore exhaustible, and therefore that it would be foolish to allow the withering of the region's permanent economic base in pursuit of a rich but transient industry. From this perspective, it would be better to mandate that new water demands be met from the unused stocks of groundwater even with their correspondingly higher cost.

A different argument arises out of concern for the relatively low average income levels in the Southwest. A common aspiration of many of the people in the region is for substantial economic improvement, and that aspiration implicitly requires that the scarce resources of the region, including water, should be allocated to their most economically valuable uses. For proponents of this view, an inflexible system of water allocation may be a serious obstacle to improvement of their living conditions. From this perspective, the existing system for managing water allocation is excessively cumbersome and complex, and it perpetuates economic inefficiency by maintaining existing patterns of water use when economically more attractive reallocations could be made. Succinctly stated, the management issue questions the extent to which the water management system in the region should be refashioned to permit more flexibility in the movement of water from one use to another and yet retain social and political acceptability. It overlaps and cuts across the equity issue, which refers to a conflict between three societal groups over the right to decide upon water allocations. The management issue is faced at the national level and also within each group; for example, Indian farmers and miners may have opposing viewpoints on water allocation, as may Anglo farmers and miners.

Any water management scheme must take into account the widely held belief in the Southwest that water, unlike other scarce commodities, is owned by society as a whole. Indigenous westerners of all cultures are affronted by the wasteful use of water in any activity, public or private, and the notion of public ownership is a fundamental element in regional water law. An individual appropriator of water never obtains a right to the water itself, instead, he establishes a right to *use* the water contingent upon his putting it to "beneficial use" as defined by the laws of society. Although this distinction has the appearance of legal hairsplitting, it accurately reflects the societal attitude toward water. Appropriators technically relinquish their rights to use water should they fail to continue putting the water to beneficial use for a specified period, as legislated by each of the states. This notion of public ownership seems to arise from the common perception that water is fundamentally the most essential commodity without which life cannot be sustained. As a consequence, public ownership of water is asserted as a means of preserving its accessibility to each and every person.

Numerous examples of the management issue are being contested now within the region. The cities of Tucson, Santa Fe, and Denver have recently experienced hotly argued conflicts over the extension of water services to new users and the pricing of those services. Jurisdictional conflicts between the Middle Rio Grande Conservancy District and the state engineer of New Mexico have placed a potentially expensive legal cloud over future transfers of water rights in that basin. Arizona laws designed to protect agricultural water users place costly restrictions on further expansion of nonagricultural uses in many areas of that state. The sheer number of local, state, regional, Indian, and federal organizations having authority over some aspect of water management threatens the efficient use of the resource. As more and more basins reach a condition of full appropriation, the management issue will increase in importance, and instances of conflict will become correspondingly more numerous.

The Environmental Quality Issue

The issue of environmental quality, as it relates to water, may be divided into two subquestions: (1) the quality of the water itself, and (2) the quality of the watercourse. The term "water quality" is most frequently used in the Southwest in connection with the problem of increasing salinity in the region's streams and rivers. Increased brackishness of the water leads to decreased productivity in almost all water uses and in irrigated agriculture in particular. This effect has been especially severe in the lower Colorado River and, as mentioned, has caused significant problems for U.S. relations with Mexico. Although the United States has a firm treaty commitment with Mexico regarding the quantity of Colorado River water to be delivered to Mexico, the increase in salt concentration that has occurred over a number of years has significantly adulterated the value of the water delivered. This saline condition of substantial proportions has created considerable debate over appropriate salinity abatement policies. In a broader sense it raises the standard environmental economics question: What degree of quality is optimal for society to maintain?

The question of degree of quality preservation is currently debated in the Southwest more frequently and hotly in connection with the quality of the watercourse than with the water itself. Water development projects disturb the natural scenery and habitat. The Colorado River is no longer the watercourse that John Wesley Powell described so eloquently in the nineteenth century. Rivers that once flowed freely through steep canyons are now dammed, slack bodies of water. The battles over the once proposed hydroelectric dams on the Colorado in the Grand Canyon provided clear illustration of the conflict between preservation and water development. More recently, the case *Friends of the Earth* v. *Armstrong*,[5] exemplified the conflict between water development and environmental preservation as the waters of the man-made Lake Powell backed up into Rainbow Bridge National Monument in southern Utah. In the Grand Canyon example, environmental interests proved dominant, while in the Rainbow Bridge case, federal courts eventually permitted the extension of Lake Powell into the national monument.

Even apart from the conflicts over water development projects, the preservation issue is contested in debates over (1) the legality of allocating water for "instream uses," such as the maintenance of aquatic life and the scenic quality of the stream; and (2) various proposals to eradicate scenic vegetation along watercourses. In the latter case, the argument is made that vegetation draws water from the watercourse and transpires it into the atmosphere, hence reducing the availability of water for other uses. The question here involves a societal choice between continued use of water exclusively in municipal, agricultural, industrial, and other consumptive uses and the development of a new category of "beneficial use" that is to a large extent aesthetic in nature. The benefits from instream uses are not exclusively aesthetic, of course, since they also provide tangible economic benefits through the revenues derived from tourism, fishing, and other recreational enterprises. One state in the Southwest—Colorado—has modified its water law to legitimize these instream uses; others have not. This facet of the environmental quality issue may be succinctly stated in the following question: What is the optimal combination of environmental preservation and water development?

---

[5] *Friends of the Earth* v. *Ellis L. Armstrong*, Commissioner of Reclamation, Department of Interior, et al., Doc. A-1111, U.S. Sup Ct. 411, US. 980, May 14, 1973.

*The Water
Development Issue*

As mentioned earlier, the water development issue was given considerable prominence in early 1977 by President Carter's attempt to cancel seventeen water development projects around the nation, many located in the West. This attempted cancellation of large water development and diversion projects, though later compromised, met with a strong reaction from western political leaders. Ever since the construction of Hoover Dam on the Colorado River early in the twentieth century, the practice of providing federal funds for large water development projects had become almost ritualistic. This practice has been particularly cherished in the arid West, and for many western leaders the controversy sparked by the Carter action was perceived not as a simple skirmish over congressional pork barrel privileges, but rather as a fundamental assault on the traditional way of conducting water business in an arid environment.

In the face of conflicting demands for water, the easiest political course always has been to find or acquire new water sources, rather than to be forced to choose between one or another of the conflicting demands. Thus, as adjacent rivers reach full appropriation or underground aquifers begin to be mined, political attention quite naturally focuses on more distant sources of water that may possess unused surpluses. Physical acquisition of these more distant resources commonly requires interbasin, or even interregional, construction projects to divert the water from its distant source. Historically, these diversion or storage projects, which are expensive investments, have been funded by the federal government in pursuit of the "reclamation ethic," which has sought "to make the desert bloom." In recent years, as the search for new sources of water has moved farther and farther afield, and at the same time construction costs have steadily increased, the price tags on these water development projects have soared. As an example, the Texas State water plan proposed a multibillion dollar diversion of Mississippi River water to the high plains of Texas and eastern New Mexico. That plan has been rejected twice by Texas voters but still retains many strong proponents. The high cost of these development projects has become inescapably a principal factor in the water development issue.

In the following sections we return to the equity and management issues to develop them more fully. Case studies are presented to illustrate concretely the many aspects and complexities of these issues.

THE EQUITY ISSUE: DIVIDING A GRANT FROM NATURE

The foregoing discussion summarized the equity issue in the practical terms in which the issue currently is being debated. In many water basins of the West there have arisen a number of claims and potential claims to the water resources of the basin which taken together exceed the available resources. The claimants include the federal government, Indian tribes, and established right holders who have put water to beneficial use under prior appropriation doctrine. We expressed the issue succinctly in question form: Which claimants are entitled to the water of the region and to what extent? It is in terms of this entitlement or right to water that the issue is currently argued in the courts, in Congress and state legislatures, in federal and state bureaucracies, and before the public.

To fully understand the issue, however, and appreciate the strength with which the various positions on the issue are advocated, it is necessary to set aside temporarily the expression "water rights." Although a water right is well defined legally and may even be embodied in words on an adjudication decree, the emotional and financial resources that have been committed to the struggle for the water rights cannot in this instance be explained simply by a few words on a piece of paper. Moreover, the term has become rhetorically ambiguous. In one usage its meaning may be confined to its narrow legal definition as a water counterpart to a deed for land, while in another context its meaning may rise to a position parallel with the inalienable rights espoused in the Declaration of Independence. To clarify the issue, attention must focus on the actual objectives of the parties at interest. These objectives may be quite distinct from the ownership of water rights per se. For example, if the objective is simply a secure physical supply of water, the ownership of rights may be an unnecessary step in reaching the objective. Farmers in many conservancy districts have irrigated land for years without ever "owning" a right to the water they use. Ownership has rested, instead, with the conservancy districts themselves. A guaranteed physical supply of water can be established without actual ownership of water rights.

The objective sought may also be intangible. Instead of the water itself, the objective may be a degree of control over the use of the water. For example, if the federal government in its policy-making role should assign a high priority to making western water available for particular energy projects, then the simplest and cheapest alternative may be a strengthening of the private market institutions in the various basins rather than outright ownership of water rights by the government itself. In this strategy, it is virtually certain that energy companies would outbid other users of water and acquire the desired rights. In this case, actual ownership of water rights may be inordinately expensive when compared to other methods for achieving the desired degree of control. The dispute may ultimately be resolved by an allocation of water rights, but the basis for that settlement will be dictated by the individual objectives and the motive strength with which those objectives are pursued. Accordingly, we shall examine each of the principal parties to the issue in order to delineate clearly their objectives and provide some assessment of their tenacity of purpose.

THE PARTIES AND THEIR PURPOSES

The individual parties to a water rights dispute will generally be different for different water basins. However, previously we classified these claimants into three categories based upon a commonality of purpose and circumstances. These categories are labeled: (1) established appropriators, (2) Indian users, and (3) federal users. Each of the categories will be examined separately.

Established Appropriators

These claimants include farmers, conservancy districts, municipalities, mining companies, ski resorts, manufacturing concerns, land developers, energy companies, and a large collection of small businesses and individual homeowners. Their claims are alike in two important respects. First, each party currently uses water beneficially. Accordingly, their claims do not seek a future or potential right to put water to beneficial use but are concerned instead with support for their current activities. Second, the claim of each party in this class is based on the legal doctrine of prior appropriation. The parties will differ in the degree to which their appropriative right has been perfected, but in the final analysis, the security of their claim to water rises or falls with the security of the appropriation doctrine itself. Many, possibly most, of the parties in this category do not expect to be forced to defend their continued use of water. Certainly they are not in court actively "claiming" their right to continued use of water, except in those circumstances when another party has forced the issue upon them. The notions of prior appropriation and beneficial use are so embedded in the consciousness of most appropriators that it would come as a severe shock were the appropriative system to be superseded.

Since all of these appropriators are current water users, a settlement of the equity issue would affect them only if it weakened their claim to water. If a settlement recognized new claims, then a weakening would be unavoidable in any basin which was already fully appropriated or in which the newly recognized claims exceeded the remaining unappropriated water. As a practical matter, the weakening could be felt in several ways. Most obviously, the right of an established appropriator might be reduced in seniority. As long as newly recognized claims remained paper rights and were not exercised, then the water practices of an established appropriator could continue unaffected. Whenever the new rights were exercised, however, then many established appropriators would find themselves physically short of water, just as has been the drought-year experience of many current junior appropriators. One likely implication of such a settlement, then, would be an increase in the number of right holders who are physically short of water in any given year. There are other possible implications, however.

In the case of a conservancy district or other appropriator who possesses rights to use large quantities of water, the introduction of further conservation practices might alleviate the problem of actual physical shortages. Alternatively, an appropriator may buy up the rights of other similarly affected appropriators, thereby reducing the demands on the available supply and ensuring a continuity of his own supply. Both of these alternatives, however, effectively increase the cost to an established appropriator of maintaining his physical supply of water. Thus, increased operating costs would be an almost certain implication of any newly recognized claims to water rights.

There is a third possible implication. A water right is closely akin to a dividend-paying share of common stock in that the owner of the water right or common stock is entitled to receive certain benefits each year arising from his ownership. In the case of the stock, the benefit is generally provided directly in monetary terms; whereas, in the case of the water right, the owner is entitled to use a certain quantity of water that he may convert into economic benefit to himself. In the case of the stock, a reduction in the expected stream of future dividend payments reduces the value of the stock itself. An analogous situation exists with the water right, at least in those states that allow the buying and selling of water rights. Although many current water right holders may have no intention of selling their right in the foreseeable future, there would nevertheless be a reduction in the asset value of their water rights arising from any settlement that recognized new claims and thereby reduced the future quantities of water likely to be available for their use.

Any of these possible effects would be damaging to an established appropriator. The last two are expressible directly in monetary terms, either as an increased operating cost or as a reduction in asset values. For some appropriators, water functions exclusively as an ingredient in a production process whether it be manufacturing, energy production, or tourism. Consequently, although their damages may be large, they are conveniently summarized in monetary terms. For other appropriators, the possible physical loss of their customary access to water may not be easily translatable into monetary terms. The best example here is the individual farmer whose life-long routine has included use of irrigation water. If his use of water were marginal in economic terms, he might not be able to sustain financially any solution that entailed increased costs. At the same time, the decline in the asset value of the water rights would prevent a comfortable move from irrigated agriculture that would otherwise be available through sale of his rights. The social and psychological damages to this individual undoubtedly would transcend the more limited economic costs incurred.

The distinction between these two cases is important. In both cases, the interest of the parties is in preventing or reducing the damage that a settlement would produce. However, the potential losses that they seek to minimize are not the same. In one instance the loss is purely economic, while in the other case it is the threatened loss of the physical water itself and a way of life that has accompanied this access to water. All appropriators face the possibility of economic loss arising from any reordering of claims, while a subset of them faces the possibility of psychologically disruptive reworking of their basic way of life. Any successful resolution of this issue must address these differing basic interests.

It is important to recognize one other conclusion of this analysis; namely, the basic interests of established appropriators—whether they be purely economic or water itself—could be met in some cases without their retaining legal title to the water rights themselves. If the loss were purely economic, then a compensation scheme should suffice. If the prospective loss surpassed economically quantifiable damage, it could still be ameliorated (albeit at a possibly higher cost) through a guaranteed access to water via a leasing arrangement even though the property right itself were lost.

It is difficult to overestimate the intensity with which current appropriators will advocate their interests. The current political clamor in some quarters for final quantification of Indian water rights, or even dissolution of Indian reservations, is one indication of the strong emotions attached to this issue by established rightholders. In this regard, two statements made at the beginning of this discussion deserve reemphasis. In the conflict over this issue, current appropriators will be battling for something that they have rather than something that they want. In other words, in their view they are the defenders. What is more, the cornerstone of their defense is the prior appropriation doctrine itself, which is the established legal doctrine in the western states. So these are not individual solitary defenders fighting a crusade; instead they have considerable social, legal, and political support behind them.

Indian Users   The volume of literature on Indian water rights is considerable. Much of it is concerned with legal analysis of the basis of Indian rights, possible procedures for quantifying those rights, or the politics of the issue. It is difficult to glean clear notions of Indian objectives and motives from this welter of opinions, analyses, and emotional arguments, and, moreover, the objectives may vary from tribe to tribe. Nevertheless some conclusions can be substantiated and others hypothesized.

Indian claims to water rights cannot credibly be separated from the subject of Indian aspirations generally. Irrespective of whether these aspirations are expressed in such words as "equal justice," "equal opportunity," "equal footing," or an "equal standard of living," they arise from the stark economic condition of many of the Indian peoples of this country when contrasted with the status of most of American society. Yet, as is commonly the case with distant goals, the desired status escapes exact definition. Several American presidents have attempted to lend the concept more precision. In a message to Congress, President Lyndon Johnson stated, "Our goal must be: a standard of living for the Indian equal to that of the country as a whole." However, Indians themselves in describing their hopes for the future use expressions such as "equal footing," "justice," "opportunity," words which are much less specifically economic in content than the expression "standard of living." This difference in terminology may reflect an Indian concern with noneconomic goals such as acceptance and respect, or it may reflect an Indian perception that the economic standard of living of modern society has only been achieved at significant cost both socially and psychologically. Approaching the future from a distinctly different cultural history and perspective, the Indian may be instinctively seeking a different path along which he can gather some of the fruit of economic improvements without paying so high a social cost. In either case, it is difficult to define his vision of the future in concrete terms. Instead, a more specific definition of equivalent status will evolve through future events and actions.

Indian plans for achieving equivalent status—however that expression is defined—place great emphasis on water and water rights in fulfilling their aspirations. Indians, as well as many Westerners generally, perceive inadequate supplies of water as being a critical factor limiting economic development, and there have been sizable Indian commitments of financial and human resources to the battle over water rights. Even apart from its direct use in assisting Indian economic development, ownership of water rights is perceived to be a potential revenue generator for tribal governments which often are short of funds to support long-term investments as well as current operations. If clear title to quantities of water rights could be coupled with legal authority to lease the water obtained through exercise of those rights, then the tribes could realize a stream of annual receipts from the lease of any water that is surplus to the tribes' own current internal needs. Unlike the energy resources of the western tribes, surface water supplies are a renewable resource. Moreover, as demand for water in the West has increased, the market value of this resource has steadily increased also. As a result, the potential revenues from leasing surface water could be expected to continuously increase in value until such time as the tribes converted the water to internal use.

Both of these purposes—economic development and revenue generation—have been asserted as principal concerns of the Indian tribes in the water rights issue. However, neither of these two purposes goes to the heart of the Indian interest and accordingly, leaves implicit a fundamental principle essential to any stable solution.

Water rights appear to have become a symbol to American Indians with an importance akin to that attached to the American flag by the many generations of Americans who have fought beneath it. Just as the flag burnings of the 1960s incensed these Americans far beyond the actual physical damage inflicted by the destruction of the piece of cloth, so too the Indian interest in water rights far exceeds the economic value of the water itself. An alternative illustration is provided by the successful fight of the southern Blacks for the right to sit in the front of the bus, an achievement whose tangible benefits were minute when compared to its spiritual and psychological value. For centuries Indians experienced a steady erosion of their land holdings as they were appropriated by the dominant society. In their view, the same conflict now has shifted to the water rights arena. They are determined that in this case the outcome will be different.

In this perspective the Indian interest becomes clear. Were water rights less than a symbol to the Indians, then the tangible fulfillment of that interest might be met with less than the water rights themselves. The economic development and revenue generation purposes could be achieved through means other than outright ownership of rights. But the symbolic nature of the rights permits no other interpretation of the Indian interests. It is water rights they desire, and that desire is fervently held. Quantitative definition of the rights that they seek, however, must be derived from the revenue generation and economic development purposes since symbols do not lend themselves to quantification. It is clear, however, that any agreed-upon criteria for quantifying the Indian water rights should be future oriented in keeping with the nature of the economic development and revenue generating purposes. As the future remains uncertain, so too does the quantification of the sought-after rights. It is in this quantification process that flexibility in the Indian position must be found. For the symbolic nature of the water rights seemingly will permit no compromise on the mode of settlement itself.

Federal Users   As a preface to the discussion of the federal interest in water rights, we recall the several ways in which the federal presence within the region is connected with water. First, as the largest single landowner in the region, the federal government operates numerous installations and reservations, including national laboratories, wilderness areas, forests, parks, monuments, and military facilities. In these activities the federal government is a water consumer similar to many other water users within the region. Second, the federal government owns and operates many of the water storage and delivery systems within the region, particularly the larger ones such as the Colorado River Storage Project. Third, the federal government is the mortgage holder for many other systems. The federal role here is that of a water manager, or in its mortgage holder capacity, the role is that of a party with a significant financial stake in water management. The fourth role filled by the federal government in the West is that of trustee to the numerous Indian tribes. Finally, the federal government has an important stake in water as it relates to its own national policy-making role. The recent "water for energy" debate is a good indicator of the attention that must be focused upon water in the arid West whenever it is expected that this region will be critical to the policy under consideration. In short, water must be viewed as a constraint upon national policy in a western regional context.

As is commonly the case with federal involvement in an issue, its several roles produce a diverse collection of federal interests that, moreover, may be in significant conflict with one another. There is conflict within the trustee role itself in those instances in which two or more tribes may have competing claims to waters of the same basin. More broadly, the opportunities for conflict among its policy-making, consumer, and trustee roles are many. Historically, part of the equity issue itself had its origin in a conflict between the federal trustee and policy-making roles. In adopting a policy that allowed the development of the prior appropriations doctrine of water rights within each state before it had adequately met its trustee responsibilities and secured Indian water rights, the federal government sowed the seeds for this modern dispute.

It is not possible to identify a single dominant federal interest as was the case for the appropriators and also for the Indians. Each role produces a distinct federal interest that will be advocated by some portion of the federal bureaucracy. As a water consumer, the interest is in an assured supply of water adequate to meet federal needs. As a trustee, the interest is in fulfilling its *fiduciary* responsibility to the Indian tribes which should imply strong pursuit of the Indian interest discussed earlier. As a policy maker, its interests will be as diverse as the policies that it seeks to follow. Finally, as a manager, its interest should be in the *efficient* fulfillment of the several objectives (agricultural, municipal, industrial, and the like) that western water is capable of serving. This last task is formidable, if not impossible, owing to the numerous and often conflicting objectives of the various parties with an interest in water.

In addition to these parties who are primary to the societal dispute over water rights, there are numerous secondary interests that occupy various roles in the drama. For example, a state water administration may seek to maintain an orderly process in which a dispute can be resolved. However, this same administration must inevitably represent the dominant political force in the state which in turn generally reflects the sentiment of established appropriators. Hence, there is an inherent conflict in this state role, with the likely consequence that state water administrators become narrowly confined to a procedural function in resolving the dispute. Other examples of interested parties include water lawyers, agricultural specialists, realtors, and merchants whose business is closely involved with the existing pattern of water use. Their influence may be decisive at critical junctures.

Table 4-1 summarizes the principal parties to the dispute, their array of interests, and the emotional character of those interests. This information should be considered as constituting the basic parameters of the dispute against which any proposed solution must be measured for fit. Unless a trial solution takes account of these interests and the intensity with which they are espoused, it is unlikely to have universality or permanence.

THE INGREDIENTS OF A SOLUTION

From this welter of conflicting interests in a highly charged, emotional environment, it is possible to discern a few principles upon which a sustainable solution could be constructed. We will discuss them in sequence.

First it is essential that the origin of the problem be recognized and accepted for what it implies. Society acting through its political agent, the federal government, has historically endorsed two fundamentally distinct sets of rules for dividing the water resources of the West. On the one hand Congress has confirmed, both explicitly and implicitly, the notion that an equity interest in water can be acquired by capturing a water supply and putting it to beneficial use. This doctrine has been further extended by assigning a higher claim to those appropriators who put the water to beneficial use at the earlier chronological time. The established appropriators of today are descendants, in property right, of individuals and organizations who took productive action based upon this set of societal rules.

On the other hand, society, acting through the federal judiciary, confirmed a different legal means for establishing an equity interest in water for the Indian tribes in the West by making water rights riparian,

Table 4-1.   Social and Political Parameters of the Water Rights Dispute

Party to dispute	Interests or objectives	Emotional intensity of interest
Established appropriators	• Prevention of economic loss (all appropriators)	→ Commercial interest, diligently protected.
	• Maintenance of physical availability of water and associated way of life (e.g., small farmers)	→ Fervent defense of home and life-style.
Indian	• Economic development	→ Fundamental and tangible interest, strongly advocated.
	• Revenue generation	→ Budgetary interest, administrative convenience.
	• Symbol of Indian aspirations	→ Overriding interest, compelling and considered worthy of great sacrifice.
Federal	• Expansion of water supply for federal installations	→ Program level necessity, partial alternatives possible.
	• Trustee responsibility to Indians	→ Persistently advocated within those governmental agencies and divisions to which responsibility assigned; degree of intensity varies with individual.
	• Water manager and financier	→ Bureaucratic purpose with strong political overtones.
	• Policy making	→ Varies with degree of national resolve.

tied to the land, in the manner of the prevailing legal doctrine in the eastern United States. Modern Indians simply seek to exercise these inherited rights. However, their assertion of these Winters rights commonly arises in geographical areas in which appropriative rights have already captured the reliable surface flows or groundwater stocks of water.

The fundamental fault for this conflict, however, lies not with the current advocates of either appropriative or Winters rights, but instead it rests with their forefathers and the society of that era which failed to address the fundamental discrepancy between the two separate systems for establishing claims to water. It was left to smolder for decades until the modern period in which resolution has become much more difficult because of the higher rate of utilization, and hence higher value, of water supplies.

Once this historical basis for the dispute is understood and accepted, then the argument can no longer be cast in terms of "legitimacy" or higher legal right. *Both* positions have legitimacy against the background of societal actions. Two contributing ingredients to a solution flow from this analysis. First, there is no purpose served in an exhaustive effort to determine which of the most important parties to the dispute—Indians and established appropriators—are "right." Both of the parties should accept the notion that the other side was historically granted society's blessing for its position and instead concentrate on what practicable solutions can be found in the current environment. The second ingredient is the recognition that since society created the dispute, society will have to pay at least part of the cost of settlement including any compensation to those who must relinquish claim to water as part of the settlement.

If these two principles were accepted by all parties to the dispute, then the outlook for a sustainable solution would be significantly enhanced since it would then become possible to focus attention on finding a solution that meets the interests of the parties as described in table 4-1. At this point in the analysis we attempt to distill the "core" interests from the earlier table. By core we refer to those essential interests that, if left unmet in an imposed solution, would continue to fester until the dispute exploded once again. All of the interests described above are pertinent to the dispute, but only a few could wreck a proposed solution if left unfulfilled. What are these core interests?

We suggest the following. (1) Established appropriators must have *water* (at least for the lifetime of individuals who currently have access to water) and compensation for any loss of equity. (2) Indians must have *water rights* and sufficient control over the resource to allow their economic improvement. (3) The federal government must be able to ensure that national policy objectives are met. This analysis has, admittedly, become speculative in that it has proceeded several major steps beyond the existing debate and litigation over the water rights issue. Consequently, there is little value in extending the analysis much farther until it is determined whether the interests we have labeled core actually prove to be so. However, we conclude the analysis by proposing the form of at least one solution that recognizes these core interests and meets them.

THE FORM OF A SPECULATIVE SOLUTION

There are three elements to this potential solution.

1. The appropriative doctrine is confirmed as the prevailing legal system and the last vestiges of riparian law in the West are eradicated. Since water and water rights are transferable under the appropriative system, this step ensures that the federal core interest is met because water will move to the use of highest priority but in a voluntary manner. It also means that Indian rights become alienable and not attached to the land.

2. The federal government, as trustee for the Indians, purchases water rights in the marketplace for use in any Indian economic enterprise that meets the test of beneficial use and an adequate benefit–cost ratio, the latter *without reference to the cost of water*. Corollaries of this element include:

A. The federal trustee holds the rights for the Indians until such time as the Indians and Congress jointly agree to the dissolution of the trusteeship, at which time the rights are relinquished to the Indians.

B. In the event that insufficient rights are for sale in the marketplace, two options that are available are purchase of rights under a leaseback arrangement to the established appropriator or, similarly, purchase of the right in the present but with the effective date in some future year.

3. By use of the marketplace, established appropriators are not coerced into giving up their rights and are compensated for any loss of equity.

Current events and arguments surrounding this equity dispute do not offer many optimistic grounds for a successful resolution of the issue in the near term. Tension and controversy seem to be growing rather than diminishing. Perhaps the recognition and acceptance by all parties of the core interests of the other parties is infeasible without an initial period in which positions are hardened and harsh public postures are adopted. If so, then the social and human damage may be great.

MANAGING A SCARCE PUBLIC RESOURCE

The genesis of the water management issue lies with the fact that the states of the region have reached or are nearing the point at which their water supplies have been fully appropriated. There are precious few locations left in the Southwest in which an usufructuary right to water can be established simply by filing notice, diverting a surface stream or sinking a well, and putting the water to beneficial use. Though there still remain groundwater basins that are largely untapped, these commonly are in remote areas distant from major water users, or the water is very deep and may be of such low quality that it can only be prepared for use at costs which make it economically unsuitable for many uses.

In these circumstances, it has become clear that the water future of the West will impose increasing demands on the *transfer* of water from one use, or location, to another. This prospect should not be exaggerated as was the case in the immediate flush of the energy crisis following the oil price rise of 1974. Not only is demand not increasing as rapidly as some originally forecast, but possible alternatives to transfers do exist, such as streamflow augmentation and increased conservation in industrial, agricultural, and other uses. Nevertheless, in those states which permit water transfers, there is evidence of increasing use of transfer procedures where it should be expected—in those fully appropriated basins still experiencing growth in water consumption.

The growing number of transfers, coupled with the prospect that the process may be accelerated by energy events and policies, has met with increasing concern and budding resistance from a portion of the region's people. Faced with a steady decline in irrigated agriculture and the dwindling of natural streamflows, proponents of preservation seek to retain the region's natural heritage and rural, agricultural industry that has been the dominant user of water over the last hundred years.

In support of the current trend, proponents base their arguments on the national need to develop the region's energy resources and the regional need for economic improvement. In this context, the issue is the adequacy of the region's water management institutions and the extent to which they should be refashioned.

Here, this issue will be examined in the form of two questions which focus on both short- and long-run aspects of the issue. First, much has been made of institutional impediments[6] to the transfer of water between uses—impediments that either prevent the transfer altogether or impose significant transaction costs on the transfer. The important, near-term, question is whether these impediments are simply anachronisms left over from an earlier period of water surplus and will be readily resolved as the need arises *or* whether they instead represent legitimate societal interests which can only find expression through perpetuation of the impediments with the likely consequence that resistance to transfer will increase in proportion to the quantities of transfers proposed. Stated more simply, are the region's water institutions successfully adapting to its changing water needs, or are significant regional interests being inadequately addressed?

The second question concerns the eventual form to be taken by the regional institutions governing water allocation generally. Meyers and Posner[7] have argued for "improved" markets for allocating water.

[6] See, for example, Mason Gaffney, "Economic Aspects of Water Resource Policy," *American Journal of Economics and Sociology* vol. 28 (1969).

[7] C. Meyers and R. Posner, *Market Transfers of Water Rights: Toward an Improved Market in Market Water Resources* (Washington, D.C., National Water Commission, July 1971).

In contrast to market alternatives for reallocating water in the West, there is an opposing tendency toward a centrally managed water system in which water is allocated in a manner that builds upon and extends the centrally directed reservoir release procedures already employed by the U.S. Water and Power Resources Service (formerly, the U.S. Bureau of Reclamation). Despite federal disclaimers, that possibility must be considered as real. In these circumstances it is appropriate to examine the long-term prospects for institutionalizing water allocation within the region. What institutional forms are practical and which should be chosen?

INSTITUTIONAL IMPEDIMENTS

The problem of institutional impediments to transfers of water or water rights has concerned economists and lawyers for years. Their concern is easily understood. Historically the region's water institutions evolved during a period of agricultural and mineral development. The compelling objective driving this evolution was the desire to capture the naturally occurring water sources in an arid region, bend them to beneficial use by human beings, and protect the interests of those parties who succeeded in beneficial use. Preoccupied with this development need, little thought was given to the future adequacy of these institutions once capture was complete, or nearly so. Consequently, it is not surprising to find that the institutional machinery governing water is ill designed to accommodate new municipal and industrial uses by facilitating the transfer of water or water rights from old to new uses. Although the transfer mechanisms vary from state to state and even basin to basin in the ease with which a transfer may be accomplished, in only a few locations can the transfer procedures be characterized as smooth or routine. When compared to the mechanisms for transferring common stock, houses, automobiles, land, or a wide variety of other commodities, water transfer procedures must be generally described as cumbersome, ill-defined, and as consuming disproportionately large amounts of time and money. Nevertheless, the argument is made by some regional leaders that current procedures are too facile and allow transfers that are not in the public interest. We shall briefly describe the mechanics of transfers and present a few examples illustrating the difficulties that surround them.

As discussed above, a claim to water is subject to a wide variety of interpretations by Indians, federal officials, prior appropriators, and others. Similarly, the legal manifestations of these claims also assume a variety of forms. To name a few of the more common legal forms, a claim to water may be held through: (1) ownership of a perfected water right recognized by an appropriate state authority, (2) ownership of land in a state in which groundwater is legally appurtenant to the land, (3) ownership of stock in a mutual water company, (4) payment of taxes to a public irrigation or conservancy district, (5) ownership of a lease signed by a federal agency administering a reservoir or other water system, or (6) ownership of a lease agreed to by another party which itself holds a perfected right or some other valid claim to water. Of course many of these legal claims may be subject to higher claims that may emerge from court decrees regarding Indian or federal reserved rights.

Given the variety of legal forms in which a valid claim to water may be embodied, actual transfers of these claims from one use to another assume a variety of forms also. A transfer may be accomplished through: (1) legal sale of a perfected right from one owner to another, (2) sale of the land to which the water is appurtenant, (3) sale of stock in the mutual company, (4) subleasing, (5) condemnation by a public authority such as a municipality, or (6) potentially by a number of other techniques (for example, legislative dissolution of a public irrigation district and auctioning of its rights to the highest bidder). It is certain that human ingenuity will find many singular ways to achieve a transfer before regularity of procedure is established.

Although certain of the transfer procedures enumerated above inherently carry more problems than others (for example, condemnation procedures in which a reallocation is forced rather than mutually agreed to), none of the existing procedures is free of impediments. To lend concreteness to the discussion, we shall briefly describe a few examples of impediments to transfers before discussing the question in more general form.

Case A (*Tucson*). Arizona water law has made groundwater rights appurtenant to the land under which the water is confined. As a consequence, the city of Tucson has been forced to acquire agricultural land well beyond the city limits in order to obtain water to meet growing urban demand. The appurtenancy doctrine has prevented transactions involving water rights alone so that Tucson has become a landowner to an extent well beyond what it otherwise would desire, while landowners have been required to sell the land in order to realize the gain from the water rights.[8]

Case B (*San Juan Basin*). Water rights in the San Juan Basin have a degree of insecurity arising from very large, and competing,

---

[8] Depending on its location, much of this land may have little market value divested of its water rights. However, low market values of land per se challenge only the degree of burden placed upon Tucson in terms of increased expense and not the existence of an impediment itself.

Winters doctrine claims of the Navajo and Jicarilla Apache tribes. Even though non-Indian rights have been previously adjudicated, the extensive Indian claims have only begun to receive judicial review in the last several years. Any contracts between the Water and Power Resources Service and prospective surface water users require the approval of the secretary of the interior who must determine that Indian rights will not be adversely affected.[9] In at least one instance, contract approval was delayed because of this provision. It can be expected that there will be further instances in the future.

Case C (Conservancy District Powers). Meyers and Posner give a general description and Ellis and DuMars[10] a specific example of the impediments to the movement of water or water rights associated with conservancy districts and other irrigation companies. In the New Mexico example cited in the latter work, the Middle Rio Grande Conservancy District filed a protest against an application to change the point of diversion and the place and purpose of a water right previously applied to irrigation. However, the state engineer of New Mexico approved the application. The district has in turn challenged this decision in court.[11] This jurisdictional conflict provides a significant impediment to transfer in the growing metropolitan area of Albuquerque by placing potentially expensive litigation in the way of future transfers away from irrigated agriculture.

Case D (Energy Transfer). This case is actually a collection of existing and potential restrictions on the transfer of water to energy uses. Arizona, for example, has a long-established statute[12] that requires that any transfer of water for use in an electrical generation facility larger than 25,000 horsepower must be approved by the legislature directly. This is clearly a cumbersome impediment to smooth transfer and indicates that the regional concern about the effects of energy development on agriculture, fish, wildlife, and other features of the region's environment is not simply a recent phenomenon.

These cases are certainly not exhaustive, but they do illustrate the problem in a concrete fashion. Against this background we now return to the first issue posed above; namely, in each of these cases

---

[9] Act of June 13, 1962, P.L. 87-483, 76 Statutes at Large 96 (1962). This section, however, is omitted from the official compilation of the U.S. Code. It can be found in 43 U.S.C.A. Section 615 ii-yy, 620-620 f (Supp 1979).

[10] Meyers and Posner, *Market Transfers;* Willis Ellis and Charles DuMars, "The Two-tiered Market in Western Water," *Nebraska Law Review* vol. 57, no. 2 (1978).

[11] *In re Cox,* No. 7147 (D.N.M. filed September 5, 1977), appealing No. 02377A and RG-10591 (Office of N.M. State Engineer, filed December 4, 1975).

[12] *Arizona Revised Statutes* 45-146 (enacted in 1919).

what is the reason for the impediment? Is it simply a relic of the past or does it continue to reflect a strong societal interest that is not represented elsewhere in the regional water apparatus?

The Tucson and conservancy district cases are similar in that the impediments serve to protect the historical position of agriculture in the use of water. In the Tucson case, Arizona groundwater law has tied the water right firmly to the land that lies directly above the groundwater stock, a situation which is compatible with a pattern of land use that is solely or predominantly agricultural. The same water code, however, does not fit well with an urban-industrial pattern of use that must collect and redistribute the water resource in a geographical pattern of use which may be quite dissimilar from the original spatial distribution of water. This water code, then, inhibits the movement of water from agricultural to nonagricultural uses by making the transfer more difficult and expensive than it would be if the water right could be severed from the land. The Arizona legislature has recently changed this code in ways that may improve the situation.

In the specific conservancy district case cited, officials of the district are concerned with the loss of jurisdictional authority if water rights can be transferred from within the district boundaries to a use outside of those boundaries. The Middle Rio Grande Conservancy District, which was legislatively created to provide flood protection and water for irrigation to district farmers, has in recent years come into increasing conflict with the metropolitan governments that have grown significantly in size within virtually the same geographical region as that served by the district. The district is the only institution in the area which simultaneously (1) provides (as its stated institutional purpose) support for the agricultural industry and (2) has the legal and financial ability to maintain that support. Any erosion in its authority would potentially diminish the life expectancy of irrigated agriculture in the area. Yet the district's resistance to transfers impedes the development of nonagricultural activities that require water rights.

Thus, agricultural preservation can be clearly identified as one societal interest which gives purpose to one class of impediments to water transfers. In addition, the Tucson case also suggests another concern which is more prominently illustrated in other cases within the region; namely, the nature of the hydrological regimes in most groundwater basins introduces the strong possibility that a transfer of point of diversion or use, or both, may adversely affect the exercise of a neighbor's water right. This interconnection between water rights is important not only in groundwater uses but also in surface instances in which the availability of enough water to fulfill one party's right may be predicated on the return flow of a neighboring right or on the deep percolation of water on the neighboring land. If there is one principle that is common to water law throughout the West, it is the explicitly stated condition that a transfer must not injure another rightholder. Consequently, lack of understanding of these hydrological relationships makes a transfer more difficult to complete.

The San Juan case illustrates the results of a failure to resolve the basic equity issue discussed earlier. Water-related events have almost certainly moved in a different direction from what would have occurred had the issue already been resolved.

The last case, energy transfers, is in practical terms a new phenomenon although vestiges of the problem have long existed within the region as the Arizona law cited above indicates. The source of the problem here is to a large extent environmental. With full appropriation has come increased concern over the loss of natural streamflows and the drying up of fish and wildlife habitats. Only in recent years have these "natural" uses of the region's water supplies begun to be recognized as legitimate "beneficial uses" under the water laws of the states. That process, however, has not come very far, and it has apparently proved easier in some states to put obstacles in the way of water transfers for energy than to enact positive statutes (or make constitutional changes) that give instream uses the same legal standing as other beneficial uses for water.

Thus we have an answer to the first water management question: the impediments, on the whole, are not anachronisms but, to the contrary, regardless of their original purpose, they reflect significant regional interests. Agricultural preservation, environmental preservation, and Indian water rights have strong proponents within the regional society. When those forces are compounded by the incomplete understanding of the hydrological relationships that persists, it is easy to see why these impediments continue to exist.

The second part of this same question was whether these impediments would dissolve as increasing demands were placed upon the transfer process. Here the answer is less certain and depends upon the degree of success that the region will achieve in resolving the fundamental problems that underlie the retarding impediments. The pressure for resolution is increasing, motivated by events such as Tucson's accumulating stock of vacant land, a coal gasification company's desire for water rights in the San Juan, and increasing urban growth amid formerly agricultural land. Two possible extreme outcomes are for all impediments to be swept away, as in a crash energy program, or for the impediments to become rigid, seemingly immutable barriers to transfer, much as the two Colorado River compacts are viewed by most authorities today. In either of these two outcomes there would be, in fairly clear-cut terms, winners and losers. In either of these outcomes, however, the regional interest underlying the losing position is likely to be unrelenting. Eventually, after wounds are healed, it is likely to reappear as a complicating factor much like the Indian water rights issue which, left unsolved in earlier water allocation decisions, has now been thrust into the modern scene.

A better solution would seek to accommodate these various interests by (1) making instream uses legitimate beneficial uses in all states, (2) pressing for an agreed-upon division of water rights among all claimants, (3) standardizing the measurement of water use in consumptive units, (4) eliminating the last vestiges of riparian doctrine within the region, and (5) developing sophisticated hydrological models of water basins that interrelate surface and groundwater and can approximate the effect of changing uses, points of diversion, and return flows. The momentum is in the direction of this sort of solution. The question mark lies in collective impatience with change. Time permitting, the water institutions of the region can accommodate the various interests and still provide a reasonable degree of economic efficiency in the use of water. Fundamental to this accommodation, however, is the necessary recognition among policy makers throughout the region that the water circumstances of the region have themselves undergone a fundamental change. No longer can the region's water institutions have as their central purpose the capture and beneficial use of new water. The principal water task of the next century will instead be water allocation under socially acceptable practices that balance the need for economically efficient use with societal norms of fairness and equity. The water institutions themselves will, accordingly, be forced to modify their purposes and adapt to this new central task.

A FUTURE INSTITUTIONAL FORM?

The eventual form assumed by the water institutions that manage this allocation task throughout the region will be shaped from the existing array of institutions by the developing pressures. Although new, or newly named, institutions may be created through combinations of, or modifications in, the existing structures, it is unlikely that any "fresh start" approach will ever be practical. The political power of the existing institutions themselves virtually precludes such an effort. For that reason, any effort to outline a future institutional form for the allocation task must begin with the current institutions that govern water allocation. To construct that outline, we return to the list of legal claims to water enumerated earlier.

As a practical matter, these legal claims to water may be divided into two classes. First, there are those claims that arose through the historical doctrine of prior appropriation whereby a water user acquired a legal right to withdraw a certain amount of water each year by having put that water to beneficial use in accordance with the procedures established by the state in which the use occurred. The transferability of these private, appropriative rights, which in principle entitle the holder to a certain amount of water *in perpetuity*, subject only to the exercise of more senior rights, either is already established or potentially could be established in every western state. A market for these rights exists in some instances, as in New Mexico (see appendix 4-A following this chapter). In principle a sophisticated descendant of this market form would offer a decentralized, economically efficient allocation procedure in which the role of regulation could be confined to the tasks of (1) initial adjudication of all private rights to ensure title and (2) monitoring of all prospective transfers to prevent external effects upon third parties to the transaction, particularly more senior rightholders.

An even more sophisticated offspring could, of course, allow a negotiated bargain to be struck among all parties so that even the monitoring role could be reduced. In the current political climate, which increasingly emphasizes deregulation and decentralization, this institutional form would be likely to have many admirers.

The second method by which legal claim to water has been realized by final users is through a contract, explicitly or implicitly stated, between the end-user and a public or quasipublic body which actually holds the equivalent of a legal title to water rights of the appropriative kind. Familiar examples, of course, are contracts between a power company and the Water and Power Resources Service or conservancy and irrigation districts to which taxes or charges are paid by the end-user. In this category the actual user of the water does not possess a transferable title to the perpetual use of water, but instead is entitled to use water within the terms of the contract, which may be specified for only a period of time or under certain conditions such as residency within the district.

Maass and Anderson have presented a thorough comparative analysis of different regimes for allocating such "public project water" within the scope of the "project."[13] These regimes include market bidding, rotation, equal sharing of shortages, and other apportioning schemes. Within the jurisdiction of these "projects," then, various methods have been devised for taking the "public" water and dividing it among the users in a socially acceptable manner. Some of these schemes have market features; most do not. In fact most of these

---

[13] Arthur Maass and Raymond L. Anderson, ... *And the Desert Shall Rejoice— Conflict, Growth, and Justice in Arid Environments* (Cambridge, Mass., The MIT Press, 1978).

projects or districts in the West must be classed as centrally managed institutions which divide the water among users on an operational basis. Although political authority within the project may or may not be fragmented and diffused among all users, there is little question that from a managerial standpoint these organizations are not decentralized and that they make small use, if any, of market signals.

These organizations differ greatly in size, importance, and degree of success in efficiently fulfilling the organizational objectives. At one extreme there are small irrigation districts that have exhibited only slight change in managerial practices over time. At the other extreme are large districts whose managerial skills rival those of the most sophisticated corporations. The large river water storage systems of the West must be included in this class of centrally managed water organizations even though for the most part their managers may primarily be determining reservoir releases rather than allocations to final consumers. Other prominent examples of centrally managed water institutions are the municipalities, which have increasingly come into conflict over the water management issue.

In short, western water management institutions may be divided into two broad classes: (1) decentralized, market directed allocation procedures for "private water" and (2) centrally managed procedures for "public project water." These two schemes commonly exist side by side in most basins even though they reflect radically different ways of addressing the water allocation task.

It is not possible to predict accurately the dominant organizational form that will eventually evolve within the region. That form could resemble decentralized markets, as would be the case if the centrally directed public projects gradually divested themselves of their publicly held rights either voluntarily or involuntarily through political action. Alternatively, the emerging form may resemble more closely the centrally directed projects, as more privately held rights are consolidated into larger holdings with an eventual political decision by the public to buy out the few large private holdings to avoid protracted impasse when new uses must be accommodated. Lastly, there could develop a marriage or blending of the two institutional forms as exemplified in a public agency which technically owns all rights to water but which auctions off contracted rights to private parties for specified periods of time, thereby obtaining economically efficient water allocations.

While it is not possible to predict which of these institutional forms will eventually be adopted by society, it is possible to identify the major forces and attitudes that will shape the societal decision:

1. The "essential" nature of water. There is a deeply rooted tradition in the arid West which insists that water is different from

other scarce commodities and its allocation should not be governed by purely economic motives. The evidence of this tradition abounds. Witness the usufructuary nature of a water right, mentioned in an earlier section, in which the public retains the ultimate ownership of water while appropriators obtain only the right to use the water. Witness the requirement in all state water codes that the appropriator continuously put the water to beneficial use with the threat of forfeiture should he discontinue his use or attempt to hold the right for a speculative economic purpose that is explicitly excluded as a beneficial use. Witness the hydrologically impossible attempt by states to guarantee water for domestic purposes to all new entrants even when a basin is already fully appropriated. At the heart of this tradition lies the notion that water is "essential" to life itself and that access to it must be guaranteed to everyone, economic criteria notwithstanding. Although economic criteria may be tolerated, and even applauded, in determining water allocations, this societal tradition dictates that these criteria must remain subservient to the rule of guaranteed access to all.

2. Economic improvement. Despite the constraint on economic motives just stated, there can be no question that the desire for improvement will be a strong force in the shaping of future water management institutions within the region. This force will be especially prominent in the case of those subsocieties within the region which, in relative terms, are poor. It would be very difficult for localities with large numbers of unemployed to resist a large new water user who brought jobs even if the new entrant would require a substantial reallocation away from existing uses.

3. Federal pressure. The time has passed when the region could conduct its water business in relative isolation from any national considerations apart from the federal budget. Events have focused attention on the region and that attention can only increase. For the time being, the federal government has repeatedly disclaimed any intention of usurping the historical role played by the states in water management. However, those disclaimers should accurately be viewed as a temporary abeyance of federal initiative rather than as a permanent disavowal. Within the federal system, sustained national needs and policy will ultimately prove irresistible.

The states have been granted a period of time within which they may fashion a water management system that will both accommodate new needs and protect legitimate regional interests. Although some compromise among these conflicting objectives will be necessary, a workable system can be evolved which gives sufficient weight to all objectives. Some of the elements of such a system were developed in the earlier portions of this chapter. The forces pushing toward a renovation of the existing institutional management scheme continue to build (1) from within the states, for example, the consolidation of private rights in the hands of a few owners; (2) among the states, for example, the increasing concern in the Lower Basin of the Colorado about the approaching prospect of actual Upper Basin utilization of its entitlement under the compacts; and (3) on the states, for example, federal energy legislation. The process of revision will be slow and sometimes painful, but it will occur. For the near term, the opportunity to fashion a new management system will rest with the states. If they fail the task will shift to the federal government.

APPENDIX 4-A
WESTERN WATER
RIGHTS MARKETS

Documentation of water rights markets and water rights values in the West is sparse because there is no organized reporting or collecting of this information on a regular basis. In a New Mexico study Khoshakhlagh, Brown, and DuMars reported a range of prices for which water rights were selling in several water basins in that state. These appear in table 4-A-1. These prices are for the right to consume one acre-foot of water per year in perpetuity. Considerable care must be exercised in comparing water values since there are a number of opportunities for confusion including: (1) failure to distinguish between the value of a physical stock of water that may be sold in any given year and the value of the legal right to water that exercises perpetual control over a given stock of water and (2) failure to distinguish among the various physical units in which a water right may be described. In the latter case a water right may be costed in terms of the number of acres to be irrigated (with the volume per acre a matter of recognized practice but left unstated); the amount of water which may be diverted to the land (in acre-feet per year or cubic feet per second); or the consumption right, which is the diversion less the return flow.

In the report, the authors concluded that "the relative price" of water rights, then, in the different basins does provide a good indicator of the demand for water in those basins and the supply of that water, even though the market for these water rights is extremely rudimentary when compared to more sophisticated markets which exist for other commodities.[1]

_____

[1] Rahman Khoshakhlagh, F. Lee Brown, and Charles DuMars, *Forecasting Future Market Values for Water Rights in New Mexico,* Water Resources Research Institute Report No. 092 (Las Cruces, N.M., New Mexico State University, November 1977), p. 141.

Table 4-A-1.   Price Comparisons of One Acre-Foot of Consumptive
Water Right in Five Major River Basins in New Mexico

Basin	Price of right (dollars)	Year
San Juan	72	1970
	171	1972
Roswell/Artesia	238	1970
	628	1976
Rio Grande (excluding Santa Fe)	250	1969
	532	1975
Gila	657	1971
	1,610	1976
Santa Fe	3,733	1969
	10,909	1975

Source: Rahman Khoshakhlagh, F. Lee Brown, and Charles DuMars, *Forecasting Future Market Values for Water Rights in New Mexico,* Report No. 092 (Las Cruces, N.M., New Mexico Water Resource Research Institute, New Mexico State University, November 1977) p. 140.

III AIR QUALITY AND OTHER ENVIRONMENTAL ISSUES

5 SKETCH OF NATIONAL AIR QUALITY LEGISLATION

In the previous chapters we examined the complex array of policy issues surrounding a condition of fully allocated water supplies in the water-scarce Southwest. While some major issues remain unsolved, from our analysis it does not appear that water scarcity as such will be an impenetrable barrier to further development of the area's natural resources to meet regional and national demands if the region's water institutions can respond to the situation with a degree of flexibility. But from studies performed by the Southwest Region Under Stress Team it seems likely, perhaps surprisingly, that air quality considerations will have a much greater bearing upon both the level and the pattern of future resources development than will water scarcity.

The atmosphere of this region of deserts and mountains is especially delicate. This is because there are long periods of poor ventilation and inversions are frequent. As a result, even cities of modest size and great charm and beauty, such as Santa Fe and Aspen, occasionally already have air pollution episodes. The largest cities have persistent and sometimes severe air quality degradation.

The air quality problem in the Southwest region is the result of two major types of emissions. The first is discharges from giant heavy industry sources, power plants, copper smelters, and potentially, synfuel plants and oil shale facilities. The second is a very large number of small sources—automotive vehicles. The former produce a number of ill effects, perhaps the foremost of which is periodic visibility reductions over vast areas. The latter, given the meteorological characteristics of the Southwest, easily produce thick smog in the major metropolitan areas. Even now, Denver's air is said by the newspapers to be "the second dirtiest in the nation."

In the case of water issues, the primary policy questions relate to the functioning of the state, regional, and interstate institutions responsible for water allocation, although as we saw, federal policy also has a major bearing. With respect to air quality preservation, federal policy has clearly been the dominant force up to now. This is true in regard to stationary sources, although the states play a substantial role in the execution of federal policy, and even more so with respect to mobile sources. Accordingly we begin, in this chapter, with a review of how federal policy came to be the way it is. Subsequent chapters discuss the situation in regard to both stationary and mobile sources, implications for future resource development, weaknesses of federal policy in the Southwest context, and suggest policy actions by state and local governments in the region.

NATIONAL AIR POLLUTION LEGISLATION

Early History

In 1950 researchers at the California Institute of Technology established a link between automobile emissions and photochemical smog in the Los Angeles Basin. A short time later the Los Angeles Air Pollution Control District began calling for action from the automobile companies and the state government. Despite company claims that the requisite technology was not available, a study group was set up under the auspices of the Automobile Manufacturers Association and reached a cross-licensing agreement for emission control devices. Over the same period a number of resolutions were introduced in the Congress, though not passed, calling for federally sponsored research on the air pollution problem. Senators Thomas H. Kuchel of California and Homer E. Capehart of Indiana took a leading role in this new effort; in 1955 Senator Kuchel introduced legislation authorizing a federal program of research, training, and demonstrations. In the meantime, President Eisenhower had received a report from an interdepartmental study committee recommending the same steps. Congress passed the legislation and the president signed the first federal law on air pollution in July 1955.[1] The level of activity authorized by the 1955 Air Pollution Control Act, however, was very low—$5 million annually for five years to support all its functions.

By this time the problem in California had worsened, and the state took the initiative in establishing automobile emission controls. A new law requiring recirculation of crankcase blow-by (reducing hydrocarbons by about 20 percent) on new 1963 cars induced the industry to begin installing the simple crankcase device on some 1961

---

[1] P.L. 84-159.

models. In 1963, over the objection of the automobile industry that such technology did not exist, California legislation required exhaust control devices on vehicles once two such devices were approved by the State Motor Vehicle Control Board. When four devices produced by independent manufacturers were approved in 1964, the industry discovered that it could indeed introduce its own devices on cars sold in California starting with the 1966 model year. In that year, the first California emission standards were set.

Meanwhile, back in Washington, things were rather quiet. The main reason was that air pollution was at the time widely regarded as an exclusively state and local problem, as exemplified by the official position of the Department of Health, Education and Welfare (DHEW) toward the 1955 act. Accordingly, eight years elapsed between this act and the first permanent air pollution legislation, although in 1959, the 1955 act was extended for four more years.

In 1962 President John Kennedy asked the House of Representatives to pass a bill sponsored by Senator Kuchel that had passed the Senate in 1961. It authorized the surgeon general to hold hearings on particular interstate air pollution problems. Certain features relating to the research program and grants to state and local governments were added. The House deferred action. Meanwhile, another major incident, a deadly smog that hit London in the winter of 1962, underlined the dangers of air pollution.

A recommendation by the administration in February 1963 finally produced legislation signed by President Lyndon Johnson in December of that year. This law for the first time gave the federal government enforcement powers. They followed closely the pattern of the procedures earlier legislated for water pollution. At the request of a state, DHEW could call a conference on air pollution problems in a particular region or airshed; then hold hearings; and if no satisfactory result followed, finally bring court action. In interstate cases, DHEW could act on its own initiative. The bill also specifically mentioned the need for additional attention to the automobile exhaust problem.

Hearings held in 1964 by the Senate Public Works Subcommittee on Air and Water Pollution underlined the inadequate attention that had been given to automobile emissions in federal legislation. The Johnson Administration held that voluntary cooperation should be sought from the industry, and so it opposed enforcement legislation proposed by Senator Edmund S. Muskie of Maine in 1965. But this position was widely denounced in the press, leading to a reversal by the Administration. Thus, a second title to the 1963 act was passed in 1965 as the Motor Vehicle Air Pollution Control Act authorizing DHEW to set emission standards for automobiles as soon as practicable.[2] The first standards were for 1968 models and were roughly the same as those applied in California in 1966. Many people felt that the federal program was unimaginative and lagged behind the progressive California program.

Exacerbating the matter, the automobile industry took a series of bewildering actions that destroyed—almost as if intentionally—the favorable public image that it had so long held. An attempt by General Motors to intimidate consumer advocate Ralph Nader backfired spectacularly, and its president was forced to apologize before a congressional committee and a national television audience. During the same period the Los Angeles County Board of Supervisors charged that the Automobile Manufacturers Association committee, established ostensibly to exchange emission control information, was really a setting for collusion to prevent or delay controls. They cited evidence and asked the attorney general to take action. The ensuing Justice Department investigation ended in 1969 with a consent decree providing for an end to possible conspiratorial activities while not officially conceding their existence.

The year before, representatives of the industry had given testimony on alternatives to the internal combustion engine which, to put it mildly, was inaccurate.[3] The image of the industry had hit rock bottom. These events contributed heavily to the political climate in which the 1970 act, which is still the governing law, was passed. But first it is useful to look briefly at the 1967 Air Quality Act which was the basis for the far-reaching amendments enacted in 1970.

The 1967 Air Quality Act   In the move toward control of air pollution, a dramatic incident once again proved to be a factor. A four day inversion episode in New York in 1966 was estimated to have caused eighty deaths. A month later a National Air Pollution Conference was held that DHEW hoped to use as a stimulus to new legislation embodying regional control organizations and national emission standards. Senator Muskie, chairman of the Pollution Subcommittee at that time, conceded that stronger legislation was needed but opposed national standards. In 1967 President Johnson delivered a message to Congress dealing primarily with air pollution matters and, despite Muskie's opposition, proposed legislation including national emission standards for major industrial sources and establishment of regional air quality commissions for enforcement.

---

2 P.L. 89-272.
3 *Automobile Steam Engine and Other External Combustion Engines,* Joint Hearings before the Senate Committee on Commerce and the Subcommittee on Public Works, 90th Cong., 2 sess., 1968.

After hearings that reinforced Senator Muskie's reluctance about national emission standards, the Senate Public Works Committee delayed a decision and reported a bill that provided for a two year study of such standards and that transformed the regional agencies from devices to enforce them into organizations involved with the states in setting them. The Department of Health, Education and Welfare was charged with issuing "criteria" which set forth the relationship of concentrations of specific pollutants in the atmosphere to damages to "health and welfare." Ninety days after publication of the criteria, each state had to file a letter of intent that within six months it would establish standards for ambient air quality and, within six more months, implementation plans for each of those pollutants in the airsheds over which it had jurisdiction. The secretary of DHEW could establish such standards himself if the state failed to comply. The final version, which left these elements intact, was passed and signed by the president in November 1967 as the Air Quality Act.[4] The act also authorized a greatly expanded research effort and for the first time set national standards for automobile emissions.

The Department of Health, Education and Welfare was slow to provide the criteria that were the first step in the state and regional approach dictated by the act, and the states in turn were slow to act once criteria were issued. By 1970 not a single state had a full-scale plan of standards and implementation in effect for any of the pollutants, and a Ralph Nader study estimated that the process would not be concluded until well into the 1980s.[5] The report on this study not only roundly condemned DHEW's National Air Pollution Control Administration and all its works but also contained an attack on the Subcommittee on Public Works. Other senators and committees were trying to push into the environmental arena, and the president boarded the now fast-rolling environmental bandwagon. Nineteen seventy was the year of Earth Day. The credibility of the automobile industry was shattered. This was the dramatic political setting for the Clean Air Amendments of 1970.[6]

By 1970 congressional framers of legislation had come to the conclusion that motor vehicle emissions would not be lowered to levels

The 1970 Amendments on Automotive Emissions

[4] P.L. 90-148.

[5] John C. Esposito, ed., *Vanishing Air* (New York, Grossman Pubs, Inc. for the Center for the Study of Responsive Law, 1970) p. 158. An informative discussion of enforcement problems in the air pollution field is found in U.S. General Accounting Office, *Assessment of Federal and State Enforcement Efforts to Control Air Pollution from Stationary Sources,* Report to the Congress by the Comptroller General of the United States (Washington, D.C., GPO, 1973).

[6] P.L. 91-604.

sufficient to protect public health unless Congress specifically established emissions standards and set schedules for obtaining those standards. The congressional standards set in the amendments of 1970 were intended to ensure attainment of health-related air quality levels according to calculations supplied by the National Air Pollution Control Administration in the Department of Health, Education and Welfare. The deadlines for meeting those standards were the 1975 and 1976 model years. This gave some recognition to the need of the industry for lead time to develop the necessary control technologies and equipment. The standard for automobiles sold during model year 1975 and thereafter called for a reduction in hydrocarbons and carbon monoxide emissions of 90 percent from levels produced by 1970 cars, which already had achieved a modest degree of control. Similarly, in model year 1976 a 90 percent reduction in nitrogen oxide emissions was required by the act compared to the 1971 standard. As we will see later, delays and new legislation have caused these requirements not to be met.

The 1970 Amendments and Stationary Source Emissions

The 1970 Clean Air Amendments sharply expanded the federal role in setting and enforcing standards for ambient air quality. The act embodies the concept of a "threshold value"—a level of ambient concentration below which it is assumed that no damage occurs to health. Materials subsequently designated to have threshold values include the main pollutants by mass: sulfur dioxide, carbon monoxide, nitrogen oxides, particulates, and oxidants. The notion of threshold value can be regarded as a politically convenient fiction which permits the law to appear to require pollution damage to health to be reduced to zero.

Congress directed the Environmental Protection Agency to use scientific evidence to determine threshold values for pollutants assumed to have them. Those values minus an adequate margin of safety became primary standards. Those standards that relate to injury to human health were to be met first. More rigorous standards, to be met later, relate to public welfare and aim to protect property, crops, public transportation, and aesthetics from pollutants. The states were to prepare implementation plans ensuring that the primary standards would not be violated anywhere in the state after mid-1975. The act also expressed the intent that the quality of the air be maintained or enhanced. This has since been interpreted by the courts to mean that no new source is permitted to degrade significantly air quality anywhere. This is the so-called Prevention of Significant Deterioration (PSD) doctrine.

Congress did not rely solely on the established standards for ambient air quality to control stationary source pollution. It also gave the Environmental Protection Agency (EPA) power to set specific limits on emissions of certain kinds of pollutants. It recognized a category of substances called "hazardous pollutants" which are considered to have especially serious health implications (some of the heavy metals are examples). The EPA was directed to prepare a list of such substances and to issue regulations limiting their emissions, by both new and existing sources. These standards were to be enforced at the federal level. Very little progress has been made in implementing this part of the act.

The act also directed the administrator of EPA to set new source performance standards which limited the emissions of pollutants from new industrial plants to an amount no greater than that obtainable with "the best adequately demonstrated control technology."

Implementation and enforcement of national clean air policy, with the exception of automotive emissions control, is primarily the responsibility of the states. Their performance in carrying out this mandate has been variable but generally weak, judged in terms of the objectives of the Clean Air Act, and none of the goals of the act has been fully met.

The 1970 act is still the basic law governing air quality policy in the United States. The act has been amended several times, most recently in 1977. These amendments may have an important bearing on resources development in the Southwest Region, and they are best discussed in connection with current air quality issues there. We turn first to stationary sources.

6 OPERATION OF STATIONARY SOURCE REGULATIONS AND A POLICY ALTERNATIVE

As discussed in chapter 5, national law endeavors to lay two types of restrictions on the discharge of residuals to the atmosphere: emission regulations and ambient standards. Emission regulations prescribe the allowable emission rate from the source, usually in relation to the amount of input material used by the source. Thus a power plant may emit some number of pounds of sulfur dioxide for each million Btus of heat input. Examples of emission regulations are the federal New Source Performance Standards (NSPSs) mentioned in chapter 5. States also have NSPSs that in many, but not all, cases are equal to the federal standards.

Under federal law, states are also required to establish compliance plans pertaining to existing sources. These involve emissions regulations which in some instances are more restrictive than federal emissions standards or which apply to existing sources not covered by these standards. For example, in the Southwest, New Mexico's new source standards are far more restrictive than the federal standards or those of other states in the region.

As contrasted with emissions standards, ambient standards specify the allowable concentrations of pollutants in the atmosphere at ground level for various time periods. The major goal of the federal Clean Air Act is to achieve ambient air standards and to prevent deterioration of air quality. Although in practice only loosely linked, if at all, to ambient conditions, emissions standards are the policy tools intended to achieve this objective. Related to the ambient standards are "nondeterioration increments." These are defined under the prevention of significant deterioration doctrine as permissible increases in the ambient air concentrations associated with new industrial sources, increases that are taken to be consistent with nondeterioration

111

of air quality. The increments are different for each geographical area classification.

Under present interpretation of the law, a geographical area may be classified as Class I, II, or III. All areas are initially classified Class II, except for areas specified Class I in the legislation. Class II designation is presumed to permit moderate growth of polluting industries. Class I areas are places such as national parks of over 6,000 acres, and wilderness areas and international parks of over 5,000 acres. In such areas, small changes in air quality may be highly detrimental and industrial facilities are presumed to be inconsistent with current land use. The 1977 Amendments to the Clean Air Act for the first time established the protection of visibility in designated Class I areas as a national goal. As we shall show, this new goal may have very far reaching implications for resource development in the Southwest region. The amendments also provided for procedures involving permits and modifications to state implementation plans to attain the goal. In addition, the administrator of the Environmental Protection Agency must report to Congress on methodologies that might be used to meet the visibility nondegradation goal.

Human activities have already contributed substantially to the reduction of visibility in the Southwest. This is dramatically illustrated by the fact that visibility readings at airports in the region improved substantially during the 1967–1968 industry-wide copper strike.[1]

Exactly how the visibility provisions of the 1977 amendments will be implemented was not clear as this was written. One indication of the potential importance of the visibility amendment to development in the region is shown in figure 6-1. It indicates the Class I nondegradation areas in the Southwest. It is the densest concentration of such areas in the nation.

To summarize, the present regulatory approach designed to achieve ambient standards is based on two main components: (1) emission restrictions under state law for old plants in addition to restrictions on new plants under federal law (or under state law) as just discussed, and (2) construction permits under state law for new plants. In the case of the latter, in principle no new plant may be constructed if its operation will result in a violation of ambient standards or if its emissions will aggravate an existing violation of ambient standards. Thus, in theory, emission regulations for existing sources (in addition to emissions control and siting considerations for new sources) are designed to meet ambient standards.

---

[1] John Trijonis and Kung Yuan, *Visibility in the Southwest: An Exploration of the Historical Data Base* (Research Triangle Park, N.C., U.S. Environmental Protection Agency, 1978).

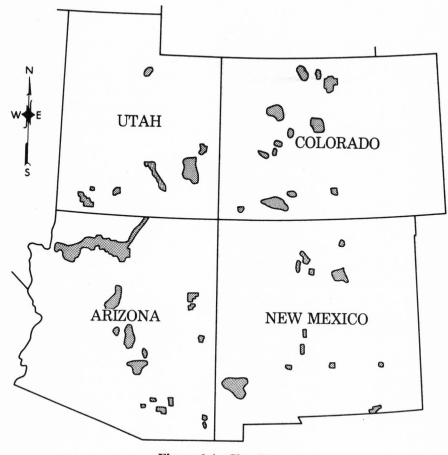

Figure 6-1. Class I areas

In practice, both technical and legal difficulties have limited effective implementation of this principle. For example, there is an important question about whether state agencies may control existing sources to levels better than ambient standards in order to permit location of other sources in the interest of economic development. In New Mexico an appellate court struck down regulations applicable to existing coal-fired power plants because the regulations were designed to provide room for new sources. The New Mexico State Supreme Court upheld the appellate court decision. A proposed amendment to the state's clean air act to deal with the question was defeated in the state legislature.

For new sources, emission regulations at the federal level (New Source Performance Standards) are supposed to represent the best available control technology for the type of source in question. However, NSPSs have rarely been revised, and since they are usually set for the worst combination of plant type and coal, frequently they do not represent the best available control technology at a given time for a source with anything but the worst of conditions.[2] These emission regulations are set without regard to plant size (the larger the plant, the greater the permissible emissions), meteorology, existing ambient air quality, or terrain. Thus, compliance with New Source Performance Standards does not guarantee compliance with ambient standards, and indeed, there is no logical connection between them. Efforts to implement NSPSs with respect to sulfur compounds have resulted in a standoff between industry and the regulators about what devices are "technically feasible."

For a source where nondeterioration is pertinent, the existing air quality is not a consideration as long as the air quality is better than the standards minus the allowable increment. In this case, the relevant question is whether or not the proposed new source plus all other new sources that were not under construction by 1975 will produce increases of the pollutant in question by more than the permissible increment.[3] In this context, any point, no matter where located, which may reasonably be expected to receive significant pollution from this source must be considered. In some cases the source may be in an area classified in one fashion while associated air quality effects may be in an area classified in another fashion. When this happens, the source is still required to meet the increment appropriate to the point where the increased concentrations are expected. Thus with Bryce Canyon classified Class I and with a hypothetical plant located on the Kaiparowits Plateau classified Class II, the plant would in principle not be permitted to produce concentrations beyond the Class I increment at Bryce Canyon.

For any new source, the effective criterion is whether or not a computer model of the distribution through space of the emission from the proposed source (called an air dispersion model) predicts a violation of the ambient standards or the nondeterioration increments. In the case of the ambient standards, actual measurements may be used to confirm the modeling predictions, but there are few locations where monitoring networks are adequate for this purpose. If the standards are predicted to be exceeded, further control may be required.

Even with existing sources, air dispersion modeling plays an important role in relating emission regulations to ambient standards. For

---

[2] See Allen V. Kneese and Michael D. Williams, "Air Quality Issues and Approaches in the Southwest," *Natural Resources Journal* vol. 19, no. 3 (July 1979).

[3] U.S. Environmental Protection Agency, Office of Transportation and Land Use Policy, "Guidelines on Reclassification of Areas Under EPA Regulations to Prevent Significant Deterioration of Air Quality" (Washington, D.C., June 1975).

point sources whose emissions are expelled far above the land surface and therefore spread out over large areas, it is costly to put enough monitors in the field and operate them for long enough periods of time to determine the actual highest short-term concentrations that may occur. Because of this, modeling is frequently used to extend monitoring results in both space and time.

Air dispersion modeling is at best a rather imprecise science. This is especially so in the mountainous West where high terrain may be affected by emissions. Taking account of other than flat terrain greatly complicates air dispersion models but predictions which do not consider high terrain may be greatly in error. Experiments by members of the Southwest Project team have shown that flat-terrain models may dramatically underestimate actual concentration.[4] For this reason, the team developed a high-terrain dispersion model to analyze regulatory alternatives. The modeling of the case study presented in the following text was accomplished prior to the passage of the 1977 Clean Air Act amendments, which designate certain areas pertinent to the analysis as Class I areas. Some of the results might be changed if this were taken into account. However, the examples are used merely to illustrate the interrelations among development, control technology, and environmental impact. As well as being complex, dispersion models have difficult data input problems. A discussion of how these were handled is found in appendix 6-A.

To examine some of the implications of various regulatory options, we have taken the San Juan Basin in northwestern New Mexico as one of our case studies. This area has large coal resources and available water. Currently there is one 2,175-megawatt (Mw) coal-fired plant (the Four Corners Power Plant) and a 660-Mw-coal-fired plant (New Mexico Public Service Company's San Juan Power Plant). The San Juan Plant will have another 1,000 Mw added to its capacity. Construction permits have been obtained for the new units. In addition, four coal gasification plants with a total output of 1,750 million cubic feet (mcf) of syngas have been proposed.[5] If constructed, the first plant, owned by WESCO (Western Coal Gasification Company), will

THE SAN JUAN BASIN EXAMPLE

---

[4] Michael D. Williams and Robert Cudney, "Predictions and Measurements of Power Plant Plume Visibility Reductions and Terrain Interactions," paper presented at the Third Symposium on Atmospheric Turbulence, Diffusion, and Air Quality, Raleigh, N.C., October 18–22, 1976 (Boston, American Meteorological Society).

[5] U.S. Department of the Interior, "Draft Environmental Impact Statement WESCO Gasification Project and Expansion of Navajo Mine by Utah International Inc., San Juan Basin, New Mexico" (Washington, D.C., December 1974); U.S. Department of the Interior, "Draft Environmental Impact Statement El Paso Coal Gasification Project, New Mexico" (Washington, D.C., July 1974).

be composed of two 250-mcf-per-day units located south and slightly west of the Four Corners plant. The regulations for WESCO I have lapsed and must be reconsidered from scratch. Although the San Juan permits are active, they were granted under the assumption that high-level sulfur dioxide (SO_2) control was required at Four Corners (the regulations struck down by the appellate court) and thus their status is not clear. A second plan consisting of two 250-mcf-per-day units is planned about 5 kilometers to the northeast. The second plant does not have a new source construction permit. There are two plant

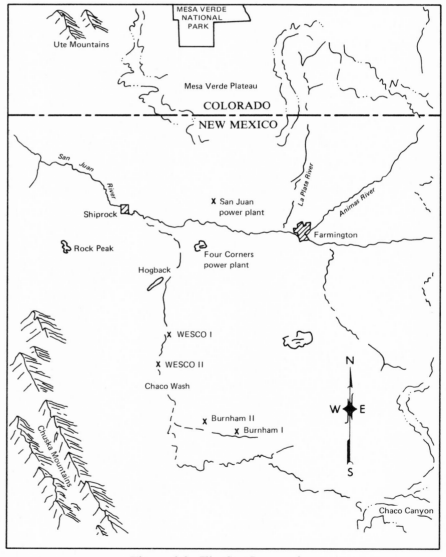

Figure 6-2. The San Juan region

sites proposed by El Paso Natural Gas Company located east of the WESCO sites. There are no construction permits granted for these sites except for small pilot units. Figure 6-2 shows pertinent features of the San Juan region together with proposed developments.

Prominent high-terrain features virtually surround the area. The Chuska mountains form a barrier on the western side of the basin which is broken only at the northern end where the San Juan River flows out. To the north, the foothills of the San Juan Mountains include the Mesa Verde Plateau, a national park. On the southern and eastern borders there is also high terrain although not as steeply rising nor as high as that which forms the western and northern boundaries.

The actual and projected situation with respect to the regulation of emissions and plant siting in the San Juan Basin is rather intricate. We therefore have decided, for reasons of space, not to include detailed discussion of the regulatory assumptions of the modeling of various alternatives in this chapter. The interested reader can find a discussion of them in appendix 6-B. In general, the initial modeling assumes that state and federal emissions standards are met by all new sources, that the sites of such sources can be effectively controlled, and that retrofitting at all existing sources can be instituted in an effective and timely manner. This is a strong set of assumptions, indeed, in view of the historical record of regulation. Figure 6-3 schematically sketches the range of physical legal assumptions currently tenable and their range of implications.

Under these assumptions we explore how much development could occur in the basin without violating existing established standards and, to the limited extent possible, what other environmental consequences related to emissions might be associated with such development. Later, we explore the situation that might prevail if existing regulations are violated.

It appears that the San Juan and Four Corners power plants, four coal gasifications plants, plus an additional seven new 2,000-Mw plants could be accommodated without violating primary ambient standards in the region. This is roughly comparable to the level of development contemplated in scenario D, our highest development scenario. The proposed WESCO II facility would have to be resited because of contributions to excessive nitrogen dioxide (NO_2) levels on the Mesa Verde Plateau. Furthermore NO_2 standards would be exceeded on the Hogback, a promontory in the region, and the Mesa Verde Plateau. Nonetheless, the new sources would make no significant contribution to the excessive levels. This analysis assumes that Four Corners' SO_2 would be cleaned up enough to meet standards at all points. If existing

When Existing Ambient Standards Are Met

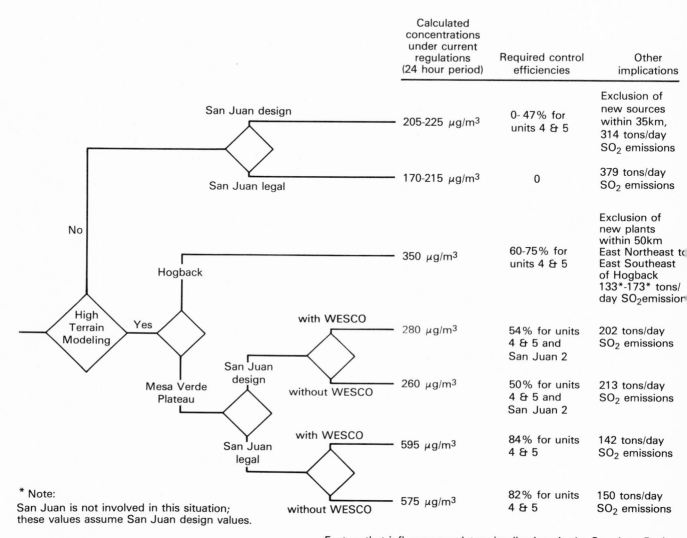

	Calculated concentrations under current regulations (24 hour period)	Required control efficiencies	Other implications
San Juan design	205-225 μg/m³	0-47% for units 4 & 5	Exclusion of new sources within 35km, 314 tons/day SO₂ emissions
San Juan legal	170-215 μg/m³	0	379 tons/day SO₂ emissions
Hogback	350 μg/m³	60-75% for units 4 & 5	Exclusion of new plants within 50km East Northeast to East Southeast of Hogback 133*-173* tons/ day SO₂emission
with WESCO	280 μg/m³	54% for units 4 & 5 and San Juan 2	202 tons/day SO₂ emissions
without WESCO	260 μg/m³	50% for units 4 & 5 and San Juan 2	213 tons/day SO₂ emissions
with WESCO	595 μg/m³	84% for units 4 & 5	142 tons/day SO₂ emissions
without WESCO	575 μg/m³	82% for units 4 & 5	150 tons/day SO₂ emissions

* Note:
San Juan is not involved in this situation; these values assume San Juan design values.

Factors that influence regulatory implications in the San Juan Basin

I. Legal assumptions
  A. Modeling is done with or without the WESCO facilities.
  B. Modeling is based on legally permissible emissions at San Juan or modeling is based on design emissions.

II. Physical assumptions
  A. With or without high terrain.
  B. If high terrain is considered, is Hogback appropriate or Mesa Verde appropriate?

Figure 6-3. Implication tree for restrictions on SO₂ emissions posed by ambient standards

emissions at this plant were permitted to continue, an effective block on development within tens of miles of the plant would be occasioned because any new source might aggravate an existing violation. As explained earlier, there is at present no legal basis for requiring the Four Corners plant to clean up.

There is one circumstance which has not been modeled that may prove very important—air stagnation. This occurs when a high pressure system is stationary over an area and one or more day's emissions may be trapped within a confined area. Light and variable winds slosh the pollutants around but they are not carried out of the basin. Unfortunately there are no generally accepted models to deal with this circumstance. But stagnation does occur and could result in severe violations of standards.[6]

Other possible implications of development include acid rain, elevated sulfate concentrations, elevated nitrate concentrations, and severe visibility reductions that would conflict with the visibility maintenance goals of the 1977 amendments. In addition, trace element deposition and contribution to downwind ozone production are also potential areas of concern. All this while existing ambient standards are being met.

With respect to visibility, the principal effects within the basin would be expected during low wind speed, stable conditions.[7] Under these circumstances, a significant plume would probably be visible as one looked across the basin. With low wind speed conditions and winds out of the west an observer looking to the NNE from the southwestern corner of the basin would be unable to see beyond the plumes. With higher wind speeds and winds out of the east, an observer near the southeastern corner and looking NNW would be able to see only about 60 kilometers (about 35 miles) as opposed to a normal pre-power plant background range of 160 kilometers (about a hundred miles). The result will be a striking brown plume as seen against a bright blue sky. Such plumes have been observed to be associated with the Navajo Power Plant. During startup when the particulate emissions are greatly increased, the adverse effects would occur under a greater variety of conditions.

---

[6] It should also be noted that the modeling assumes normal plant operation, whereas during a cold start up of operations, emissions are many times higher. Thus, the model does not capture the extreme events that could occur. Cold starts occur eighteen to twenty times per year and last eight to ten hours.

[7] A major enterprise of the Southwest Project was to develop improved methods for visibility impact analysis, including a unique computer photograph simulation technique. Because an exposition of this technique would require an extensive photographic display, we have not included it here. The interested reader should consult the list of publications resulting from the Southwest Project, which appears at the end of this book.

It is also possible that significant effects on visibility and elevated nitrate and sulfate levels may occur outside of the basin. For example, with winds out of the west in the early evening, the pollutants could probably be transported to the Rio Grande Valley with little loss of pollutants to ground uptake. Visibilities would be significantly reduced, probably to 50 to 60 kilometers or less in the valley.

When Ambient Standards Are Relaxed

So far we have been considering the case where ambient standards have been essentially met. We now consider what happens if ambient standards are relaxed and emission regulations are also relaxed, or as an equivalent, if the administrative legal process is not successful in implementing the standards. Under these conditions, the SO_2 from Four Corners would probably remain at its present 328 tons per day. If the Public Service Company of New Mexico stopped its control, the level of SO_2 emissions would probably reach 330 tons per day from the San Juan units. The coal gasification units would also have increased SO_2 emissions of perhaps 200 tons per day. In addition, another new 2,000-Mw plant would probably produce emissions of 400 tons per day of SO_2. These levels would total over 1,200 tons per day of SO_2 emissions. Maximum SO_2 concentrations would reach approximately 1,100 micrograms per cubic meter for a 24 hour average on the Mesa Verde Plateau. This is approximately *five times* the New Mexico standard and about three times the federal standard. Near Hogback the values would be 550 to 750 micrograms per cubic meter for a 24-hour average. In addition, on flat terrain, values of 335 to 420 micrograms per cubic meter of SO_2 would be expected.

Total nitrogen oxides (NO_x) emissions would probably also increase as measures required to minimize NO_x formation were dropped. This would probably mean increases in the order of 30 percent in the NO_x emissions. Nitrate levels would increase correspondingly.

Particulate emissions would also be increased. The exact level is difficult to specify, but current particulate emissions from Four Corners are about 90 tons per day as opposed to the 5 tons per day assumed in the analysis of the case where existing ambient standards were met. In the case of San Juan, because the equipment is already in or under construction and there is little energy penalty associated with it, the values would probably only increase to 5 or 6 tons per day. It is also possible that Four Corners would decide to stop using the existing scrubbers on units 1 through 3 with consequent large increases in particulate emissions. Visibility effects would extend to a greater variety of circumstances, and effects would be severe on distant locations.

Thus, large-scale energy development in the San Juan will have severely adverse effects on the environment unless both emissions and site locations are carefully and successfully controlled. Even with such controls, development keyed to existing ambient standards could cause serious environmental deterioration, especially in terms of visibility deterioration, acid rain (which could adversely affect aquatic and terrestrial life), and deposition of hazardous materials.[8]

The dramatic impact which even small (compared with ambient standards) amounts of atmospheric particulates can have on the Southwestern landscape is illustrated by the accompanying photograph (figure 6-4). The view is from Los Alamos across the Rio Grande Valley to the Sangre de Cristo mountains.

As noted above, even meeting the federal primary ambient standards in the region, much less protecting against visibility deterioration and other ill effects, would place heavy demands on the regulation process. Careful location of activities with implied land use planning and precise programs of control, including successful and timely retrofitting of existing facilities, would be required to do the job. In practice the regulatory process has been cumbersome, slow, and litigation-ridden and, rather than inducing technological innovation, has spawned endless arguments about the availability of control technologies. In light of this, it is hard to be optimistic about how successful and efficient the regulatory process can be in the region, especially if pressure to develop energy resources continues to remain strong.

Moreover, as the earlier discussion indicates, the effects on visibility, on the acidity of rainfall, and possibly on the dispersal of toxic substances of large emissions in the Southwest region may extend over great distances. These effects are only partially covered by existing legislation but they point to the need for effective control at all sources, and especially at the largest sources, if the quality of the atmosphere is to be protected.

Many students of environmental policy have concluded that the system of regulation must be changed if we are to have a more successful environmental policy.[9] The suggested way of doing this is to levy a regulatory fee on polluting residuals that are released to the environment. The idea is to make it in the economic interest of the industrial enterprise—be it an old or a new plant—to control the discharge of pollutants to the environment rather than to discharge freely as is now the case. Such a fee also has the effect of inducing the

AN ALTERNATIVE TO REGULATIONS

[8] Additional case studies further confirming these general conclusions were conducted by the Southwest Project. See Kneese and Williams, "Air Quality Issues," pp. 537–585.

[9] See Allen V. Kneese and Charles L. Schultze, *Pollution, Prices, and Public Policy* (Washington, D.C., The Brookings Institution, 1975).

Figure 6-4. Effect of small amounts of atmospheric particulates on the Southwestern landscape. *Source:* Los Alamos Scientific Laboratory, *The Atom* (Los Alamos, N.M., December 1968)

highest degree of control at those sources where control costs are lowest. Frequently these are the largest sources. At those facilities where control costs are low, it will pay to control to a high degree and avoid paying a fee on those units not discharged. Where control costs are high it will pay to control emissions to only a lesser extent. A number of studies have shown that when such a pattern of control occurs, a given ambient condition can be obtained at a much lower cost to society than when uniform requirements are laid on all dischargers to the environment.[10] Moreover, and perhaps more important, the profit will be taken out of polluting the environment and the powerful system of economic incentives will work for the environment rather than against it, as is now the case when the valuable environmental resources of the region are used at zero price.

This being the case, the states of the Southwest region should consider implementing a system of emission fees for polluting substances which are discharged into their atmospheric environment (1) to supplement efforts to enforce regulations already in effect, (2) to compensate for social costs imposed upon their citizens, (3) to provide a continuing incentive to the industries of the region to use clean technologies and to control the discharge of polluting substances which are nevertheless generated, and (4) to provide an economic incentive to develop more cost-effective control technologies.[11]

A Sulfur Emissions Fee

The best place to start is to establish emission fees for the discharge of sulfur compounds. There are two reasons for this. (1) Sulfur compounds are discharged to the Southwest's atmosphere in very large amounts by industries whose products most often are almost entirely exported, and there is evidence that they are the dominant contributor to visibility reduction as well as causing acid rain and possibly health problems.[12] Therefore, under the present system, the uncompensated social costs are imposed heavily on Southwesterners, although others enjoying the Southwest environment bear them too, while beneficial products are in most cases enjoyed by others. (2) The monitoring which would need to be done to effectively implement a discharge fee is considerably simpler for sulfur compounds than for most other polluting substances discharged to the environment.

[10] See Allen V. Kneese and Jennifer Zamora, "Quantitative Comparison of Policy Instruments for Environmental Improvement," in *Decision Making in the Environmental Protection Agency,* Volume 11b (Washington, D.C., National Academy of Sciences, National Research Council, 1977).
[11] The Navajo Tribal Council enacted a sulfur emissions fee in 1977.
[12] See Trijonis and Yuan, *Visibility*.

Before proceeding to a discussion of how such a fee could be designed and implemented, it is useful to examine whether there exists a defensible legal basis for such fees at the state level.

A State's Authority to Levy a Sulfur Emissions Fee

The threshold legal question concerning a state sulfur fee is whether the state has legal authority to make such a levy.[13] States do have such authority under the police power and probably also under the taxing authority.

First consider the police power. It is well established that the police power provides authority for a state to take steps to control air pollution. The U.S. Supreme Court has said that a state effort to combat air pollution "clearly falls within the most traditional concept of what is compendiously known as the police power."[14]

Given the authority of the state to combat air pollution, the question remains whether a regulatory sulfur emissions charge is an appropriate exercise of the police power to this end. There appears to be no reason why it would not be. For instance, the Oregon Supreme Court upheld a law setting a mandatory deposit on returnable beverage containers (in effect a charge on failure to return the containers) as a valid exercise of the state's police power. The court stated:

Selection of a reasonable means to accomplish a state purpose is clearly a legislative, not a judicial function, to which the admonitive language from *Firemen* v. *Chicago R. I. & P. R. Co., supra,* 393 U.S. at 136 and 138–9, quoted above is clearly applicable. In particular, the courts may not invalidate legislation upon the speculation that . . . additional and complementary means of accomplishing the same goal may also exist. The legislature may look to its imagination rather than to traditional methods . . . to develop suitable means of dealing with state problems, even though their methods may be unique. Each state is a laboratory for innovation and experimentation in a healthy federal system. *American Can Company* v. *Oregon Liquor Control Commission* 517 F.2d 691, 4 ELR 20218, 20221, 1973.

The question of whether the courts of the relevant state (for example, Utah) have taken a broad view of the legislature's freedom to experiment with innovative techniques under the police power has to be addressed in each individual case by someone familiar with relevant state law.

As for the taxing authority: the states, like the federal government, have the authority to lay and collect taxes. The primary pur-

---

[13] See Frederick Anderson, Allen V. Kneese, Phillip Reed, and Serge Taylor, *Environmental Improvement Through Economic Incentives* (Baltimore, Johns Hopkins University Press for Resources for the Future, 1978).
[14] *Huron Cement Co.* v. *Detroit,* 362 U.S. 440, 442 (1960).

pose of taxation is to raise revenue, but a number of federal and state taxes have been upheld that have a regulatory purpose as well. The leading federal cases in this area are *Sunshine Coal* v. *Adkins,* 310 U.S. 381 (1940) and *U.S.* v. *Sanchez,* 340 U.S. 42 (1950). New York courts upheld a tar and nicotine tax designed to create an incentive to smoke less harmful cigarettes. *Long Island Tobacco Co., Inc.* v. *Lindsay,* 348 NYS 2d 122. The Vermont Supreme Court upheld a tax on land sales designed to deter speculation in rural land. *Andrews* v. *Lathrop,* 315 A. 2d 860, 4 ELR 20571 (1973).

The question then arises, is it preferable to base the sulfur levy on the police or the taxing power. While bills which have proposed emissions fees have usually referred to the proposed fees as "taxes" (for example, the bills introduced in New Mexico in 1972 and in Montana in 1974), it appears to be preferable to set up the program as a regulatory charge rather than as a tax. The following discussion of legal constraints on state sulfur emissions charges indicates, among other things, whether the constraints apply to a tax, a regulatory fee, or both. The potential problems with the tax approach are significantly greater.

Possible Constraints

1. The constitutions of the United States and nearly all states require that excise taxes (a sulfur tax would fall into this category) must be levied uniformly within the relevant jurisdiction. The purpose is to prevent discrimination against one or more states or regions by the federal government or against one or more localities by a state government. It is not necessary that the same tax rate apply to everyone, but rather that any differences in rate must be based on reasonable, nondiscriminatory grounds.

A state scheme would not have a uniformity problem if set up as a tax so long as all sources of a given type would pay at the same rate or according to the same schedule, wherever they are located in the state.

2. Some state and local governmental functions are immune from federal taxation. This suggests that they may also be immune from state taxation. Whether this is true in a given state would have to be researched if the charge were to be a tax and were to be applied to any state or municipally owned sources. A state sulfur tax aimed only at very large sources would not affect such smaller sources. There is a related question, however, that warrants attention at the level of each state. Are there limitations in state law on the power of the state to tax public utilities? If so, there could be a problem, because power plants are very major sources of sulfur emissions.

3. Generally, tax legislation must originate in the lower house of state legislatures and in finance-oriented committees that in some states, at least, are hostile to tax programs with regulatory purposes.

4. The improper delegation of authority to the executive branch, which stems from the separation of powers doctrine, affects both tax and regulatory charge programs, but creates more serious problems for the former. Under federal law, Congress cannot delegate to an administrative agency the authority to set a tax rate. The same requirement may apply to a state legislature under state law. If so, there is some problem. It might be desirable to delegate the setting of the rate to an agency which would take into account technical and economic considerations that bear upon whether the charge will be effective in cutting emissions or internalizing external costs. Economists refer to costs (such as pollution damage) generated by an economic entity but not borne by it as "external costs."

A regulatory charge scheme would also have to clear certain delegation hurdles. So long as the charge were not held to be a criminal penalty (a problem discussed below), there is probably no reason why a legislature could not delegate to an agency the power to select the charge rate or schedule. This question should, however, be given some attention by someone familiar with the law of the relevant state. Furthermore, it is important to be sure that draft emissions charge legislation complies with state law in terms of the extent to which powers can be delegated to an agency and the standards prescribed for the exercise of those powers.

5. It is very important that the fee, whether a charge or a tax, not be set up so that a court might consider it to be a criminal penalty. Federal law prohibits Congress from enacting a penalty under the label of a tax. *U.S.* v. *Constantine,* 296 U.S. 287 (1935). A regulatory charge held to be a criminal penalty would be unconstitutional unless it provided for elaborate procedural safeguards. This is an area in which the law is not clear and should be investigated within the affected state.

It should be fairly easy to avoid the "criminal penalty" trap in drafting a charge proposal. Courts have often wrestled with the question of whether a penalty in a statute is criminal or civil in nature, and although no clear-cut rules emerge from these decisions, it is clear that a well-drafted charge system would not be considered a criminal penalty.

To avoid the criminal penalty problem, the charge rate should be set on the basis of reasonable criteria such as internalizing external costs or achieving desired levels of abatement. A charge on all emissions from a source avoids several possible problems, but a charge on emissions over a standard would not be a problem if the rate were rationally based on the costs of achieving the standard and were designed to be a reasonable approximation of the minimum necessary to achieve compliance.

6. Any emission charge legislation enacted by a state must meet due process standards in the Fourteenth Amendment to the U.S. Constitution and, in all probability, similar provisions in the state constitution. The basic due process requirement of the Fourteenth Amendment is spelled out in *Nebbia* v. *New York*, 291 U.S. 502 at 525 (1933).

The Fifth Amendment, in the field of federal activity and, the Fourteenth, as respects state action, do not prohibit governmental regulation for the public welfare. They merely condition the exertion of the admitted power by securing that the end shall be accomplished by methods consistent with due process. And the guaranty of due process, as has often been held, demands only that the law shall not be unreasonable, arbitrary or capricious, and that the means selected shall have a real and substantial relation to the object sought to be attained.

The Supreme Court has found this to be a very limited restriction on otherwise valid state action. There only needs to be some rational basis for the legislation and the court does not look into whether the particular measure enacted is the wisest or most appropriate response that is possible for the particular problem addressed. *Olsen* v. *Nebraska ex rel. Western Ref. and Bond Ass'n,* 313 U.S. 326 (1941).

A sulfur emission charge not set with complete indifference to its effect on abatement or to the external costs generated by sulfur emissions would clearly pass this test. It would be wise, however, to make sure that the charge scheme satisfies the specific due process requirements of the state constitution as well.

7. The charge (or tax) scheme must also satisfy the requirement of the Fifth Amendment (and the state constitution), that "nor shall private property be taken for public use, without just compensation." There is no property right to discharge pollutants into the air. While "taking" has not been clearly defined, the most common test is whether a regulation causes a drastic reduction in the economic value of property. Further research on the exact criteria for taking under federal and state law would be useful, since a charge might drive some marginal firms out of business.

8. The equal protection claim of the Fourteenth Amendment prohibits states from implementing legislation that discriminates unfairly against certain classes of persons (corporations included). The state constitution probably contains a similar provision. Legislation does not violate this requirement if statutory categories are based on differences that are reasonably related to the legitimate purposes for which the statute was enacted. The courts generally allow a great deal

of leeway except where particularly suspect classifications, such as race, or nationality, are involved. Any reasonable basis for a classification will be upheld. See *Allied American Co.* v. *Commissioner,* 219 Jd. 607 (1971). The Vermont Land Gains Tax, which provided for a variable tax on sales of land depending on the length of time it was held; the Oregon bottle bill, which banned nonreturnable beverage containers and required a deposit on returnables, and the Illinois sanitary ordinance levying a sewer surcharge only on industrial users were all upheld as not in violation of the equal protection clause. See *Andrews* v. *Lathrop,* 315 A.2d 860 (1973); *American Can Company* v. *Oregon Liquor Control Commission,* 517 F.2d 691 (1973) and *Chicago Allis* v. *Sanitary District,* 4 ERC 1642 (1972).

There is some possibility that a sulfur emission charge scheme that applied only to one class of source, for instance power plants, and not to smelters or the other large sources, might run afoul of the equal protection clause. Is there a rational basis for such a distinction? It appears that political feasibility alone would not suffice. The reason should relate to the aims of the statute, that is, to control sulfur pollution or internalize its costs. Thus a cut-off at a rational size limit emission would cause no problem. This is an area that needs substantial research if smelters or other very large sources are to be exempted.

9. An emission charge or tax enacted by state must not unduly interfere with interstate commerce. The basic commerce clause test is spelled out in *Pike* v. *Bruce Church, Inc.,* 397 U.S. 137 (1970).

... where the [state] statute regulates evenhandedly to effectuate a legitimate local public interest, and its effects on interstate commerce are only incidental, it will be upheld unless the burden imposed on such commerce is clearly excessive in relation to the putative local benefits. If a legitimate local purpose is found, then the question becomes one of degree. And the extent of the burden that will be tolerated will, of course, depend on the nature of the local interest involved, and on whether it could be promoted as well with a lesser impact on interstate activities.

In the case of a state sulfur emissions charge or tax, the validity of the local purpose of controlling air pollution is well recognized. The effect on interstate commerce (higher costs on sources that sell their products in other states) is incidental—that is, it is not related to the main purpose of the legislation. Thus, a court will look to see how heavily the program burdens commerce and balance that against the demonstrably strong interest in controlling sulfur emissions. The latter should prevail, especially since alternative means of achieving the goal have been tried without success and do not seem to involve any less a burden on interstate commerce. Furthermore, the main evil protected against by this application of the commerce clause—

state programs designed to favor instate business at the expense of out-of-state business—is not present. In New Mexico the charge, for instance, would apply to two large power plants both located in the state, one selling electricity in New Mexico and one selling it elsewhere. It should be noted that if the charge applied only to businesses selling out of state, there could be commerce clause problems.

10.   A final legal constraint is the emissions monitoring necessary to implement a tax or a charge. Self-monitoring requirements might violate the Fifth Amendment protection against self-incrimination. This protection does not apply to corporations nor does it "require records" for business, however. Furthermore, the protection does not apply where there are no applicable criminal sanctions for the activity about which self-monitoring information is required. It is possible that the Fourth Amendment prohibition against unreasonable searches and seizures might require warrants for administrative monitoring inspections. (This protection, unlike that against self-incrimination, applies to corporations.) While the law in this area is not entirely clear, warrants have been held to be unnecessary where administrative inspections were required as part of a valid regulatory (as opposed to penal) program and would not be effective if warrants were required. *United States* v. *Biswell,* 406 U.S. 311 (1972). This is another area where research into specific state law would be useful.

11.   The final constraint appears to apply only to a regulatory charge scheme. It is the question of whether federal legislative action in an area in which the federal government and states have concurrent authority (such as pollution control) has preempted state action. It is clear from the Clean Air Act and regulations adopted under that act that the states have not been preempted from establishing sulfur emission charge schemes. The act leaves the states a great deal of leeway to enact measures to control emissions except in specified areas not relevant here (section 116). In 40 CFR 51.1 (n)(2), the Environmental Protection Agency (EPA) included federal or state emission charges or taxes among strategies which could be used to implement federal air quality standards.

In summary, states have a clear legal basis for enacting charges systems. It is probably better to use the police power rather than taxing power as such a basis. Carefully drafted legislation should not run into legal or procedural difficulties.

How high would a charge have to be to provide a genuine incentive to control emissions? We use some examples from New Mexico to estimate the needed level of the charge.

During August 1974 the New Mexico Environmental Improvement Board held a hearing on SO_2 regulations for coal-fired power plants. An expert, Milton Beychok, who is frequently employed by industry, testified that 90 percent control of SO_2 at Four Corners would cost 4.5 to 3.7 mills per kilowatt hour, a figure which includes capital costs.[15] The higher figure amounts to 34 million dollars a year for units 4 and 5 while the lower amounts to 23 million dollars a year. Arizona Public Service Company estimates of operating costs were apparently about the same[16] as the upper value used by Beychok, and their estimates of capital costs were perhaps slightly lower. With a 70 percent load factor, total Four Corners emissions would be about 84,000 tons per year. These values could be increased slightly with higher sulfur coals (such as exist in the field being mined for the plant) or decreased with the lower sulfur coals in the field. The emission of units 4 and 5 comprise 82 percent of this total, or 68,800 tons per year. Thus a charge of 350 to 550 dollars per ton of SO_2, or 18 to 28 cents per pound of SO_2, would probably induce cleanup of units 4 and 5. Significant cleanup of units 1 through 3 would probably occur at a lower value.[17]

Arizona Public Service (APS) has fought two major court actions to prevent any cleanup. Currently they are required to clean up about 35 percent of their potential emissions from units 4 and 5 and 65 percent of the emissions from units 1 through 3. They currently remove about 40 percent of the SO_2 emissions from units 1 through 3 as a by-product to particulate control. Thus under current regulations they would emit 44,720 tons per year from units 4 and 5 and 8,866 from units 1 through 3. At 25 cents per pound this would produce revenues of 26.8 million dollars per year from Four Corners. The Environmental Protection Agency has ruled that 35 percent control on units 4 and 5 is inadequate to achieve ambient air standards. Thus, further regulations can be expected; however, based on past history it is likely that Arizona Public Service will attempt to delay enforcement of any new regulations. It should be stressed that at present levels of emissions, a regulatory fee would yield substantial revenues. But the primary purpose of a fee is not to yield revenues but to induce abatement action. Thus, the revenues from a well-designed fee system should drop drastically as companies like Arizona Public

[15] This value is taken from the transcript of the August 1974 New Mexico Environmental Improvement Board hearings on regulations 602 and 504 held in Farmington, New Mexico, p. 616.

[16] This value is from p. 775 of the transcript that is a supplement to the testimony of Thomas Woods of Arizona Public Service Company.

[17] Testimony at the hearings indicated that cost is approximately linear with control efficiency up to about 90 percent.

Service find it in their economic interest to stop fighting regulation and get on with the job of emission control.

The other major coal-fired power plant in the San Juan region is Public Service Company of New Mexico's (PSCNM) San Juan plant. Apparently the sulfur content of its coal is slightly higher than that of Arizona Public Service so that total emissions from a 1,660 Mw plant (to be completed in 1983) would be about 84,300 tons per year at a 70 percent load factor.[18] However, PSCNM is committed to control 90 percent[19] of its SO_2 emissions. Thus PSCNM would emit only 8,400 tons per year while APS under current regulations would have emissions of 53,600 tons per year. Thus PSCNM's emissions would be only 16 percent of APS's emissions. A fee of 25 cents per pound on PSCNM's San Juan plant would net only 4.2 million dollars per year. Furthermore, PSCNM is in the process of installing equipment on its units while APS continues to stall. The much lower payments which PSCNM would have to make would be an economic reward for its much stronger commitment to control while the fact that it would still have to pay for all units discharged would provide a continuing incentive to do better and some compensation for the external costs associated with even the controlled level of emissions.

The other major set of sources of sulfur emissions in the Southwest is the large copper smelters scattered through the region. In a percentage sense, high level control of sulfur emissions from smelters can be achieved much more cheaply (on a per pound basis) than is the case for power plant emissions. Mead and Bonem[20] have done some estimates of copper smelter emission fees that would produce high percentage control. At charges of 0.6¢ (6 mills) per pound of SO_2, smelter emissions would be reduced by about 60 percent (as compared with an uncontrolled situation). Charges of 0.8¢ (8 mills) per pound of SO_2 would result in reduction of emissions by about 95 percent. These estimates are in 1975 dollars. It should be pointed out that there are reasons to believe that these estimates are somewhat low; in fact, an emission charge of 1½ to 2¢ per pound of SO_2 might be required to reduce smelter emissions by 90 percent. Even if the actual charge needed were double this amount, it would still be small when compared with that needed for power plants.

---

[18] The sulfur value is reported in a booklet, "San Juan Generating Station," by the Public Service Company of New Mexico and the Tucson Gas and Electric Company, which also gives 180 tons per hour coal assumption for a 330 Mw unit out of a total of 1,660 Mw.

[19] The booklet also describes 90 percent control of SO_2.

[20] Richard Mead and Gilbert Bonem, "Residuals Management in the Copper Industry," draft (Albuquerque, N.M., University of New Mexico, Department of Economics, June 1976).

The large discrepancy between required emission charges for smelters as opposed to power plants is the result of copper smelters having very large sulfur emissions, most of which can be controlled by process changes involving the recovery of sulfuric acid. But uncontrolled emissions from a large smelter are perhaps 6 to 8 times as large as those from a 400 to 500 megawatt power station, and this means that a high level of control in percentage terms still leaves a large amount of emissions in absolute terms.

Furthermore, to achieve sulfur emission reductions above 90 to 95 percent appears to be extremely costly. For copper smelters, very high sulfur reduction levels can be achieved only by methods such as installing a two-stage sulfuric acid plant instead of a one-stage plant; or by using limestone to scrub tail gases from an acid plant. Kellogg and Henderson estimate that the removal efficiency of a single-stage acid plant on a converter might be 97.3 percent and for a two-stage acid plant, 99.3 percent.[21] But the two-stage acid plant uses 40 percent more power (electric requirements in acid plants are quite high) and requires a capital outlay at least 50 percent higher than a single-stage plant. Putting limestone scrubbing on the tail gas from an acid plant would probably involve even larger costs. Consequently, at high removal levels, costs of treatment are high, probably comparable to those from a power plant.

In summary, it appears that a regulatory fee of about 25¢ per pound of SO_2 would provide a strong incentive to both power plants and copper smelters in the Southwest to clean up to a high degree. Of course, given the rapid cost escalation that has occurred in recent years, the fee would have to be moved up over time to account for inflation.

Monitoring Emissions

A prerequisite for any sort of reasonably accurate emissions control system, whether it be based upon standards or charges, is a suitable means of monitoring emissions. There are two major questions in this respect: (1) Who will do the monitoring? and (2) Is an acceptable technology available for making the measurements?

One of the first questions that must be answered in designing a monitoring scheme is whether the initial burden of making the quantitative and qualitative measurements on which the charges are to be based will lie on the discharger or on the charging authority. When one considers the expense and the practical difficulties of allocating the entire measurement task to the government, the answer comes rather

---

[21] H. Kellogg and J. Henderson, "Energy Use in Sulfide Smelting of Copper," in J. Yannapoulos and J. Agarwal, eds., *Extractive Metallurgy of Copper* (Baltimore, American Institute of Mining Engineers, 1976).

easily. The bureaucratic burden that would result from exclusive reliance on monitoring carried out by the regulators would be enormous, but fortunately this is a problem that is easily avoided by requiring each major pollution source to monitor and report its own discharges. Moreover, equity and economic efficiency suggest that the costs of monitoring be imposed on the sources of the problem rather than on the public at large.

But would not self-reporting provide too great a temptation for underreporting? Is it realistic to expect dischargers to be completely honest in their measurements? What happens when the measurement device breaks down (either accidentally or with some outside assistance) and produces no data about pollutants? The answers to these questions are not so difficult as they may seem. To begin with, there is a precedent for the viability of a self-reporting approach in the income tax system. While it cannot be denied that there is some income tax cheating, the majority of business tax returns are entirely honest; the amount of false reporting is not nearly great enough to threaten the viability of the system. The application of a self-reporting system to charges would require occasional verification by the authorities (analogous to income tax audits) and penalties for intentional misreporting, but such provisions are hardly novel to our legal system. They might be supplemented in the environmental field by provisions for "bounties" to private citizens who developed evidence leading to the exposure of a polluter for false reporting.

Nevertheless, no matter who does the monitoring, the government agency or the discharger, someone must produce acceptable estimates of emissions. In general, the measurement of gaseous discharges from large stacks is rather tricky but instrumentation does exist, and for large sources, such as would be involved in sulfur emissions fees in the Southwest, the cost is relatively small.

One of the reasons for starting with sulfur components in the development of a regulatory fee approach is that a very simple method can be used for monitoring emissions. It is a simple matter to determine by chemical analysis the sulfur content of a fuel, and the sulfur content of the ash material and therefore the proportion going up the stack. If a plant installs abatement equipment to remove sulfur from the stack gases, it is again a relatively simple matter to determine the amount removed and deduct that from the total sulfur burned to arrive at the amount that goes up the stack.

Concluding Comments

The studies done by the Southwest Project show that air quality considerations may constitute the most severe constraint on the development of energy conversion facilities in the Southwest region. Such considerations appear more likely to set severe limitations on development than the lack of water. If the 1977 Clean Air Act Amendments, including visibility provisions, are stringently interpreted and enforced, it is hard to see how any major new development of power plants, gasification plants, and oil shale facilities could take place.

Such a situation was foreshadowed by the cancellation of the proposed Kaiparowits Project in 1976. This project was intended to use the abundant coal resources of the Kaiparowits Plateau in southern Utah to meet projected power demands in southern California. Although the efforts of the design engineers to control emissions were substantial, the amounts of airborne pollutants produced by the project would nevertheless have been large because of its awesome size.

The plant was designed to produce 3,000 megawatts of electricity, more than the power consumption of the entire state of Utah, and operating at full capacity would have consumed about 33,000 tons of coal per day and would have produced almost 2,500 tons of fly ash per day. M. D. Williams of the Southwest Project Study Team pointed out, based on his atmospheric modeling work, that, combined with existing emissions from the nearby Navajo Plant, total emissions of SO_x would have been about half of the total Los Angeles Basin emissions and about one-third of the NO_x emissions in that highly polluted area. He predicted that resulting levels of NO_x in Bryce Canyon National Park, designated Class I in the 1977 amendments, would at times have exceeded the present adverse levels in California.

There are many and complex reasons for the cancellation of the Kaiparowits Project. But prominent among them was the inability to resolve the visibility issue, especially in view of intimations that the national parks would be classified as Class I areas.

At present it appears that no power plants of such enormous scale can be contemplated in the region with present technology. Does this mean that the coal of the region cannot be used? It is too early to tell for sure but it appears that the emerging pattern is to mine coal in the region and ship it to less sensitive locations for conversion, probably in smaller facilities. For example, Nevada Power Company will transport coal by slurry pipeline to a plant near Las Vegas. Other similar projects are contemplated.

But complacency is not in order. It is not yet clear how stringently the 1977 amendments will be interpreted and enforced. Air quality in the region has been degraded substantially already by, sometimes recalcitrant, existing sources, and there are still plans on the books of the utilities for large new power plants in the region. If coal gasification and oil shale conversion develop, they will most likely be done on site, and if these processes become a significant part of the energy picture, the scale will be enormous.

In view of this, and the cumbersome and slow process which the regulation and enforcement approach to air quality management has turned out to be, the states of the region would be well advised to consider an alternative approach. Emissions fees could be used to turn the economic incentive system in favor of environmental protection. There is a clear legal basis for such an approach at the state level. The best residual to start with is sulfur emissions, both because of the mass of destructive material involved and because emissions of this substance are relatively easily monitored.

APPENDIX 6-A.
INPUT DATA FOR THE DISPERSION MODEL

A key factor in air dispersion modeling is the data put into the model. In the present study we were particularly interested in the case of stable conditions with wind moving toward high terrain. Under these circumstances, the relevant windspeed and direction is that which is at effective stack height. Effective stack height is the height above the earth at which the hot gases level off. Frequently this is 1,000 feet or more above the actual stack top. During stable conditions, wind may vary greatly in speed and direction within a few hundred feet vertically. Rarely are actual measurements of windspeed and direction available over appropriately long periods at actual effective plume height.

Typically the problem of the paucity of actual wind data is avoided through the use of scenario development. In this way, postulated combinations of windspeed, wind direction, and atmospheric stability are used. For short periods of time, three hours or less, a short-term calculation (10 minutes to one hour) is made and the result is adjusted to a three hour or one hour value with a relationship of the form [1]

$$X_T = X_{T_1} \left(\frac{T}{T_1} \right)^{-P}$$

where X_T is the average concentration of the pollutant over time T and X_{T_1} is the average concentration over time T_1. For longer periods of time where the atmospheric conditions cannot be presumed to be relatively constant, a different approach is required. In the case of a 24 hour average, a frequently used approach is to adjust the one hour average by a factor based on experience. For example, the Tennessee Valley Authority (TVA) uses a factor of five to scale from one hour to the 24 hour average.[2] This procedure applies only to those cases where there is a single isolated source.

---

[1] D.B. Turner, *Workbook of Atmospheric Dispersion Estimates* (Washington, D.C., U.S. Department of Health, Education and Welfare, 1969) p. 38.

[2] T.L. Montgomery, W.B. Norris, F.W. Thomas, and S.B. Carpenter, "A Simplified Technique Used to Evaluate Atmospheric Dispersion Emissions from Large Power Plants," *Journal of the Air Pollution Control Association* vol. 23 (May 1973) pp. 338–394.

In the analysis relevant to this volume, the concern was with concentrations that are the result of two or more sources. Thus, we developed a scenario that supplies a consistent set of winds for an entire 24 hour period. The 24 hour period is used, because frequently the limiting standard in western states is based on this time period. The desired scenario is achieved by simulating the winds that result from a circular high pressure pattern that is presumed to move through the area at a speed consistent with those found in experience.[3] The gradient wind for both speed and direction is then calculated for each 4 hour period. A drainage wind is also sometimes used to make up a small portion of the 24 hour period. In this formulation, the winds are dependent on the intensity of a pressure disturbance and the distance and direction to its center.

[3] Thomas A. Blair and Robert C. Fite, *Weather Elements—A Text in Elementary Meteorology* (Englewood Cliffs, N.J., Prentice-Hall, 1965) p. 216.

APPENDIX 6-B. ASSUMPTIONS ABOUT REGULATIONS

The actual regulatory situation with respect to air pollution in general is complex and somewhat confused. Clear-cut regulations under New Mexico state law have been established for new sources including coal-fired power plants and coal gasification facilities.[1] For coal-fired power plants, new sources are limited to 0.05 lbs per million Btu of total particulates (of less than 2 microns aerodynamic diameter). Sulfur oxide emissions are limited to 0.34 lbs per million Btu, while NO_x emissions are limited to 0.45 lbs per million Btu.

In the case of existing coal-fired power plants (all of Four Corners plus unit 2 of San Juan, which is the first one constructed), the smaller units at Four Corners must control 65 percent of the input sulfur, which corresponds to approximately 0.54 to 0.57 lbs per million Btu (based on 8,000 to 9,000 Btu per lb with 0.7 percent sulfur). At full load these emissions correspond to about 34 tons per day of SO_2. Permitted NO_x emissions are 0.7 lbs per million Btu, while particulate emissions are governed by the same restrictions as those on new sources.

For the large units at Four Corners and unit 1 at San Juan, much more restrictive regulations were adopted by the New Mexico Environmental Improvement Board. These regulations specified 85 percent control (0.23 to 0.24 lbs per million Btu based on 0.7 percent sulfur and 8,500 to 9,000 Btu per lb) by 1977, with the level rising to 90 percent in 1979 (0.15 to 0.16 lbs per million Btu). The effect of these regulations would be to reduce the existing 270 tons per day of SO_2 emissions from Four Corners units 4 and 5 to 28 tons per day by 1980.[2] However, Arizona Public

[1] New Mexico Environmental Improvement Agency, *Ambient Air Quality Standards and Air Quality Control Regulations* (Santa Fe, N.M., 1976).

[2] This value is based on the full-load coal consumption as reported in U.S. Department of Interior, "Draft Environmental Impact Statement, Proposed Modifications to the Four Corners Power Plant and Navajo Mine, New Mexico" (Washington, D.C., July 1975). With the additional assumption of 0.7 percent coal (the 1974 value was 0.197 S) p. 1.14 and p. 1.45.

Service Company (the operator of the Four Corners Power Plant) and Public Service Company of New Mexico (the operator of the San Juan Plant) sued to have the regulations struck down on the grounds that the regulation was established to provide room for additional development rather than merely meet ambient standards. The appellate court ruled in favor of the utilities, and the court was subsequently sustained by the State Supreme Court. An attempt is being made to amend the legislation to permit the New Mexico Environmental Improvement Board to pass more restrictive regulations than currently required to meet ambient standards to allow for construction of new sources.

As a result an earlier regulation specifying 1.0 lbs per million Btu remains in effect in these units. This would produce emissions of approximately 175 tons per day of SO_2 from the large units at the Four Corners Power Plant. Total SO_2 emissions from the entire facility would be 209 tons per day. Still, this less stringent regulation has been ruled by EPA as inadequate to meet federal ambient air standards. For this reason further regulatory activity is expected.

Regulations on the books restrict NO_x emissions to 0.7 lbs per million Btu and particulate emissions to the same levels as required of new sources. However, the particulate regulations will not be applied until the SO_2 situation is resolved. Currently, SO_2 emissions total 368 tons per day, while particulate emissions are approximately 90 tons per day at full load. The vast bulk of this (97 percent) is from Four Corners units 4 and 5. NO_x emissions will probably total approximately 165 tons per day.

Unit 2 of San Juan is governed by the same regulations for SO_2 as are the large units at Four Corners; however, SO_2 removal equipment is currently being installed that should have removed 90 percent of the SO_2 by the time it became operational in June 1977. Unit 1 is a new source; nonetheless, the same equipment is being installed in it. Without the planned control, the two operating units would emit 130 tons per day.[3] With the control, the units would release 13 tons per day. Without controls, the total for all units would be 330 tons per day versus 33 tons per day with controls. The control levels correspond to 0.17 lbs per million Btu. Under current regulations (that is, 1.0 lbs per million Btu for unit 2 and 0.34 lbs per million Btu for units 1, 3, and 4), emissions of 120 tons per day would be permitted.

Permitted particulate emissions for the San Juan plant would be about 10 tons per day. Actual emissions would probably be somewhat lower because high-efficiency particulate control equipment normally releases primarily very fine particulates. For this reason, 90 percent of the particulate emissions may be fine particulates so that only an average of 0.022 lbs per million Btu of total particulates will be released if the fine particulate regulation of 0.02 lbs per million Btu is met. In this case only 4.3 tons per day of particulates would be released. Current plans include a minimum of 99.5 percent control prior to entering a scrubber, which is then expected

[3] The sulfur value and coal consumption are reported in a booklet, "San Juan Generating Station" by the Public Service Company of New Mexico and the Tucson Gas and Electric Company.

to remove an additional 90 percent of the particulates.[4] This would correspond to 99.95 percent overall control and emissions of only 0.009 lbs per million Btu. For the newer units, the emissions will be further reduced through the use of more efficient first stage collectors with unit 1 having 99.8 percent as a first stage and units 3 and 4 having 99.93 percent as first stage particulate collectors.[5] Total emissions in this case would be about 1.6 tons per day.

Table 6-B-1.   Applicable Ambient Air Standards in the San Juan Basin, New Mexico

Time period	SO_2	Particulates	NO_2
3 hour	1300 $\mu g/m^3$	—	—
24 hour	0.1 ppm	150 $\mu g/m^3$	0.1 ppm
Annual	0.02 ppm	60 $\mu g/m^3$	0.05 ppm

Note: $\mu g/m^3$ = micrograms per cubic meter; ppm = parts per million.

Table 6-B-2.   Class II Increments Applicable to New Sources

Time period	SO_2	Particulate matter
3 hour maximum	700 $\mu g/m^3$	—
24 hour maximum	100 $\mu g/m^3$	30 $\mu g/m^3$
Annual mean	15 $\mu g/m^3$	10 $\mu g/m^3$

Table 6-B-3.   Class I Increments Applicable to New Sources

Time period	SO_2	Particulate matter
3 hour maximum	25 $\mu g/m^3$	—
24 hour maximum	5 $\mu g/m^3$	10 $\mu g/m^3$
Annual mean	2 $\mu g/m^3$	5 $\mu g/m^3$

Total NO_x emission would be about 98 tons per day under the regulations which restrict San Juan unit 2 to 0.7 lbs per million Btu and units 1, 3, and 4 to 0.45 lbs per million Btu.

For the first of the gasification plants, WESCO I and II, the emission would be about 2 tons per day of particulates, 35 tons per day of NO_x, and 30 tons per day of SO_x.[6]

[4] Public Service Company of New Mexico, "San Juan Unit No. 1 Briefing" (Albuquerque, N.M., April 6, 1973).

[5] Public Service Company of New Mexico, "Permit Application for San Juan Unit No. 3," January 1975.

[6] R.W. Beck and Associates, "Cumulative Air Quality Impact at Four Power and Coal Gasification Facilities in the Northwest Corner of New Mexico," U.S. Department of the Interior, Bureau of Reclamation, Upper Colorado Regional Office, Denver, Colo., May 1974, p. 22.

The first El Paso Natural Gas facility (Burnham I) would have particulate emissions of 1.4 tons per day, NO_x emissions of 8.1 tons per day, and SO_x emissions of 8.3 tons per day.[7] The second facility (Burnham II) would have particulate emissions of 2 tons per day, NO_x emissions of 11.5 tons per day, and SO_x emissions of 11.8 tons per day.

The entire area modeled is now considered Class II, except that one interpretation would hold that existing standards are being violated and thus nondeterioration does not apply. Table 6-B-1 gives the relevant ambient air standards.[8]

There is also a federal primary standard of 365 micrograms per cubic meter ($\mu g/m^3$) for 24 hour average SO_2, and 80 $\mu g/m^3$ annual arithmetic norm for SO_2. The New Mexico standard of 0.1 parts per million (ppm) corresponds to 215 $\mu g/m^3$ at 25°C and 5,500 feet. At a lower temperature, 0°C, the value would be 235 $\mu g/m^3$. These values are described as levels not to be exceeded. The NO_2 value of 0.1 ppm would be 155 $\mu g/m^3$ at 5,500 feet and 25°C and would be 170 $\mu g/m^3$ at 5,500 feet and 0°C.

In addition to the ambient air standards, nondeterioration increments will also have to be met. This is because SO_2 and particulate concentration probably did not exceed federal ambient standards over 75 percent of the country in 1974. These standards were not "previously exceeded" and nondeterioration regulations apply.[9] Under these circumstances new sources must meet the increments detailed in table 6-B-2.

These increments are relative to concentrations existing in 1974. Thus, if concentrations of SO_2 at a point in time were 250 $\mu g/m^3$ for a 24 hour average in 1974, values as high as 350 $\mu g/m^3$ would be permitted at a later date. The total of 350 could include any combination of existing and new sources. Thus, if Four Corners were responsible for a given level, say 250 $\mu g/m^3$ in 1974, and reduced its emission to the point that only 150 $\mu g/m^3$ are found at the same point in 1985, a new source or combination of new sources would be permitted to produce 200 $\mu g/m^3$ at the same point under federal nondeterioration regulations. Of course, if the 1974 concentrations were less than an increment different from the ambient standards, the total would be restricted by the ambient standards rather than the increment.

It is also possible that Mesa Verde National Park might be made Class I, and in this case the permitted increments are in table 6-B-3.

Taking account of this complex array of restrictions, we have modeled the impact of the aforementioned facilities. We have also investigated the impact of a number of new 2,000 Mw plants meeting New Mexico's new source regulations as described above. Such sources would have particulate emissions of 5 tons per day, NO_x emission of 101 tons per day, and SO_2 of 77 tons per day.

---

[7] Ibid., pp. 23–24.

[8] New Mexico Environmental Improvement Agency, *Ambient Air Quality Standards.*

[9] U.S. Environmental Protection Agency, Office of Transportation and Land Use Policy, "Guidelines on Reclassification of Areas Under EPA Regulations to Prevent Significant Deterioration of Air Quality" (Washington, D.C., June 1975).

The model used to investigate the implications of the various development scenarios is a Gaussian dispersion model using Turner dispersion parameters.[10] Limited mixing is treated through the series formulation of Bierly and Hewson as reported by Turner.[11] For high terrain and limited mixing, the effective mixing depth is given by the height of the mixing layer minus the height of the terrain, unless this value is less than a specified minimum value (usually 200 meters). For other conditions, the terrain height is subtracted from the plume height; however, the ground reflections are eliminated.[12] Thus for the case of plume height terrain, the concentrations are one-half of those which would be calculated for a ground level source. The modeling suggests a number of circumstances in which ambient standards might be exceeded.

In the case of SO_2 with Four Corners emissions of 209 tons per day, there are two circumstances of particular concern. First, with a high pressure system WNW of the Four Corners area, winds carry the plume from the Four Corners Power Plant toward a local promontory, the Hogback, southwest of the plant. From the Four Corners Plant alone, a concentration of 350 $\mu g/m^3$ for a 24 hour average would be expected. A 3 hour value from this source of 2,085 $\mu g/m^3$ would be expected. The ratio of 3 hours to 24 hours is in part an artifact of the modeling assumption. Based on field experience near the Navajo Plant, the actual value may be as much as 480 $\mu g/m^3$.[13] On this basis, the Four Corners emission would have to be reduced to 100 to 140 tons per day. If this control were applied to large units only, 60 to 75 percent control would be needed to just reach ambient standards.

If the Four Corners plants were controlled to just barely meet standards, this situation would preclude the siting of another plant within 50 kilometers or more east (from ENE to ESE) of the Hogback. This is because a new source emitting 805 grams per second, or 77 tons per day, would be expected to frequently produce concentrations of 10 $\mu g/m^3$, or more, for a 24 hour average on Hogback. Since this case would be associated with a 4 hour duration of drainage winds,[14] it might be expected to occur during the same 24 hours as the impact from the Four Corners Plant.

Another circumstance of interest is the case where a high pressure is situated at east or east southeast of the Four Corners Area. In this case, winds would carry the emissions from the Four Corners Power Plant, the WESCO units, and the San Juan Plant to approximately the same point on

[10] D.B. Turner, *Workbook of Atmospheric Dispersion Estimates* (Washington, D.C., U.S. Department of Health, Education and Welfare, 1969).

[11] Ibid., p. 36.

[12] Michael D. Williams and Robert Cudney, "Predictions and Measurements of Power Plant Plume Visibility Reductions and Terrain Interactions," paper presented at the Third Symposium on Atmospheric Turbulence, Diffusion, and Air Quality, October 18–22, 1976 (Boston, American Meteorological Society, 1976).

[13] Rockwell International, Air Monitoring Center, Meteorology Research, Inc., Systems Applications, Inc., *Navajo Generating Station Sulfur Dioxide Field Monitoring Program, Vol. I, Final Program Report* (report of contractors) (n.p., September 1975).

[14] R.W. Beck and Associates, "Cumulative Air Quality Impact," p. 14.

the Mesa Verde Plateau. In this case, of a total of 280 μg/m^3 for a 24 hour average, 76 are attributable to San Juan, 184 to Four Corners, and 20 to the WESCO facilities. The corresponding 3 hour value would be 1,210 μg/m^3. In this instance, Four Corners emissions would have to be reduced to 158 tons per day to permit all four facilities to meet standards. This would require 54 percent control on unit 1. If, instead, the control on Four Corners is limited to values which can meet standards without consideration of the proposed WESCO II facility, the Four Corners emissions would only have to be reduced to 169 tons per day. With 50 percent control of units 4 and 5, this level could be achieved.

The foregoing analysis assumes that San Juan will indeed achieve design control levels. Thus, the fact that Four Corners needs to reduce sulfur emissions by only 54 percent from units 4 and 5 is clearly the result of high level control (90 percent) applied by San Juan. The level of control assumed for San Juan is not required by existing regulations. If one uses the San Juan emissions required by law (170 tons per day), the resulting 24 hour ambient value is 595 μg/m^3, of which 391 are contributed by San Juan and 184 by Four Corners. If one chose then to make each of the Four Corners units and San Juan reduce their contribution to the ambient concentration proportional to that required to meet standards with no further control at WESCO I and II, Four Corners emissions would have to be reduced to 78 tons per day and San Juan to 64 tons per day. In the case of San Juan, this level could not be achieved without further control on units 1, 3, and 4. Then, the Four Corners 84 percent control on the large units would be adequate. This analysis assumes that the 65 percent control on units 1 through 3 would not be changed because this level is readily attainable without the major capital expenditures that higher levels of control would require. This is because existing particulate controls can be modified to provide SO$_2$ control.

Another area of concern would be near the Four Corners Power Plant, during very unstable conditions. This circumstance is a fairly frequent summer phenomenon. On certain days of this type, one could probably expect a significant contribution from San Juan. Levels of 170 to 215 μg/m^3 would be expected for 24 hours. Under these circumstances, the 0.1 ppm would correspond to about 215 μg/m^3. There might also be other contributions during the same period, such as a drainage wind down Chaco Wash from WESCO I and WESCO II. However it is difficult to assess the frequency of such a condition; that requires three different wind situations within a 24 hour period. These conditions are not inconceivable, however, and each situation is associated with what might be expected at different times of the day. It is also possible that under these conditions the Four Corners contribution could be significantly greater than that assumed here.

Under these circumstances if San Juan released its legal entitlement of 170 tons per day, the combination would lead to 205 to 255 μg/m^3 for a 24 hour average. To achieve standards with the higher value, both San Juan and Four Corners would have to reduce emissions to 83 percent of the level modeled (209 tons per day at Four Corners and 170 tons per day at San Juan). For Four Corners 4 and 5, this would imply control levels of 47 percent.

This analysis assumes only San Juan and Four Corners are involved. Instead of San Juan another source could be involved. For example, with emissions of 77 tons per day versus 33 for San Juan, a new source could produce a similar impact unless it were more than 35 kilometers away.

The foregoing suggests that if regulations were to be adopted that would ensure that standards are met, control levels of approximately 84 percent would be required of two large units at Four Corners with an overall control of 82 percent at San Juan. The latter would imply some revision of current new source regulations. If only actual design values are used at San Juan, the limitation would be 54 percent, based on the circumstance to the north of the San Juan plant. This assumes that WESCO II will be built; control of only 50 percent would be required if allowances were not made for WESCO II. In this case a 4 percent control makes the difference between building WESCO II and not building it.

The particular scenario here is one the Environmental Protection Agency has suggested in their deliberations on required control level. It is also a reasonable extrapolation of the experience at the Navajo site in Arizona. The latter is the only comprehensive measurement program which examined impact on high terrain. However, the state of New Mexico is not currently using full-terrain height models, although they have been making progress toward the use of such models. Since only state standards are involved, the option is theirs.

To meet nondeterioration Class II standards, no new source could be added which produced an additional 100 $\mu g/m^3$ over and above the concentrations produced from sources existing or under construction in 1974. In areas unaffected by Four Corners, a new plant with emissions of 77 tons per day could be located at a distance of 21 kilometers from high terrain. If the maximum were at a point significantly impacted by Four Corners, the source could be located much closer. Nonetheless, location at 21 kilometers would not permit siting any other plants on a line between the source and nearest high terrain. At a distance of 25 kilometers, the sources' contribution would be 80 percent of the increment.

The other standard of interest is the New Mexico NO_2 standard. In the case of winds traveling toward the Hogback, a maximum NO_x of 275 $\mu g/m^3$ would be expected. Experiments near the Navajo plant suggest that 88 percent of this might be in the form of NO_2, or 235 $\mu g/m^3$.[15] Thus, the standard of 120 would be exceeded. A more severe case would be with the plumes of San Juan and Four Corners traveling to the north northeast. In this case, the expected total NO_x would be 395, with 335 of it in the form of NO_2.

For particulates, there is one major question. In most areas of the West, the 24 hour secondary standard is probably exceeded by wind-blown dust. Thus, strictly speaking there should be no significant increases in particulate concentrations permitted. Normally this fact is ignored by all interested parties, industrialists, regulatory personnel, and environmentalists.

[15] Williams and Cudney, "Predictions and Measurements."

In part, this is because the highest contribution from elevated sources is not apt to be coincidental with high levels of wind-blown dust. Furthermore, with the control levels discussed here, direct fly ash emissions usually produce relatively low concentrations. For example, on the Hogback, ash concentrations would be 8 $\mu g/m^3$ for a 24 hour average. On the Mesa Verde Plateau, the levels would be 10 to 17 $\mu g/m^3$. On flat terrain near Four Corners, values of about 6 $\mu g/m^3$ would be expected. Direct ground level concentrations of total suspended particulates would probably be much more influenced by such things as waste piles, dirt roads, and strip mining. None of these is usually considered in the siting of new facilities.

Particulates could play a more important role in the case of prevention of significant deterioration. In Class II areas, the total addition is restricted to 30 $\mu g/m^3$, which could be approached in some circumstances if one considers the fly ash, the sulfates, and the nitrates. However, in the San Juan Basin, with the high existing emissions that are programmed to be cleaned up, this does not appear to be a significant restriction.

7 MOBILE SOURCES AND POLICY ALTERNATIVES AT THE STATE AND LOCAL LEVEL

In the introduction to this part of the book, we mentioned that air quality degradation in the Southwest comes from two main sources. One consists of a relatively few but very large industrial emitters. The other is a multitude of small emission sources—automotive vehicles. Unless effective action is taken, the latter as well as the former will become worse as resource development, general population growth, and economic development proceed. We now turn to a discussion of automotive emissions. In the introduction we also outlined the early history of federal legislation pertaining to mobile sources of airborne residuals. Before turning to a discussion of the specific problem in the Southwest, we fill in the more recent history of federal regulatory efforts for automotive emissions.

Prior to the passage of the Clean Air Act of 1970, federal legislation had very little effect on emissions from cars. By 1970, Congress had come to the conclusion that emissions would not be lowered to levels sufficient to protect public health unless Congress specifically established emissions standards and set tight schedules for reaching those standards. The congressional standards set in the amendments of 1970 were intended to ensure attainment of health-related air quality levels according to calculations supplied by the National Air Pollution Control Administration in the Department of Health, Education and Welfare. Later the Environmental Protection Agency was formed, and the enforcement of standards became its responsibility. The deadlines for meeting the standards set forth in the 1970 amendments were 1975 and 1976 model years, which gave some recognition to industry's need for lead time to develop the necessary control technologies and equipment. The standard for automobiles sold during the 1975 model year and thereafter called for a reduction in hydro-

145

carbon (HC) and carbon monoxide (CO) emissions of 90 percent from levels emitted by 1970 cars, which already had achieved a modest degree of control. Similarly in the 1976 model year, a 90 percent reduction in nitrogen oxide (NO_x) emissions was required compared with the 1971 standard.

Congress also authorized the administrator of the Environmental Protection Agency to grant a one year delay of these standards, which he did. Thus, the 1975 requirements for HC and CO control were pushed back to 1976, and the 1976 requirement for NO_x control was pushed back to 1977. When the administrator granted this one year delay, he set interim standards for 1975 as required by law. One set of standards was set for forty-nine states; a more stringent standard was in effect for California in 1975; and both were more lenient than the full 90 percent reduction requirement.

In June 1974, Congress amended the Clean Air Act by adopting the Energy Supply and Environmental Coordination Act. That act further delayed new car emission standards; the interim standards prescribed by the administrator were carried over through the 1976 model year; and in addition, Congress authorized the administrator to grant an additional one year delay of the HC and CO standards to model year 1977. Furthermore, Congress postponed the full 90 percent NO_x reduction requirement until the 1978 model year. The automobile industry thus received a moratorium of three years through 1978 from the initial compliance date written into the 1970 act. This came as a consequence of both legislative and administrative actions. In 1977, the Congress once again amended the Clean Air Act, further weakening standards and delaying deadlines.

As part of the hearings on new amendments to the Clean Air Act, an air pollution bill giving the automobile industry more time to meet the strict emissions standards originally set forth in the 1970 amendments was passed by both houses of Congress and signed by President Carter on August 8, 1977. The new timetable for emissions standards calls for still another extension of the current 1977 standards for two more years, followed by stricter HC and CO standards in 1980, and further tightening of the CO and NO_x standards in 1981 and beyond. The original NO_x emissions goal of 0.4 grams per mile (gpm) was retained as a research objective. The administrator of the Environmental Protection Agency subsequently used the discretion given him under the act to further delay the standards. At present (1981), further amendments to the act are being debated in Congress.

The Clean Air Act also specifies that a fine of up to $10,000 per vehicle be levied on any manufacturer who is not in compliance with the standards. This extreme penalty, which, if applied, would shut down the industry, has been one of the reasons that there has been a reluctance to enforce deadlines. Furthermore, the control that has been achieved up to this point has come at the cost of fuel penalties vis-à-vis the mileage that could be achieved presently if such controls were not implemented. If the original 1976 NO_x requirement were implemented now, it appears it could be achieved, if at all, only at the cost of substantial further fuel penalties.

Since the 1970 amendments there have been several detailed studies of government policies toward automotive emissions control. These are carefully and thoroughly reviewed in a paper by Edwin S. Mills and Lawrence J. White, "Government Policies Toward Automotive Emissions Control."[1] The authors conclude that although a certain amount of progress has been obtained in emissions control, it has been a slow and costly process involving tinkering with present technologies rather than any substantial change in the basic technology that would lead to automobile power plants inherently low in emissions. Several such technologies have been known since the 1920s and 1930s: the stratified-charge engine, Stirling and Rankine cycle engines, fuel-injection, the diesel engine, lean-burn engines, and various other devices that can be employed to regulate the combustion process more precisely. More recent developments include the use of sophisticated electronics and computer technology. The succession of gradually tighter, year-by-year requirements in the current legislation has encouraged small modifications of the standard internal combustion engine rather than more fundamental changes. There is another well-documented aspect of the current situation (see Mills and White) which is related to what has just been said, and which is very pertinent to the situation in the Southwest; that is, that automobiles meeting the test requirements of the legislation in their prototype stage do not do nearly so well on the road. In part this is because the manufactured models cannot perform as well as the prototype, but even more important is poor maintenance and tampering with control devices.

THE SITUATION IN THE SOUTHWEST

In some areas of the Southwest, both new and old cars have failed to achieve the new car standards because of the high altitude. Altitude also aggravates the production of oxidants through increased ultraviolet radiation, which speeds chemical reactions. The relatively rapid growth of Southwestern metropolitan areas tends to more than negate any gains made in emission reductions. Furthermore, the meteorology of the western mountain valleys is marked by frequent and strong inversions that further aggravate the situation. At the present time,

[1] In Ann F. Friedlaender, ed., *Approaches to Controlling Air Pollution* (Cambridge, Mass., The MIT Press, 1978).

newspapers are reporting Denver to be the second most polluted city in the country, and all the other urban places of any size in the Southwest have more or less severe smog, more or less often.

To illustrate the relatively high rate of emissions in the Southwest region, table 7-1 shows emissions from 1966–72 automobiles in use in six cities. In 1973, more than half of the 1972 vehicles in five cities failed either the HC or the CO test; only 39 percent passed both. In Denver *only 3 percent* passed both.

Table 7-1.   In-Use Emissions from 1966–72 Automobiles in Six Cities

Model year	Number of autos	Average mileage	Hydrocarbons			Carbon monoxide		
			Federal standard	Mean emissions	Estimated standard deviation of mean	Federal standard	Mean emissions	Estimated standard deviation of mean
			(—grams per mile—)			(—grams per mile—)		
1966–67	140	69,300	—	8.67	0.59	—	93.5	3.39
1966–67 Denver only	35	65,300	—	11.91	1.41	—	141.0	9.30
1968	105	59,300	5.9	6.34	0.50	50.8	63.7[a]	3.29
1968–Denver	21	51,400	5.9	6.89	0.81	50.8	101.4[a]	14.36
1969	110	50,900	5.9	4.95	0.31	50.8	64.2[a]	3.25
1969–Denver	22	46,100	5.9	5.97	0.27	50.8	97.8[a]	8.13
1970	135	37,500	3.9	5.24[a]	0.41	33.3	58.3[a]	3.30
1970–Denver	27	31,600	3.9	5.56[a]	0.30	33.3	87.5[a]	6.01
1971	150	27,300	3.9	3.95	0.18	33.3	52.8[a]	2.88
1971–Denver	30	18,200	3.9	5.19[a]	0.32	33.3	80.3[a]	6.80
1972	175	15,400	3.0	3.13	0.21	28.0	28.8[a]	1.84
1972–Denver	35	14,100	3.0	4.75[a]	0.41	28.0	80.4[a]	5.49

Note: Dashes = not applicable.
Source: Bernard Donovan and H.T. McAdams, "Automobile Exhaust Emissions Surveillance: Analysis of the FY 1973 Program" (Ann Arbor, Mich., CALSPAN for the U.S. Environmental Protection Agency, July 1975) p. 57.
[a] Significantly above the applicable federal standard at a 95 percent confidence level.

A combination of high emissions and fragile atmospheric conditions is producing a notable, and highly noticeable rapid deterioration in urban air quality in several Southwestern cities. The situation in Albuquerque (population about 300,000), while not as bad as that in larger cities in the region, is illustrative. According to the summary of recent federal primary ambient standard violations in table 7-2, the city was in violation of federal CO standards for 149 days in 1975.

Because it is believed that transportation generates approximately 95 percent of the CO emissions and 60 percent of the HC emissions in Albuquerque, the Environmental Protection Agency has required Albuquerque to implement a strategy for the control of automotive air pollution. Consequently, an air quality plan devised by TRW Industries under an Environmental Protection Agency contract addressed methods for minimizing automobile-engendered pollution. A key program involved retrofitting air pollution control devices to older cars and periodic inspections of them. Subsequent to this, however,

Table 7-2.   Primary-Standard Violations in Albuquerque
(number of days in which violations occurred)

Year	CO [a]	Ozone [b]	NO_2 [c]	Particulates
1975	149	57	0	n.a.
1974	55	8	0	4
1973	86	109	0	4

Note: n.a. = not available.

Source: Tom Busch, Air Quality Control Division, Albuquerque Environmental Health Department.

[a] In 1975 there were three stations measuring CO. In 1974 and 1973 there were two stations measuring CO.

[b] The 1975 figure is for 7 months at one station only. 1974 and 1973 figures are for 3 stations.

[c] The 1975 figure is for 6 months.

the funding for inspection stations was defeated in a bond election and the state government has shown little interest in funding the program. This leaves utilizing transportation planning to improve air quality at an impasse.

In fact, in Albuquerque, functional transportation planning (planning to meet projected demands to relieve bottlenecks) is oriented toward expanding access points and the capacity of the interstate highway I-25, which runs North–South and I-40, which runs East–West. Additional near-term highway planning includes pieces of a beltway that will eventually circumvent the presently developed portions of the city to service developing or planned scattered subdivisions in the southwestern, western, and northwestern portions of the city as well as the continuous expansion of numerous smaller scale subdivisions to the northeast. These piecemeal highway developments are a replacement for an inner beltway that was never implemented. This piecemeal policy of an outer loop will result in further encouragement of low-density sprawl, making any efficient mass transit system a virtual impossibility. This sprawl configuration is universal among the newer cities in the Southwest.

Accordingly, an important issue is whether the configuration of a Southwestern city has any major bearing on its air quality. To shed some light on this question the Southwest Project team did a case study of Albuquerque, in which six different urban forms for Albuquerque in a 21 by 19 mile study area were projected for the year 2000.[2] These urban-form scenarios were called Trend, Sprawl, Hot Spot, Checkerboard, Concentrate, and Linear.

The Trend scenario represents an attempt to continue past development patterns by means of (1) nonconstraining zoning and (2)

[2] The Albuquerque study was very detailed and is reported in Albert M. Church, Patrick Burnham, Diana Jones, Gary Peterson, Barbara Sanders, and Allen V. Kneese, *The Effect of Local Government Policy Tools on Land Use and Environmental Quality: A Case Study of Albuquerque* (Washington, D.C., U.S. Environmental Protection Agency, 1976).

fixing utilities at their 1970 level of availability. In the Sprawl scenario, public policy encourages more dispersed development through construction of a circumferential freeway and making utilities available to any site in the study area. In the Hot Spot scenario, the areas adjacent to the known air quality problem areas (the central business district, the University of New Mexico, and the regional shopping center) are zoned to prohibit further development. In the scenario termed Checkerboard, a zoning policy restricting development to alternating one square mile grids is implemented in 1970. In the Concentrate scenario, utility and zoning policies are formulated to restrict new development to an area 13 miles east to west and seven miles north to south centered on the existing urban core. The east–west Linear scenario represents the result of utility and zoning policies that restrict growth to an area 19 miles east to west and 4 miles north to south in an effort to capitalize on prevailing northerly winter winds during the inversion season.

To develop these urban forms, the forecasted population and employment growth from 1970 through 2000 were converted into land use requirements for each of eight land uses. These land use requirements were then fitted into each of the above urban forms by developing vacant square-mile grids of land using the eight land uses based on the restrictions placed on each urban-form scenario. To isolate the effects of urban form on air quality, population and employment were held constant for each scenario, as were land use requirements for five of the urban-form scenarios. In the Concentrate scenario, it was necessary to accommodate the same population and employment in a housing mix in which two-thirds of the projected growth of single-family and mobile-home units are replaced with multifamily units.

The primary air quality problems in Albuquerque consist of carbon emissions and ozone concentrations was considered because More than 50 percent of the particulate emissions come from unpaved roads. And since the number and location of unpaved roads are not in general related to urban form and land use, particulates were not considered in the Albuquerque study. Carbon monoxide and ozone were investigated, however. To compare CO and ozone concentrations in the six urban-form scenarios, first, emissions of the residuals from each grid square in the study area were estimated and then the resulting ambient concentrations were calculated. Although ozone concentrations are a complex function of nonmethane hydrocarbons, NO_x, and other elements in the atmosphere, only the relationship between hydrocarbon emissions and ozone concentrations was considered because of data limitations.

Airborne residual emissions come from point, line, or area sources. According to the 1975 emissions inventory for Albuquerque, there were no point sources of CO and less than one percent of the total

HC emissions came from point sources. It was assumed that this trend would continue in the future. Therefore, no point sources of CO or HC were considered.

In contrast, line sources (transportation) are the major source of airborne residual emissions in Albuquerque. For example, in 1975, approximately 96 percent of the CO emissions and 89 percent of the HC emissions were from transportation sources.[3] Therefore, modeling of transportation sources of emissions was of primary concern. To estimate transportation emissions from each grid square in the study area, vehicle miles traveled (VMT) and speed must be estimated, and then EPA emission factors can be applied to these estimates to calculate emissions of CO and HC.

Predictions of VMT and speed were based on a model developed by the Metropolitan Washington [D.C.] Council of Governments.[4] In that study, VMT was predicted by using regression analysis techniques. A similar model was applied to Albuquerque data to derive an equation estimating average daily VMT per grid square.

Area source emissions (emissions from space heating, neighborhood fuel marketing, fireplaces, and the like) of CO and HC from each grid square were based on per capita emission factors. These factors were derived by dividing the emissions from all nonpoint stationary sources of CO and HC in Albuquerque in 1975 by the corresponding population. The average population for the land use type in each grid was then multiplied by the per capita factor to derive area source emissions per grid square. It should be noted that these factors implicitly assume that adequate supplies of natural gas will be available in 2000 because natural gas is the primary fuel used in domestic and commercial heating in Albuquerque.

After summing emissions from line and area sources for each grid square, ambient concentrations were derived for ozone and CO. Because until now no generally applicable sophisticated dispersion model has been developed for determining ozone concentrations, ambient concentrations of ozone were calculated by using a simple rollback model applied to a central location (that is, a model which assumes concentrations are proportional to emissions). The climatological dispersion model (CDM) was used for determining CO concentrations at existing "hot spots" and at the center point in other grid squares.[5]

---

[3] Albuquerque Environmental Health Department, Air Quality Division, "1975 Emission Inventory" (Albuquerque, N.M., July 1, 1976).

[4] Sidney D. Berwager and George V. Wichstrom, *Estimating Auto Emissions of Alternative Transportation Systems,* DOT-05-2004 (Washington, D.C., U.S. Department of Transportation, April 1972).

[5] Adrian D. Busse and John R. Zimmerman, *User's Guide for the Climatological Dispersion Model* (Research Triangle Park, N.C., U.S. Environmental Protection Agency, 1973).

Comparison of air quality in the six urban-form scenarios was based on the ozone concentration, CO concentrations at existing problem areas, and a population exposure index for CO. The population exposure index was calculated by weighting the CO concentration in the center of each grid square by the average population in that grid square and summing over all grid squares in the study area.

Taking the Trend scenario as the standard of measure for comparing the population exposure index, the percentage of Trend's index was for Linear about 80 percent, for Concentrate about 80 percent, for Checkerboard about 90 percent, for Hot Spot nearly 95 percent, and for Sprawl 100 percent. The estimates of ozone concentrations were roughly similar to the population exposure index in their ranking and percentage differences.

Critical air quality problems will most likely remain at the "hot spot" areas existing in 1975: the regional shopping center, the central business district, and the University of New Mexico. Based on the climatological dispersion model, the only strong relative improvements in CO concentrations in these areas came from the Concentrate scenario. This result is significant and is confirmed by the population exposure index and the ozone concentration rankings of the various scenarios. Although the Linear scenario ranks close to the Concentrate scenario, it also represents a concentrated rather than sprawled development. Overall, then, from the standpoint of air quality, a more concentrated development appears to be the best form for future growth in Albuquerque.

It also appears that urban forms which encourage less travel, such as Concentrate or Linear, lead to fewer vehicle emissions and better air quality. It should be noted that these results are based on the air shed characteristics of Albuquerque and may not apply to other areas. But with respect to air quality, many cities in the Southwest do have similar characteristics.

Based on the above results, the main policy implication of the Albuquerque study is that air quality should be considered in land use planning for cities in which transportation is the major source of airborne residuals. But the only large improvements result from radical restructurings that it may be impossible to accomplish or that may not be desirable for other reasons. The chief hope for maintaining or improving air quality in the urban areas of the Southwest remains emissions reduction. The problem of poor emission performance from vehicles already in service is a central one in this regard.

AN ALTERNATIVE TO THE PRESENT FEDERAL APPROACH

How then to solve the two problems of ensuring the maintenance of automobile and emission control equipment and stimulating new, less polluting, automotive technology?

Fifteen years ago economists at the Rand Corporation proposed an answer which, administrative and income distribution problems aside, appears to be the economically ideal solution.[6] The proposal is that cars in service be tested periodically and assigned a smog rating indicated by a seal or coded device attached to the car. Then, when the driver purchases gasoline, he would pay a fee over and above the basic gasoline tax that would vary with this smog rating. Placing the charge on the final user of the car has the advantage that it stimulates responses all along the chain from driver to the manufacturer. Individuals could reduce their smog tax bill in several ways:

1. Tuning or overhauling the engine to reduce emissions and obtain better gas mileage is an economical alternative to paying the tax.

2. Driving fewer miles per year by living closer to places of employment, using mass transit, or participating in car pools are clear options. Standards based on emissions per vehicle mile do nothing whatsoever about miles driven, but a smog fee could affect these extremely important variables as well as emissions per mile.

3. Install control devices on older cars. In a 1970 market test, General Motors offered control kits for pre-1968 models at about $20.00 installed, but no one bought them. Clearly it was not sensible to expect anyone to make this investment because without assurance that others would also make it, any one person's effect on the situation would be negligible. A smog fee would introduce a new persuasive element into this calculation.

It is unlikely and, for various reasons, perhaps undesirable, that a pure full-scale smog fee system of the type proposed will ever be enacted. But in the Congress there is evidence of strong interest in the use of economic incentives for automotive emissions control, led by senators from the Southwest region, and there are initiatives the states could effectively take along these lines.

As a result of frustration with the present approach to automotive emissions control, an effort was made to embody some sort of emission fee on new cars in the 1977 Clean Air Act Amendments.[7] The attempt failed. In any case it would not have helped with the problems of existing vehicles. The states have a real opportunity to innovate in this area, a crucially important one to the major urban places in the Southwest.

---

[6] D.N. Fort, and coauthors, "Proposal for a Smog Tax" reprinted in tax recommendations of the President, hearings before the House Committee on Ways and Means, 91st Cong., 2 sess. (1970) pp. 369–370.

[7] Letter from senators Peter Domenici and Gary Hart to President Jimmy Carter, January 5, 1977.

WHAT THE STATES
COULD DO

As a first step the states could levy an emissions fee on new cars that would amount to several hundred dollars on the dirtiest models currently being sold. This fee would be payable at the time of registration and would be levied on average emissions of a particular vehicle type as determined by the testing of prototype fleets that the Environmental Protection Agency is doing now. The fee would be based on emissions of hydrocarbons, carbon monoxide, and oxides of nitrogen. Mills and White's report, based on rough damages data and an assessment of control costs, suggests that the total fee, based on a per-unit-of-emissions assessment, for uncontrolled cars in a high damage area should be about $900.[8] Applying the same fee schedule to an automobile meeting the 1975 interim standards would yield about $400. If emissions are less than these standards, the total fee would be proportionately lower. Such a policy would encourage persons to buy the lower emissions models and give a powerful marketing advantage to those producers able to beat the federal standards. It should be possible to control the bootlegging of new cars from other states through the registration process.

For the existing population of cars, a pure smog fee applied to all vehicles based on tests performed at the time of vehicle inspection and taking into account the mileage driven (a variant of the smog tax discussed above), would, as mentioned, have some highly desirable features. But there are some potential weaknesses too. First, there may be a substantial time and inconvenience cost to automobile users in administering a program of fees on automobiles already in use. Second, since it is probably true that poorer people drive older, more polluting cars, the effect of fees on the automobile users will be at least somewhat regressive with respect to income. There are several ways one could attempt to come to grips with these problems in framing legislation. One alternative to direct fees on automobiles in use would be to levy a pollution surcharge on the sale of gasoline and provide rebates to those who offer their vehicles for inspection and meet emission standards specified for cars of a particular age. A surcharge of, say, 10¢ a gallon, on the average would yield revenues of $100 per vehicle. Since not all automobile owners would find the time and inconvenience cost of bringing cars in, keeping necessary documents, and so forth worth the rebate, the actual amount available for rebates would be in excess of a $100 per car, minus administrative costs. This would cover the cost of major tune-ups and, with a time perspective of several years, major overhauls. It could also result in significant gasoline savings that might more than recover the surcharge paid. The noncoercive aspect of this proposal is attractive.

---

[8] Mills and White, "Government Policies."

Since in general it would seem that poorer people would be more willing to incur the time and inconvenience cost of bringing their cars in for inspection, the program would most probably be progressive in its cost incidence vis-à-vis a pure smog charge. The problem of the oldest cars that cannot be brought into compliance without a very large expenditure of funds could be handled by initially making the emission standard zero for cars beyond some age, say, eight years. But the age of cars to which standards apply should be increased progressively to encourage emissions reduction techniques that have high durability.

In addition, an emission fee based on a somewhat reduced scale from that applicable to new cars could be levied at the time of sale of every used car from an organized dealership, the purpose being to make it economically worthwhile for dealers to sell only cars that have been tuned and repaired. Moreover, such a fee program would confer higher resale value on cars containing long-lasting control technologies such as stratified-charge engines.

SUMMARY

The Southwest region faces a particularly difficult problem of air quality degradation. The two main sources of emissions are large heavy industries and automotive vehicles. In both cases, regulatory approaches based on federal and state law have met with only limited success in the region. In both cases, there are significant opportunities for the states to take major initiatives to change the system of economic incentives that now makes pollution profitable. Failure to do this implies to us that the atmospheric quality of the region will become progressively worse. If rapid development of the extractive industries occurs, it will become drastically worse.

8 EFFECTS OF ENERGY DEVELOPMENT ON RECREATIONAL RESOURCES

Energy development affects the land and associated recreational resources in many ways. Strip mining disfigures the land while it is in progress and the quality of the soil and the landscape may or may not be restorable. Transmission corridors require rights of way, and the low level electromagnetic radiation associated with them may injure plants and animals. Energy conversion facilities require sites that have effects on the landscape and displace other land uses. New service roads and other transportation corridors must often be provided.

The most neglected but perhaps most important land use effects of development, however, are related to the population shifts that accompany it. Clearly, land is needed for construction of homes and urban infrastructure. But the most destructive impacts of all may occur through increased population pressure on the limited amount of prime recreation land found in the neighborhood of the energy resources of the Southwest. To obtain some idea of the size of the problems that might occur, the Southwest team studied the potential effect of energy development on recreation areas in the Southwest.

POPULATION GROWTH AND THE DEMAND FOR OUTDOOR RECREATION

With the exception of substantial open space in which to operate dune buggies and trail bikes, the specific areas where energy resource development is likely to take place offer little in the way of outdoor recreation opportunities. The new residents will thus be drawn to the nearby mountain regions for camping, hiking, hunting, fishing, skiing, and other outdoor activities.

For example, it can be expected that a significant segment of the population that would be associated with the proposed coal gasification plants near Farmington, New Mexico, would travel frequently

157

to the more appealing surroundings of the Colorado mountains, especially to the unusually beautiful San Juan range.

The magnitude of these additional environmental pressures can be placed in perspective through the application of a recreation usage projection model developed by the Southwest Project study team. The model is specifically designed to permit projection of the effect on visitation at existing recreation sites of population migration into the Southwest. It is an adaptation of the well known Clawson-Hotelling methodology which assumes that travel cost acts as a proxy to the individual for the opportunity cost (price) of the recreational experience.[1]

The actual empirical equation adopted for this study is of the following form

$$\ln \left[VD_i \right] = B_0 + B_1 S_i + B_2 S_i^2 + B_3 C_i + B_4 C_i^2 + B_5 P_i + B_c T_i + B_7 I_i + B_8 D_i$$

In the equation i designates a specific U.S. Forest Service site (of which there are thirty-one in the sample studied). VD_i, the dependent variable, designates visitor days at recreation site i. S_i is the size of site i in acres; C_i is a measure of congestion at site i and is defined to be visitor days at site i lagged one year divided by the acreage in site i. P_i is the population per square mile of the county containing recreation site i; T_i is the average daily temperature at the weather recording station nearest recreation site i; I_i is the travel distance index defined as the sum of the population of counties within 100 miles of recreation site i divided by the distance from each particular county to the site; and D_i is a dummy variable equal to one for campsites and equal to zero for all other classifications of recreation sites (picnic areas, observation points, and boating lakes).

To illustrate the potential effect of an increase in the demand for outdoor recreation resulting from energy resource development, population estimates for energy resource development scenario C (as described in chapter 2) were used. Table 8-1 summarizes the level of energy resource development in the Four Corners States assumed under scenario C for the year 2000.

The specific facilities included in this scenario are in part based on actual planned facilities as reported by the industry in the Western Systems Coordinating Council's 1976 annual reply to the Federal Power Commission, Docket R-362. Sites for the additional electrical generating capacity and coal gasification plants, uranium oxides

---

[1] Marion Clawson and Jack L. Knetsch, *Economics of Outdoor Recreation* (Baltimore, Johns Hopkins University Press for Resources for the Future, 1967).

Table 8-1. Scenario C Energy Resource Development in the Four Corners States

Development	Projected through the year 2000
Electrical generating capacity	67,300 megawatts of electricity
Coal gasification plants	+16 (250 $\times$ 10^6 ft^3/day capacity plants)
U$_3$O$_8$ mining and milling	+24 (2,000 ton/year operations)
Oil shale plants	+20 (50 $\times$ 10^3 bbls/day plants)

Source: Alfred L. Parker, "Energy Resource Development Scenarios for the Four Corners Region," mimeo (Albuquerque, N.M., University of New Mexico, September 1978).

(U$_3$O$_8$) mining and milling operations, and oil shale plants were selected according to resource availability, market, and environmental considerations. The projected locations of these energy resource developments are indicated in figure 8-1.

The Southwest Regional Model developed by the project and described in chapter 2 was used to project population in selected years under scenario C for each of the Four Corners States. Projections for the year 2000 for scenario C are recorded in table 8-2 and were used, together with estimates of the employment associated with specific energy resource development projects, to construct county population projections.

The figures in table 8-3, which indicate the employment associated with typical energy projects, were used as the base for the projection of employment associated with energy resource development projects included in scenario C. Employment figures used in the construction of an estimate of population associated with each energy project in scenario C are shown in table 8-4.

Table 8-2. Scenario C Population Projections

State	1975[a]	2000
Arizona	2,069,000	3,734,000
Colorado	2,362,000	3,336,000
New Mexico	1,105,000	1,932,000
Utah	1,141,000	2,473,000

Source: Jeffrey D. Baxter and Mark Evans, Southwest Regional Model, developed in the Economics Department under the general supervision of Lee Brown, University of New Mexico, Albuquerque, New Mexico, 1977.

[a] Population figures for 1975 are outputs of the model, not actual data. These figures are somewhat lower than what actually prevailed for two reasons. First, control totals for 1975 reflect the national recession, but the Southwest's economy was to some extent counter to the nation's cycle. The economic model has a long-run trends and perspectives orientation, and does not attempt to represent cyclical shifts in trade coefficients. Second, immigration unrelated to economic activity is higher than anticipated by assumptions made within the demographic model.

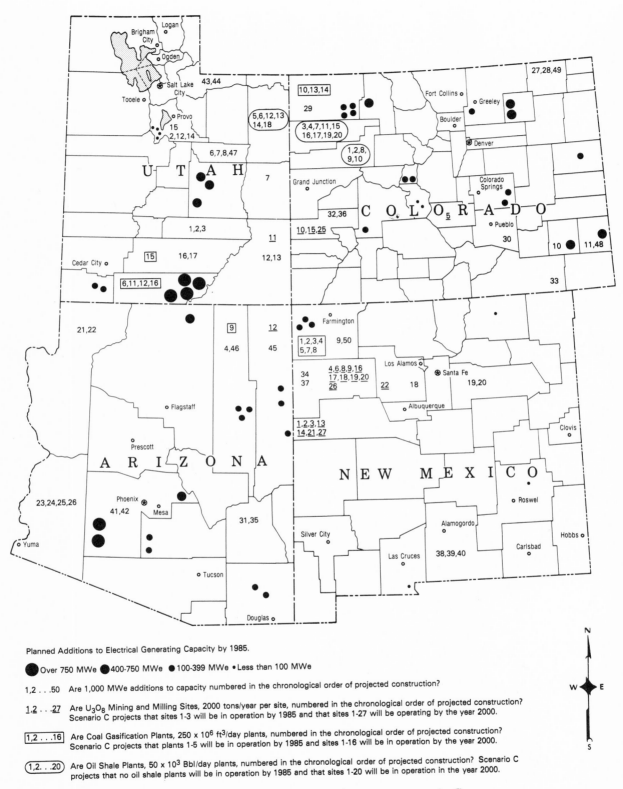

Figure 8-1. Planned and projected energy resource development—scenario C

Table 8-3. Employment Associated with Typical Energy Projects

Project	Size	Employment Peak force construction	Employment Operating force
Electric generating plant[a]	1,000 megawatts	1,500	300
Coal gasification plant[b] (includes mining)	785 million ft³/day	6,000	2,831
Uranium mining and milling[c]	10 million lbs/yr	n.a.	2,500
Oil shale plant[d]	50 × 10³ bbl/day	n.a.	1,200

Note: n.a. = not available.

[a] Approximate figures for San Juan generating plant expansion from "Status Report on Natural Resource Development Projects With Major Potential Impacts Upon San Juan County, New Mexico," prepared by staff of the secretary for the Southwest Region, Department of the Interior, Albuquerque, New Mexico, October 1975, p. 22.

[b] Figures for El Paso coal gasification complex in New Mexico from Ibid, p. 9.

[c] Estimate based on data from U.S. Energy Research and Development Administration.

[d] Estimate based on data from U.S. Federal Energy Administration, *Project Independence Blueprint Final Task Force Report, Labor Report* (Washington, D.C., November 1974) pp. 100–101.

The construction of an estimate of the population associated with an energy project is illustrated in simplified form in figure 8-2. The illustration assumes that all of the operating work force comes from outside of the community, that 85 percent will have a family (with an average family size of 3.7 persons), and that 15 percent will

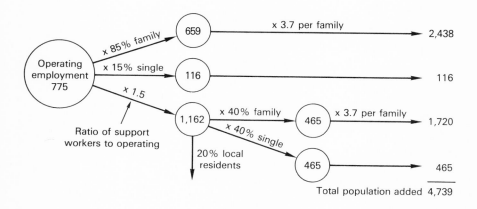

Figure 8-2. Employment and population added by operations. *Source:* U.S. Department of Housing and Urban Development, *Rapid Growth from Energy Projects, Ideas for State and Local Action: A Program Guide* (Washington, D.C., 1976) p. 6

Table 8-4. Scenario C Additions to Population Associated with Energy Resource Development Projects

State	County	Name and type of project	Size (MWe)	Operating employment by 2000	Addition to population by 2000[a]
Arizona	Apache	Coronado #1	350	309	1,508
		Coronado #2	350		
		Springerville 1	330		
		2 1,000 MWe	2,000	600	2,928
		Uranium Mining & Milling			
		1 2,000 ton/year		1,000	4,880
	Cochise	Apache Steam 2	175	105	512
		Apache Steam 3	175		
	Coconino	Navajo 3	750	225	1,098
	Graham	2 1,000 MWe	2,000	600	2,928
	Maricopa	West Phoenix CC1,2,3	225	829	4,048
		Palo Verde #1	1,270		
		Palo Verde #2	1,270		
		2 1,000 MWe	2,000	600	2,928
	Mohave	2 1,000 MWe	2,000	600	2,928
	Navajo	Cholla 2	250	255	1,244
		Cholla 3	250		
		Cholla 4	250		
		2 1,000 MWe plants	2,000	600	2,928
		Coal gasification plants			
		1 250 × 10[6] ft[3]/day plant		900	4,392
	Pinal	Montezuma #1	250	150	732
		Montezuma #2	250		
	Yuma	Axis Ct. 1	25	8	37
		4 1,000 MWe plants	4,000	1,200	5,856
Colorado	Bent	Southeastern 1	500	150	732
		1 1,000 MWe plants	1,000	300	1,464
	El Paso	Ray D. Nixon 1	200	120	586
		Ray D. Nixon 2	200		
	Fremont	Uranium Mining & Milling			
		1 2,000 ton/year projects		1,000	4,880
	Garfield	Oil shale plants			
		5 50 × 10[3] bbls/day Plants		6,000	29,280
	Gunnison	Morrow Point 2	69	21	101
	Kit Carson	Burlington 1, 2	100	30	146
	Lake	Mount Elbert 1	100	60	293
		Mount Elbert 2	100		
	Las Animas	1 1,000 MWe plant	1,000	300	1,464
	Logan	3 1,000 MWe plants	3,000	900	4,392
	Moffat	Craig 1	380	456	2,225
		Craig 2	380		
		Craig 3	380		
		Craig 4	380		
		1 1,000 MWe plant	1,000	300	1,464
		Coal gasification plants			
		3 250 × 10[6] ft[3]/day plants		2,700	13,176
	Montrose	Crystal 1	32	10	47
		2 1,000 MWe plants	2,000	600	2,928
		Uranium Mining and Milling			
		3 2,000 ton/year		3,000	14,640
	Morgan	Pawnee 1	500	300	1,464
		Pawnee 2	500		
	Prowers	Southeastern 2	500	150	732
		2 1,000 MWe plants	2,000	600	2,928
	Pueblo	1 1,000 MWe plant	1,000	300	1,464
	Rio Blanco	Oil Shale Plants			
		9 50 × 10[3] bbls/day plants		10,800	52,704

continued

Table 8-4. (continued)

State	County	Name and type of project	Size (MWe)	Operating employment by 2000	Addition to population by 2000 [a]
New Mexico	Routt	Hayden 2	250	75	366
	Weld	Ft. St. Vrain	330	99	483
	Chavez	Maddox 3	66	20	97
	Colfax	Plains Fossil Unit	180	54	264
	Dona Ana	EPE Gas Turbine	100	30	146
	McKinley	Uranium Mining & Milling			
		10 2,000 ton/year Project		10,000	48,800
		2 1,000 MWe plants	2,000	600	2,928
	Otero	3 1,000 MWe plants	3,000	900	4,392
	Sandoval	1 1,000 MWe plant	1,000	300	1,464
		Uranium Mining & Milling			
		1 2,000 ton/year project		1,000	4,880
	San Juan	San Juan 1	326		
		San Juan 3	466	377	1,842
		San Juan 4	466		
		Coal gasification plants			
		5 250 × 10⁶ ft³/day plants		4,500	21,960
		2 250 × 10⁶ ft³/day plants		1,800	8,784
		Uranium Mining & Milling			
		2 2,000 ton/year projects		2,000	9,760
		2 1,000 MWe plants	2,000	600	2,928
	San Miguel	2 1,000 MWe plants	2,000	600	2,928
	Valencia	Uranium Mining & Milling			
		3 2,000 ton/year plants		3,000	14,640
		4 2,000 ton/year plants		4,000	19,520
Utah	Carbon	4 1,000 MWe plants	4,000	1,200	5,856
	Emery	Huntington Cyn. 1	400		
		Emery 1	400	360	1,757
		Emery 2	400		
	Garfield	2 1,000 MWe plants	2,000	600	2,928
		Coal gasification plants			
		1 250 × 10⁶ ft³/day plant		900	4,392
	Kane	Kaiparowits 1	775		
		Kaiparowits 2	775	930	4,538
		Kaiparowits 3	775		
		Kaiparowits 4	775		
		Coal degasification plants			
		4 250 × 10⁶ ft³/day plants		3,600	17,568
	San Juan	2 1,000 MWe plants	2,000	600	2,928
		Uranium Mining & Milling			
		1 2,000 ton/year plant		1,000	4,880
	Summitt	2 1,000 MWe plants	2,000	600	2,928
	Unitah	Oil Shale Plants			
		6 50 × 10³ bbls/day plants		7,200	35,136
	Utah	Syar	8		
		Dyne	33		
		Sixth Water 1	45	39	192
		Sixth Water 2	45		
		2 1,000 MWe plants	2,000	600	2,928
	Washington	Warner Valley 1	250		
		Warner Valley 2	250	150	732
	Wayne	3 1,000 MWe plants	3,000 M	900	4,342

Note: MWe = megawatts of electricty.

[a] Addition to population = (.80 × Operating Employment) × 6.1. Estimates based on data from U.S. Department of Housing and Urban Development, *Rapid Growth From Energy Projects, Ideas For State and Local Action, A Program Guide* (Washington, D.C., 1976) p. 6.

Table 8-5.   Scenario C Population Estimates for Affected Counties

State	County (1)	Population 1975[a] (2)	Population estimate by 2000[b] (3)	Population change associated with energy development by 2000[c] (4)	Percent population increase associated with energy development by 2000[d] (5)
Arizona		2,069,000	3,734,000	34,069	2.0
	Apache	38,144	76,924	4,436	11.4
	Cochise	69,125	102,821	512	1.5
	Coconino	60,844	126,258	1,098	1.7
	Graham	18,793	32,841	2,928	20.8
	Maricopa	1,132,698	3,114,276	6,976	0.7
	Mohave	34,795	68,076	2,928	8.8
	Navajo	53,960	114,449	8,564	14.2
	Pinal	81,685	114,328	732	2.2
	Yuma	65,403	106,276	5,893	14.4
Colorado		2,362,000	3,336,000	137,959	14.2
	Bent	6,152	8,869	2,196	80.8
	El Paso	266,670	402,747	586	0.4
	Fremont	24,234	37,933	4,880	35.6
	Garfield	16,218	52,924	29,280	79.8
	Gunnison	9,041	11,668	101	3.8
	Kit Carson	7,084	7,571	146	30.0
	Lake	7,550	7,514	293	n.a.
	Las Animas	14,634	19,078	1,464	32.9
	Logan	17,616	29,549	4,392	36.8
	Moffat	7,643	24,791	16,865	98.3
	Montrose	18,735	36,735	17,615	97.9
	Morgan	19,947	30,692	1,464	13.6
	Prowers	12,770	23,158	3,660	35.2
	Pueblo	116,884	153,307	1,464	4.0
	Rio Blanco	4,847	58,198	52,704	98.8
	Routt	9,228	11,723	366	14.7
	Weld	100,386	151,724	483	1.5

continued

not have a family. For each member of the operating work force, 1.5 support, or secondary, workers are required. Forty percent of these support workers will have families, 40 percent will not, and 20 percent will already be local residents.

A ratio of population to operating employment of 6.1 to 1 was used in making estimates of the effect of energy resource development (specifically scenario C) on the population of affected counties. At the same time, because this standard employment multiplier is higher than that reported by the University of New Mexico Bureau of Business and Economic Research for the region and because of the relatively high unemployment rate in those counties to be most directly affected, the population projections associated with energy resource development projects have been adjusted downward. It is believed that this downward adjustment, necessary to compensate for these two regional factors, has resulted in a more accurate indicator of the demographic effect of energy resource development scenario C.

The resulting estimates of additions to population associated with specific energy projects are shown in table 8-4. Estimates of additions

Table 8-5.   (continued)

State	County (1)	Population 1975 [a] (2)	Population estimate by 2000 [b] (3)	Population change associated with energy development by 2000 [c] (4)	Percent population increase associated with energy development by 2000 [d] (5)
New Mexico		1,105,000	1,932,000	145,333	14.9
	Chavez	44,746	57,331	97	0.7
	Colfax	12,563	21,742	264	2.9
	Dona Ana	79,471	136,547	146	0.3
	McKinley	49,438	168,588	51,728	43.4
	Otero	39,641	46,170	4,392	67.3
	Sandoval	21,703	49,421	6,344	22.9
	San Juan	63,052	185,262	45,274	37.0
	San Miguel	22,886	41,331	2,928	15.9
	Valencia	44,174	108,118	34,160	53.4
Utah		1,141,000	2,473,000	91,155	6.8
	Carbon	17,867	50,752	5,856	17.8
	Emery	6,334	11,815	1,757	32.1
	Garfield	3,214	12,324	7,320	80.4
	Kane	3,309	29,901	22,106	83.1
	San Juan	10,588	39,040	7,808	27.4
	Summitt	6,239	13,635	2,928	39.6
	Unitah	16,543	114,942	35,136	35.7
	Utah	156,923	418,473	3,120	1.2
	Washington	16,259	53,279	732	2.0
	Wayne	1,513	6,272	4,392	92.3
Four-state total		6,677,000	11,475,000	408,516	8.5

[a] Population figures for 1975 are outputs of the model, not actual data. These figures are somewhat lower than actually prevailed for two reasons. First, control totals for 1975 reflect the national recession, but the Southwest's economy was to some extent counter to the nation's cycle. The economic model has a long-run trends and perspectives orientation, and does not attempt to represent cyclical shifts in trade coefficients. Second, immigration unrelated to economic activity is higher than anticipated by assumptions made within the demographic model.

[b] Estimates based on Southwest regional model projections for scenario C. The Southwest regional model, developed by Mark Evans and Jeffrey Baxter under the general supervision of Lee Brown, Department of Economics, University of New Mexico, Albuquerque, New Mexico, 1977. The development of this model was funded by research projects sponsored by Resources for the Future and the National Science Foundation.

[c] From table 8-4 in the present book.

[d] Column 4 ÷ (Column 3 − Column 2).

to population associated with energy resource development for each of the affected counties are summarized in table 8-5. These figures suggest the importance of energy development for the region. The projections provided by the Southwest regional model reflect assumptions concerning industrial growth (including energy resource development), productivity growth rates, and demographic assumptions (for example, birth rates, mortality rates, labor force participation rates, and migration relationships).

Projections for the year 2000 indicate that growth in population associated with energy resource development under scenario C represents only 8.5 percent of the growth in population for the four state area, but more than 14 percent of the growth in population in both Colorado and New Mexico. Quite significant additions to population associated with energy resource development are found in Garfield, Moffat, Montrose, and Rio Blanco counties in Colorado; McKinley, San Juan, and Valencia counties in New Mexico; and Kane and Unitah counties in Utah. These are counties that may be expected to experience boomtowns, a subject to which we return in chapter 9. Chavez county in New Mexico and Kit Carson, Lake, and Montrose counties in Colorado project a decrease in population in 1985 in spite of the addition to employment associated with energy projects.

The county population projections were used with the recreation dispersion model to estimate visitor days for the year 2000 at thirty-one U.S. Forest Service recreation sites located in southwestern Colorado and northwestern New Mexico. These estimates of visitor days provide an indication of the change in population pressure on specific recreation sites that may result from demographic changes in scenario C. The results of this analysis are summarized in table 8-6, which indicates the level of population pressure at specific recreation sites and projected changes in population pressure at those sites by visitor days for 1975 and visitor day projections for the year 2000 and by indicating "average population pressure per acre of developed acreage" (AP^3DA) in that year.

A comparison of the year 2000 visitor day projections with visitor days reported in 1975 gives an indication of those sites that will experience a significant change in the level of population pressure. A comparison of visitor day estimates with U.S. Forest Service "theoretical capacity" figures provides an indication of the site's ability to handle this additional population pressure. Two of the listed recreation sites had exceeded their "theoretical capacity" in 1975 (sites 1 and 3); however, nineteen sites are projected to exceed capacity by the year 2000.

It should be emphasized that the level of the environmental effect on recreation sites is the result of both the amount of population pressure and the ecological characteristics of the particular site. Thus, neither the projected changes in visitor days nor the level of visitation relative to "theoretical capacity" by themselves determine the level of environmental effect but they do provide an indication of the location, timing, and magnitude of additional population pressure on existing Forest Service recreation sites. Such information should clearly be of value to those responsible for the maintenance and planning for the region's recreational sites. The estimates should also be of interest, and potentially of substantial value, to those concerned with the preservation of the region's recreational resources.

The annual "theoretical capacity" estimates are based on capacity data from Recreation Information Management (RIM) Basic Address reports of the U.S. Forest Service. This Forest Service capacity con-

Table 8-6. Population Pressure on U.S. Forest Service Recreation Sites: Scenario C

Site number	Type[a]	National Forest[a]	Name[a]	County[a]	Listed[a] capacity (1)	Theoretical[b] capacity (persons) (2)	Visitor days[c] reported in 1975 (3)	Scenario C 2000[d] (persons) (4)	Percent of theoretical capacity 1975[e]	Percent of theoretical capacity 2000[f] projected	Average population pressure per acre of developed acreage 1975[g] persons	Average population pressure per acre of developed acreage 2000[h] projected persons
1	Observation	Santa Fe	Jemez	Sandoval	50	8,250	10,800	16,500 i	1.31	2.00	32.73	50.00
2	Campground	Santa Fe	San Antonio	Sandoval	180	59,400	18,500	71,280 i	.31	1.20	11.21	43.20
3	Campground	Santa Fe	Horseshoe Springs	Sandoval	15	4,950	5,400	5,940 i	1.10	1.20	10.91	12.00
4	Campground	Santa Fe	Banco Bonito	Sandoval	50	16,500	9,000	19,800 i	.55	1.20	27.27	60.00
5	Campground	Santa Fe	Las Conchas	Sandoval	60	19,800	6,800	23,760 i	.34	1.20	20.61	72.00
6	Campground	Santa Fe	Paliza	Sandoval	180	59,400	18,000	62,530	.30	1.05	10.91	37.90
7	Campground	Santa Fe	Seven Springs	Sandoval	35	11,550	4,600	9,588	.40	0.83	9.29	19.37
8	Campground	Santa Fe	Redondo	Sandoval	295	97,350	22,600	54,297	.23	0.56	5.27	12.66
9	Campground	Santa Fe	Paliza Group	Sandoval	250	107,500	20,600	90,530	.19	0.84	19.16	84.21
10	Picnic grounds	Santa Fe	Battleship Rock	Sandoval	160	31,200	22,200	46,800 i	.71	1.50	37.95	80.00
11	Picnic grounds	Santa Fe	Indian Head	Sandoval	20	3,680	1,900	3,967	.52	1.09	10.33	21.56
12	Picnic grounds	Santa Fe	Dark Canyon	Sandoval	10	1,840	1,400	2,695	.76	1.46	7.60	14.65
13	Picnic grounds	Santa Fe	La Cueva	Sandoval	50	8,250	8,100	12,375 i	.98	1.50	9.82	15.00
14	Campground	San Juan	Vallecito	La Plata	440	135,320	23,900	162,384 i	.18	1.20	15.52	105.44
15	Campground	San Juan	Kroeger	La Plata	65	20,020	6,500	13,944	.32	0.70	21.10	45.27
16	Campground	San Juan	Cimarrona	Hinsdale	75	22,950	7,300	27,540 i	.32	1.20	7.95	30.00
17	Campground	San Juan	Blanco River	Archuleta	50	19,900	5,100	7,714	.26	0.39	3.20	4.85
18	Campground	San Juan	Burro Bridge	Dolores	75	27,750	1,900	1,438	.07	0.05	1.28	0.97
19	Campground	San Juan	Sig Creek	La Plata	45	8,370	4,100	8,384	.49	1.00	11.02	22.54
20	Campground	San Isabel	Cuchara	Huerfano	145	48,720	22,200	21,028	.46	0.43	10.16	9.63
21	Campground	San Isabel	Lake Isabel	Custer	75	23,100	19,600	27,720 i	.85	1.20	25.45	36.00
22	Campground	San Isabel	Ohaver Lake	Chaffee	85	29,750	14,300	17,552	.48	0.59	7.43	9.12
23	Campground	San Isabel	Collegiate Peaks	Chaffee	145	44,660	10,800	17,975	.24	0.40	6.38	10.61
24	Campground	San Isabel	Hayden Creek #1	Fremont	55	18,480	7,900	22,176 i	.43	1.20	11.76	33.00
25	Campground	San Isabel	Parry Peak	Lake	130	40,040	17,400	48,048 i	.43	1.20	11.30	31.20
26	Campground	Rio Grande	Buffalo Pass	Saguache	150	55,500	7,600	8,024	.14	0.14	1.11	1.17
27	Campground	Rio Grande	Park Creek	Mineral	80	14,080	8,800	16,896 i	.62	1.20	14.29	27.43
28	Campground	Rio Grande	Rio Grande	Mineral	20	3,720	2,200	2,305	.59	0.62	2.96	3.10
29	Campground	Rio Grande	Conejos	Conejos	80	14,880	8,800	17,856 i	.59	1.20	9.46	19.20
30	Campground	Rio Grande	Trujillo Meadows	Conejos	105	19,530	7,400	12,710	.38	0.65	4.42	7.59
31	Campground	Rio Grande	Lake Fork	Conejos	90	17,280	8,400	10,415	.49	0.60	3.02	3.74

a "Recreation Information Management (RIM) Basic Address Record for Established Developed Sites and Dispersed Areas," U.S. Department of Agriculture, Forest Service, Washington, D.C., June 30, 1975.

b (Managed use season × listed capacity) × 2.

c "A Tabulation of Recreation Use Reported for Calendar Year 1975 on Developed Sites," U.S. Department of Agriculture, U.S. Forest Service, Regional Office, Albuquerque, New Mexico, 1976.

d Projections from "recreation model" (described herein) based on scenario C population estimates.

e Column 3 ÷ column 2.

f Column 4 ÷ column 2.

g (Column 3 ÷ managed use season) ÷ developed acreage in recreation site.

h (Column 4 ÷ managed use season) ÷ developed acreage in recreation site.

i In the construction of projections for 1975 and the year 2000, campsites were permitted to exceed the theoretical capacity (column 7) by 20%, picnic areas were permitted to exceed the theoretical capacity by 50%, and observation points were permitted to exceed theoretical capacity by 100%.

cept is not designed to reflect accurately the ecological "carrying capacity" of a particular recreation site. The capacity figures simply indicate the number of picnic tables, camping sites, or parking spaces available at the site. Although some environmental considerations were presumably involved in the design and construction of the recreation site, the ecological carrying capacity (however defined) probably differs significantly from the Forest Service capacity figures. Thus, any conclusion concerning the environmental significance of a particular site nearing its annual theoretical capacity should be limited to the environmental implications of the expansion of existing facilities, the development of new recreational sites to meet the additional demand, or both. It may be assumed that the greater the figures recorded in column 4 of table 8-6 relative to the theoretical capacity figures recorded in column 2 of that table, the higher will be the number of days that the site will be filled to capacity. Thus, the higher the number of visitor days projected relative to theoretical capacity, the higher the number of days during the managed-use season that the site will be subjected to peak population pressure.

The AP³DA recorded in columns 7 and 8 of table 8-6 may provide a more accurate indication of changes in the level of population pressure at specific recreation sites. Even these numbers, however, probably do not accurately reflect the ecological significance of such pressure. The highest average population pressure per acre of developed acreage is projected for recreation sites 1, 2, 4, and 10 in 1985 and recreation sites 1, 2, 4, 5, 9, 10, 14, and 15 in the year 2000. It does not necessarily follow that the pressures at these sites represent the greatest threat to the region's fish and wildlife and other recreation resources. The significance of these figures depends on a number of interrelated variables, including the number, diversity, and condition of the region's wildlife; the vegetation type and its ability to recover from such population pressure; the nature of the recreational experience; and more. Thus, although the AP³DA figures recorded in table 8-6 provide further insight concerning the location, timing, and magnitude of projected population pressure on existing Forest Service recreation sites, additional information is required in order to identify more accurately significant effects on recreational resources in the Southwest.

ASSESSING THE ENVIRONMENTAL EFFECT OF ENERGY RESOURCE DEVELOPMENT

The projected changes in visitor days at Forest Service recreation sites recorded in table 8-6 give an indication of the importance of energy resource development and its potential effects on the environment. The results of the analyses suggest that energy resource development may be a major factor affecting the level and scope of the so-called secondary environmental impacts associated with demographic changes in the region.

This conclusion is supported by the fact that recreation sites 18, 20, 21, 22, 26, and 27 through 31—which are generally isolated from the major energy resource development activity in northwestern New Mexico, northwestern Colorado, and southern Utah—have significantly smaller increases, or actual decreases, in visitor days projected for the year 2000. At the same time, recreation sites in the Santa Fe National Forest (sites 1 through 13) and sites 14, 15, and 16 in the San Juan National Forest—geographically located in close proximity to the major energy resource development locations in northwestern New Mexico—generally have significantly larger increases in visitor days projected for the year 2000. This evidence suggests that the level and nature of energy resource development will play a major role in determining the location, timing, and magnitude of population pressure on recreation resources.

Another important conclusion to be drawn from the preceding analysis is that there is a real danger that in examining the environmental effects of energy resource development, too much attention will be paid to the effect of a single energy project without proper appreciation of the aggregate effect of a variety of energy projects. The "one project at a time" approach is typical of environmental impact statements. The population pressure on area recreation sites of a single energy project may be accurately described as minimal. As we have seen, it does not follow, however, that the cumulative environmental impact of a variety of such energy projects will also be minimal.

Similarly, the effect on area recreational resources of a specific element of the total environmental impact may not appear terribly significant. But the aggregate effect of all the consequences of environmental changes resulting from energy resource development— including population pressure on Forest Service, Bureau of Land Management, National Park Service, and state recreation sites; population pressure on quality fishing and hunting areas; geographic and numerical expansion in the use of off-road vehicles; pressure from recreational activities on urban fringe areas; the deterioration of air and water quality associated with industrial plant operation; increased noise levels associated with plant construction and operation—may be devastating in its impact on the region's recreational resources.

It would be preferable to quantify the damages resulting from effects on recreation resources in economic terms, but, unfortunately, the discipline of economics and the data base are not ready to permit this on a routine basis. Some promising experiments in this direction were, however, conducted by the Southwest Project. They are described briefly in appendix 8-A.

APPENDIX 8-A. THREE EXPERIMENTS ON THE VALUATION OF RECREATION DAMAGE

As we have shown, many of the major recreation issues in western United States involve changes in environmental attributes resulting from energy development. For example, operation of many coal-fired electric plants in the Four Corners Region may significantly reduce visibility and disturb landscapes in addition to having possible adverse health effects. Strip mining of coal may have substantial detrimental effects on wildlife populations in addition to the expanded demand for wildlife experiences arising from a larger local population caused by the mining. The construction of large geothermal plants adjacent to existing forest recreation areas may disturb otherwise pristine, quiet recreation areas. Recreational use and benefits would be changed by these developments, but there are no existing markets to adequately price the changes. In consequence, if benefit–cost analysis is to be employed for decision making, techniques are needed to impute economic values for recreational damages. The four experiments sketched here, which were conducted over the past several years by the Southwest Project, are tests to determine the feasibility of deriving values for energy development-induced changes in outdoor recreational attributes. These are discussed in an appendix because they are experiments. Available resources did not permit full-scale benefit–cost analysis of the various recreation and aesthetic conflicts in the region. But it is very important, if recreation and aesthetic values are to be included explicitly in decision making, that methods be developed in which decision makers can have a satisfactory degree of confidence. The experiments discussed here represent some progress in that direction. It should also be noted that this appendix assumes some understanding of demand theory.

The techniques range from purely hypothetical to partially hypothetical questions posed to recreationists and others to discover their preferences. In each case, the recreationist is confronted with a possible change in an environmental attribute and asked to value it. Since the valuation is contingent on the specific hypothetical change identified (through photographs, brochures, or other means), the team refers to such approaches as contingent valuations. Within the context of contingent valuation approaches, there are numerous methods of combining hypothetical and actual responses. Recreationists can be queried as to willingness to pay, minimum compensation, evasive behavior, past experiences, current experiences, potential site or activity substitutions, potential expenditure adjustments, income compensation coupled with potential behavioral adjustments, and so forth—all of which can be coupled in theoretical structures to estimate compensated demand curves for environmental attributes. We turn now to a discussion of the various sources of possible bias.

CONTINGENT VALUATION AND BIAS

Because of the hypothetical nature of contingent valuation, several potential biases may occur. In fact, it has long been supposed by economists that valuing public goods through a direct demand-revealing process such as a bidding game would yield biased results. The principal theoretical support for this contention is the possibility of strategic bias. In spite of this, as applications of survey techniques to elicit contingent behavior or bids have become more frequent, other types of bias have come to be regarded as just as important. These include strategic bias, information bias, vehicle bias, starting point bias, and hypothetical bias. This section reviews our current understanding of such biases.

Beginning with Samuelson's seminal work on public goods, it has been supposed that direct revelation of consumer preferences for such goods would be impossible.[1] In particular, the free rider problem would give individuals incentives to misstate their preferences. For example, if nearby residents were asked how much they were willing to pay to clean up the air near a power plant and if they suspected that control costs would be borne by consumers and owners elsewhere, local residents might well have an incentive to overstate their willingness to pay. On the other hand, if residents suspected that they would be individually taxed an amount equal to their own willingness to pay, then a clear incentive would exist to understate their own true value, hoping that others would bid more.

Strategic Bias

Clearly each technique for eliciting willingness to pay will generate its own bias. Thus, if recreators are told that the average of their bids to prevent construction of a nearby power plant will be used to set an entrance fee, those individuals who suspect their bid to be greater than the average bid will have an incentive to overstate their willingness to pay. They, in fact, have an incentive to raise the average bid as close as possible to their own true bid. In other words, individuals will have incentives to misstate their own preferences in an attempt to impose their true preferences on others. Of course, if the respondents to such a survey do not believe the survey will have any impact on policy or outcome, then no incentive for bias exists. The hypothetical nature of such surveys may then, in actuality, aid in eliciting bids which are not strategically biased.

Since contingent valuation is hypothetical, it is clear that answers obtained through surveys may not be based on information as complete as that which would apply if consumers based answers on real experiences. Typically, consumers do reevaluate decisions on the basis of experience. Thus, a recreator might respond to a hypothetical decrease in environmental quality at one location with a low bid, thinking that other nearby sites would make good substitutes. However, in a real situation the recreator might have found that other sites involved more travel costs and were less satisfactory than imagined. Clearly then, the information presented to the respondent in a questionnaire relating to substitution possibilities and alternative costs may well bias the stated willingness to pay. In turn, no amount of a priori information may substitute for actual experience.

Information Bias

[1] Paul A. Samuelson, "The Pure Theory of Public Expenditures," *Review of Economics and Statistics* vol. 36, no. 4 (1954).

Vehicle Bias   It has been recognized in past studies that the mechanism used to collect the bid or pay compensation may influence its magnitude.[2] That is, if the recreationist pays a higher park entrance fee rather than another type of tax, his bid for an environmental attribute may differ. From economic theory, it should differ, provided the recreationist's substitution possibilities associated with alternative payment mechanisms are different. When a payment vehicle allows the individual to substitute over a wider range of current commodities purchased, then the bid should be higher, or compensation lower, than when the range is smaller. Ideally, the bid or compensation should be related to adjustments in disposable income or wealth, when the individual recreationist has the greatest latitude for potential substitution. Practically, however, a believable payment mechanism related to income adjustment cannot, in general, be applied. For example, surveys are often taken at recreational sites away from the recreationists' locale or state. In this case, a wage tax (or income compensation) may not be viewed as realistically payable by the recreationist. Thus, there is a tradeoff between accuracy associated with a less than ideal method of payment and the believability of the vehicle for payment or compensation. The reduction in substitution possibilities for a more believable payment vehicle is likely to reduce the contingent expenditure or increase the contingent compensation estimate.

Starting Point Bias   The contingent valuation approach commences with questions on payment, compensation, or both, for hypothetical changes in environmental attributes. In most sample surveys, it has been found that it is better to ask the recreationist a question with a "yes" or "no" answer than a question requiring explicit calculations.[3] Given that yes–no responses are desirable, it is necessary to suggest a starting bid or minimal level of compensation. The potential bias arises with a starting bid or minimal level of compensation. The potential bias arises with starting points from at least two possible sources. First, the bid itself may suggest to the recreationist the approximate range of appropriate bids. Thus, the recreationist may respond differently depending on the magnitude of the starting bid. Second, if the recreationist values time highly, he may become "bored" or irritated with going through a lengthy bidding process. In consequence, if the suggested starting bid is substantially different from his actual willingness to pay, the bidding process may yield inaccurate or only roughly approximate results. The effect of these two types of starting point biases may substantially influence the accuracy of contingent valuation and therefore the usefulness of this approach for assessment of recreationists' preferences.

---

[2] A. Randall and coauthors, "Bidding Games for Valuation of Aesthetic Environmental Improvements," *Journal of Environmental Economics and Management* vol. 1, no. 2 (1974), pp. 132–149.

[3] Ibid.; and David Brookshire and coauthors, "Economic Valuation of Wildlife," report prepared for the U.S. Fish and Wildlife Service (Laramie, Wyo., Resource and Environmental Laboratory, University of Wyoming, November 18, 1977).

The contingent valuation approach requires postulating change in an environmental attribute in such a way that it is believable to the recreationist and accurately depicts a potential change. In addition, the change must be fully understandable to the recreationist, that is, he must be able to understand most, if not all, of its ramifications. Finally, the recreationist must believe that the change might occur and that his contingent valuation or behavioral changes will affect both the possibility and magnitude of change in the environmental attribute or quality. If these conditions are not fulfilled, the hypothetical nature of contingent valuation approaches will make their application utterly useless. However, unlike other types of biases identified, it is extremely difficult to measure the extent of hypothetical bias because it depends not only on how well structured the experiment is, but also on uncontrollable factors such as attitudes, style of presentation by the interviewer, and the recreationist's mood.

Hypothetical Bias

We discuss in chronological order three studies by the Southwest team which have attempted to value recreational and aesthetic aspects of environmental quality. The first two studies, the Lake Powell experiment and the Farmington experiment, attempted to value air quality near existing or proposed coal-fired power plants. The third study, the geothermal experiment, examined the effect of proposed geothermal power plant development on an existing recreation area, calculating possible damages.

RECREATION AND ENVIRONMENTAL QUALITY: SOUTHWEST CASE STUDIES

Lake Powell, with an annual visitation now approaching two million visitor days, is an excellent example of the environment–development tradeoff. The lake was formed by the filling of Glen Canyon and retains the steep cliffs, rugged terrain features, and scenic vistas one associates with the Grand Canyon, but now available to pleasure boaters and other recreators. Construction of the Navajo generating station located at the southern end of Lake Powell was completed in 1976. Another larger power plant, the Kaiparowits Project, was also proposed for construction near Lake Powell and became an issue of substantial public concern, if not the primary issue for environmental groups in the Southwest.

During the summer of 1974, recreators at Lake Powell were interviewed by the study team in an attempt to determine the aggregate willingness to pay to prevent construction of the proposed Kaiparowits plant.[4] Photographs of the existing Navajo power plant, which all of the recreators had seen—stacks remain visible more than 20 miles up the lake—were shown to recreators both with visible pollution emanating from the stacks and with the stacks alone. Recreators were then asked what entrance fee they would be willing to pay to prevent construction of another similar

The Lake Powell Experiment

---

[4] David Brookshire, William D. Schulze, and Berry Ives, "The Valuation of Aesthetic Preferences," *Journal of Environmental Economics and Management* vol. 3, no. 4 (December 1976).

plant—first, where only pollution would be visible from the lake itself, and second, where both stacks and pollution would be visible.

The analysis of the data attempted primarily to deal with strategic bias. As noted above, if recreators believed that a uniform entrance fee might actually be set on the basis of the average bid of the sample survey to prevent construction (or believed that construction plans might be affected by the research results), then "environmentalists" might well bid very high, and "developers" might well bid zero dollars in an attempt to bias the results. A theoretical model of strategic bias was constructed to explain the distribution of observed bids that would likely be bimodal rather than normally distributed if strategic bias was present. The fact that the actual distribution of bids was normally distributed was thus taken as evidence that strategic bias was not present. It was conjectured that the absence of strategic bias was caused by the hypothetical nature of the experiment: few respondents felt that their answers would affect real world outcomes.

The average bid per family or recreator group was $2.77 in additional entrance fees in 1974 dollars, and the total annual bid—which can be interpreted as an aggregate marginal willingness to pay to prevent one additional power plant near Lake Powell—was over $700,000. Two points should be made about these results. First, they show impressive consistencies both with the one previous bidding game study[5] in the region as well as the succeeding Farmington experiment discussed below. Second, if the results are accepted as indicative of recreator preferences in general for the entire region—the canyon lands of southeastern Utah—and if the bids are extrapolated to all the affected recreation areas as well as Lake Powell, the aggregate bid would approach $20 million per year since there are some fifteen national parks and recreation areas within a 100 mile radius of the proposed Kaiparowits site.

The Farmington Experiment

The Farmington experiment attempted to establish the economic value of visibility over long distances within the Four Corners region. As explained in chapter 2, the Southwest is characterized by vast spaces and open vistas, most of which are presently relatively free of industrial and commercial development, urban development, or airborne pollutants. The major focus of the study was to establish how recreationists and residents value continuing to be able to see over long distances.

As indicated in chapter 6, visibility is emerging as the central air quality issue in the Southwest. Clearly, the ability to observe long distances is an almost pure public good. Use of this attribute by anyone does not interfere with use by anyone else. In addition, efforts were made to examine the extent of certain biases including: information, strategic, starting point, and vehicle bias on compensating and equivalent variation measures of consumer surplus. The Farmington experiment also included a first attempt to examine contingent behavior changes in response to visibility changes, that is, how people allocated time between indoor and outdoor activities.

[5] Randall and coauthors, "Bidding Games."

A survey questionnaire was given to recreators and residents in the Four Corners region of New Mexico and Arizona. The interviewee was shown a set of pictures depicting visible ranges from 25 to 75 miles and asked to bid across them. All the pictures were taken at the same location.

Two distinct methodologies were used to estimate contingent valuations for visibility. The first assumed a utility function with arguments of visibility and income and asked the respondent a sequence of questions on maximum willingness to pay and minimum compensation. The second utilized a utility function with time spent on indoor and outdoor recreation as the relevant arguments. With this function in mind, a sequence of questions was asked the respondent on adjustments in time allocations by activity where changes occurred in visibility.

As part of the contingent expenditures approach, direct tests were made for strategic bias, information bias, vehicle bias, and starting point bias. Strategic bias was evaluated by two means. First, the "game" was structured so the individual presumed that he would have to pay the "average" bid, not his own. The presumption was that if his bid were below the mean bid and he desired to increase the magnitude of the aggregate bid, he would bid higher. Alternatively, if his goal were to reduce the mean bid, he would revise his bid downward. Only in the extreme case when the individual's maximum bid is identical to the mean bid would there be no incentive for the individual to change. In addition to this process, the individual was questioned about his bid being too low. It was suggested that his bid was not sufficient to keep power plant emissions at present levels for sustained high quality ambient air and then asked if he would revise his bid. In only one case was an individual observed to be acting strategically and he turned out to be an economics professor from the local junior college. However, fully one-third revised their bids when confronted with the possibility that their bid was insufficient. Whether this latter result is indicative of the presence of strategic downward bias in initial bids or the effect of new information cannot be ascertained. Individuals may be acting strategically by subjectively forming their preferences as to the effect of their maximum bid, selecting the bid appropriately, and then not revising it. However, it appears to be an additional indication that individuals generally do not act strategically, at least in a meaningful manner, to bias the outcome of the result.

In addition to the tests on strategic bias, analysis was made of various forms of information bias, essentially trying to establish influences of various aspects of the game. It was observed the higher the starting bid suggested by the interviewer, the higher the maximum willingness to pay (equivalent variation) estimate derived from the study. Thus, if the interviewer suggested a bid of $1.00 higher, on the average individuals would bid about $.60 more at a maximum. Also, the choice of the method of payment influenced the magnitude of the bid significantly, as would be expected from economic theory. The bid should increase, the greater the number of substitutions there are in the form of the vehicle used to make payment: and this was observed in the results; that is, individuals were willing to bid higher when confronted with a "payroll tax" than with an increase in entrance fees. Finally, it was observed that whether the individual was given previous information on average bids had a substantial impact on the maximum bid. We do not wish to suggest these results indicate any final conclusions with regard to the information bias problem with the contingent valuations approach, but we do suggest that for these approaches to be accurate, one must be very careful about the vehicle used for payment and the amount and quality of information given to the interviewee upon initiation of the questionnaire.

The contingent behavior component of the questionnaire attempted through contingent changes in time allocation to infer an expenditure function and compensated demand relation for visibility. Various procedures were utilized to approximate the compensated demand curve, primarily by postulating an exact form of a utility function and estimating a time-related household technology.

The mean bid per recreationist family per month was $4.06, while their minimum compensation per month was $17.40. The compensated substitutions approach led to estimates ranging from approximately $5.00 per month for the case where the receptor had no entitlement to clean air to approximately $280.00 per month with complete entitlement. However, these estimates are not directly comparable because the contingent behavior estimates include residents in addition to recreationists, which should increase the magnitude of the estimate.

Both the Randall study and the Southwest Project study obtained only equivalent variation (EV) bids. The following comparisons are therefore limited to the equivalent variation bids. Using the sales tax as a vehicle, Randall reported yearly mean bids of $85.00 (A to C) and $50.00 (B to C) per household. The Southwest Project yearly mean bids for the most comparable situations were $82.20 and $57.00. If one considers that the Randall figures should be increased by 37 percent to account for inflation between 1972 and 1976 and that, on the other hand, the Randall figures should be higher as respondents are also bidding on spoil banks and transmission lines, these figures are very comparable.

The Farmington experiment demonstrated reasonable replicative consistency with other studies. It also demonstrated that questionnaire biases may be serious in attempting to utilize contingent valuations methodologies. Extrapolating the equivalent variation measures to all recreationists using the Navajo Reservoir, an annual estimate of $916,000 is obtained which is roughly consistent with that in the Lake Powell experiment.

Geothermal Experiment

The Jemez Mountains of New Mexico are both scenic—characterized by brightly colored rock outcroppings and forest areas—and a major recreation resource with fishing, camp grounds, hiking trails, and hot springs all located on U.S. Forest Service lands. At the same time, the Jemez Mountains also contain one of the major geothermal resources in the Southwest. Geothermal leases have been let by the U.S. Forest Service on land that is now used solely by recreators. The Public Service Company of New Mexico, together with Union Oil Company (the lease holder) and the U.S. Department of Energy are planning to construct a 50-megawatt power plant in the Valles Caldera, which is widely regarded as one of the most beautiful spots in the entire Southwest.

Both a bidding game and a site substitution approach were used to estimate environmental damages to recreators from possible geothermal development.[6] Recreators were shown both photographs of geothermal development in similar mountainous terrain and a map of the location of possible development relative to recreation areas. Noise levels and emissions characteristics were described in detail. A bidding game was then conducted that attempted to elicit a uniform entrance fee to prevent development. Alternatively, respondents were asked to indicate what their contingent recreation plan would be (what sites they would visit including new substitute sites and how often) if development were to occur. The subsample which responded to the site substitution question was then also asked what they would bid in the form of a uniform entrance fee to prevent development. Finally, starting point for the bidding game was varied from $1.00 to $10.00 in various subsamples. Thus, the study was structured to test: (1) if the bidding game and site substitution results were consistent; (2) if information on alternative new substitute sites would affect bidding game results; and (3) for starting point bias.

A set of theoretical models was constructed to estimate a consistent measure of willingness to pay to prevent development from both measures —the bidding game and additional travel costs associated with alternative recreation plans. Additionally, the model was modified to explain information bias—how changes in perceived costs of alternatives (driving costs) would affect bids; and to explain starting point bias—individuals either trade off their honest bid against the length of the bidding process *or* wish to "please" the interviewer by trading off their honest bid against what they perceive as the "desired" response.

The results of the experiment were as follows: 35 percent of the respondents indicated they would no longer visit the Jemez area if development occurred. This resulted in about a 50 percent contingent decrease in visitation. About 65 percent of the respondents indicated they would visit alternative sites more frequently, usually the Pecos Wilderness area. Bids averaged $2.35 per visitor party day, while the site substitution measure yielded a range of $2.03 to $2.84, depending on the assumed driving cost per mile. The results appear to be consistent for the two approaches and imply an annualized aggregate bid to prevent construction of about $300,000 for a 50-megawatt plant.

More surprising, however, were the results for information and starting point bias experiments. Neither bias was statistically significant. The obvious question is: Why are these results different from those of the Farmington experiment which indicated that both information and starting point would likely be serious problems? The best explanation that can be given at this point is that the value of the change in an environmental quality proposed in the two studies was more precisely perceived by respondents in the geothermal experiment than in the Farmington experiment. In other words, respondents could more easily relate the costs to themselves of "losing" in part a recreation area than they could determine the costs of a change in visibility.

[6] M. Thayer and William D. Schulze, "Valuing Environmental Quality: A Contingent Substitution and Expenditure Approach," research paper (Los Angeles, Calif., University of Southern California, 1977).

CONCLUSION   The three case studies discussed above, while still necessarily regarded as experiments, have shown an impressive consistency both in results and in the evolution of techniques to deal with the bias problem. Bias is, of course, inherent in using contingent responses to value environmental quality. It appears that problems of strategic, information, vehicle, and starting point bias are all surmountable with proper questionnaire design, modeling, and econometric analysis.

IV   WHO BENEFITS FROM ECONOMIC DEVELOPMENT?

INTRODUCTION TO PART IV

We trust that the discussion in previous chapters has made clear that the prospect of massive energy development cannot be regarded as an unmitigated boon in the Southwest—especially from the point of view of its present residents. It will strain existing public institutions which may prove inadequate to deal with its ill effects; it will, even should the best efforts to avoid them be undertaken, have destructive effects on an environment which is deceptively delicate; and it will make major demands on a resource (water) that is already in short supply. Given these circumstances, the present population of the region could be expected to put every possible obstacle in the way of such development unless the economic benefits to the region are large.

From a humanitarian and equity standpoint one would hope especially that the resource-rich income-poor Poverty Diagonal described in chapter 2 would benefit disproportionately.

We will see in subsequent chapters that the overall economic effects of such potential resource development can be significant. But the economic stimulation and employment a large energy facility provides *in the area where it is located* is not nearly so large as might be suggested by the massive investments involved (a modern power plant costs about a billion dollars). It is especially noteworthy that the existing residents of the Southwest Poverty Diagonal are benefiting but modestly and far short of their expectations. In Part IV we will also suggest some ways in which this prospect might be moderated.

To illuminate probable economic consequences to the region of the development of large energy facilities, we turn in the next chapter to a close examination of the single largest energy development that has already occurred in the region—Glen Canyon Dam and Lake Powell and the associated Navajo Generating Station (also referred to as the Navajo Power Plant) and Black Mesa Coal Mine.

BACKGROUND

9 ECONOMIC EFFECTS OF LARGE-SCALE ENERGY DEVELOPMENT IN THE SOUTHWEST

In 1956 the Colorado River flowed unimpeded from Utah into Arizona, out of Glen Canyon, and into Marble Canyon, in a nearly deserted ranching region which included a few Navajo hogans thinly scattered about on the Navajo Indian Reservation. In 1956, also, the Colorado River Storage Project Act was passed by Congress. It authorized construction of the Glen Canyon Dam, which was designated as part of a large water storage and hydroelectric system that included several reclamation projects in the Colorado River system.

Thus, after many years of discussion and study, construction began in the middle 1950s on a massive dam in Glen Canyon on the main stem of the Colorado River just below the Utah-Arizona state line, more or less in the middle of the Poverty Diagonal. It was to impound a large water body known as Lake Powell. From that time through the early 1960s, a large work force was employed in construction of the dam, Arch Bridge, below the dam and the hydro power units. Because of available cooling water and nearby coal supplies, a 2,250 megawatt power plant was constructed in the early 1970s and a coal mine was opened at nearby Black Mesa. Both the power station and the coal mine are on Navajo land. Figure 2-1 on page 9 shows what we term "the Lake Powell Region."

There are various ways of viewing the economic effect of large-scale investment in natural resources development. One is to look at the matter in terms of the broadest indicator of economic effect we possess—gross national product, or GNP. Because GNP can be broken down by state or region, we apply the concept at that level as well. In this context, it can be thought of as the gross value of all final outputs produced minus inputs purchased from outside the state or region. Associated with a production increment is an increase in employment. These aggregative measures of production and employment are called macroeconomic measures. In this chapter, we present some estimates of these indicators developed by the Southwest Project team members working under the sponsorship of the Lake Powell Research Project. Later in the chapter we take a more detailed economic look at the Lake Powell region itself, especially the economy of Page, Arizona, the settlement most closely related to the energy development.[1]

MACROECONOMIC EFFECTS

The macroeconomic methodology used by the Southwest Project team to estimate the effect of power production on GNP by region is based on a technique called the Metzler Model of Interregional Trade.[2] The effect of power production at the Glen Canyon Power Plant and at the Navajo Generating Station on the GNP by region was derived for Arizona, California, Nevada, New Mexico, Utah, and the region "rest of the United States." To analyze the economic effects of Lake Powell development, a special type of economic model was used, which is explained below.

The Metzler Model takes into account the effect on GNP of imports and exports among states and regions through multiplier (respending) effects on local external expenditures. Clearly a region which spends a large proportion of its income on imports will have a smaller multiplier effect from initial expenditures than will a more self-contained economy. The multiplier is lower because a larger proportion of initial expenditures is lost each time they are respent on imports into the region (that is, the money leaves the region). Thus, it is important to adjust for such effects when considering effects in an economically interconnected area such as the Southwest. This "leakage" of "open" economies is the key to understanding why very large capital-intensive projects may have only a modest con-

---

[1] In this chapter we are interested in economic effects but we remind the reader that Glen Canyon Dam stirred up very strong emotions among environmentalists on other grounds. This is epitomized by Seldom Seen Smith, a character in Edward Abbey's *The Monkey Wrench Gang*, who got down on his knees on the cement walkway of the bridge at Glen Canyon Dam, bowed his head, and prayed. "'Dear old God,' he prayed, 'you know and I know what it was like here, before them bastards from Washington moved in and ruined it all. You remember the river, how fat and golden it was. . . . Remember the deer on the sandbars and the blue herons in the willows and the catfish so big and tasty and how they'd bite on spoiled salami? . . . There's somethin' you can do for me, God. How about a little old *pre*-cision earthquake right under this dam? Okay?" (New York, Avon Books, 1975).

[2] For details of methodology and data, see William D. Schulze, Shaul Ben-David, David Brookshire, and Regan Whitworth, "The Macroeconomic Impact of Energy Development in the Lake Powell Area," *Lake Powell Research Project Bulletin* no. 11 (August 1975) (Los Angeles, Calif., University of California Institute of Geophysics and Planetary Physics).

tinuing stimulating effect on the general economy in the areas where they occur. This is especially so for economies like the Poverty Diagonal, which have very little industrial infrastructure. The analysis reported here estimates both the increase in GNP "induced" by the availability of the additional power and "stimulated" by the operating costs of the project.

The first step in estimating the effect of additional electrical power on GNP by region was to determine the allocation of that power and the resulting direct increase in expenditures (final demand) necessary to support such an increase in power use. To do this, energy coefficients that translate increased power use into increased dollar expenditures were derived for each state and region from input–output (I–O) data on energy consumption by industry. It was assumed that the industrial mix within each region remains proportionally similar as output expands with increased energy availability. The coefficients used to accomplish this task were derived by disaggregating national energy consumption, measured in British thermal units (Btus), into economic sectors. Then a direct correspondence between energy consumption and the economic data for each sector in the I–O table was derived. This coefficient gives the amount of energy used per dollar of sales for each sector. Thus, from increased energy purchased by region, one can derive the resulting direct expenditures. These were then "multiplied" by the Metzler Model to give total changes in GNP by region after certain adjustments were made, as outlined below, to give net direct expenditures.

Clearly, a region that experiences an increase in direct and indirect expenditures as prescribed by the Metzler Model will experience an increase in employment. Using state employment coefficients that relate total regional output to the total number of persons employed in the region, an incremental change in employment for a region can be calculated given the change in the GNP of that region. Note that we are considering the longer term employment change as a result of energy production, not as a result of initial construction of a particular power plant. We turn to an analysis of the short-term (boom) aspects later in this chapter.

To apply this methodology to obtain direct and indirect expenditures and incremental employment changes, certain assumptions were used. In 1973 Glen Canyon Dam provided 65 percent of the total power marketed by the Colorado River Storage Project. Total power included power produced and that purchased from other sources in order to fulfill existing contracts. Power production at Glen Canyon Dam for 1972 was 64 percent of the total. The allocation of megawatt hours for 1973 and 1972 was based on the assumption that 65 and 64 percent, for each respective year, of the power marketed by the Colorado River Storage Project to each region was produced at Glen

Canyon Dam. This assumption was essential because it is nearly impossible to determine where power goes once it enters the transmission grid.

The production assumptions for the coal-fired Navajo Generating Station were different, primarily because the plant was not yet in full production when the calculations were made. A probable scenario for future plant production was developed to permit the allocation of megawatt hours. Over the life of the plant (35 years), it was estimated that a plant factor of 75 percent for the station was reasonable. At this level of operation, the estimated cost per kilowatt hour would have to be 13.7 mills in order to provide full return on the investment of the participants. This is not the charge that the participants will levy on customers, but is in a sense their payment to the Navajo Generating Station to cover respective shares of capital and operating costs.

The direct expenditures resulting from increased power availability presented in table 9-1 had to be adjusted as shown in tables 9-2 and 9-3 before applying the Metzler Model. The adjustments took

Table 9-1.   Direct Expenditures Resulting from Additional
              Electric Power

Project and state	Allocation of power by state (megawatt hours)	Direct expenditures from additional power ($1,000)
1973		
Glen Canyon		
Arizona	994,854	40,136
California	139,333	5,360
Colorado	816,013	29,386
Nevada	374,970	22,774
New Mexico	377,435	8,750
Utah	913,332	26,901
Rest of U.S.	271,909	9,317
1972		
Glen Canyon		
Arizona	969,643	39,119
California	62,115	2,389
Colorado	674,614	24,294
Nevada	262,291	10,355
New Mexico	358,276	12,778
Utah	757,148	22,301
Rest of U.S.	204,532	7,008
Projected		
Navajo Plant		
Arizona	9,978,201	402,552
California	3,133,890	120,554
Colorado	0	0
Nevada	1,670,418	65,945
New Mexico	0	0
Utah	0	0
Rest of U.S.	0	0

three forms. First, the Glen Canyon Project, which the Bureau of Reclamation supervises, requires payback to the federal government; and, second, the Navajo Generating Station, which is managed by the Salt River Project in which the participants are primarily private firms, requires an allocation of the return on investment. Third, operating costs must be allocated as regional expenditures. For the Glen Canyon case, the adjustments were as follows: (1) payments for the power sold by the Colorado River Storage Project from regions to the U.S. Treasury had to be subtracted; (2) these payments were then redis-

Table 9-2. Composition of Net Direct Expenditures Resulting from Additional Electric Power, by State ($1,000)

Project and state	Direct expenditures from additional power	−	Payment to federal treasury for Glen Canyon power	+	Payment returned to states as federal expenditures	+	Operations and maintenance	=	Net direct expenditures
1973 Glen Canyon									
Arizona	40,136		6,942		184		7,623		41,000
California	5,360		799		2,685		0		7,246
Colorado	29,386		5,038		249		0		24,598
Nevada	22,774		2,088		63		0		20,748
New Mexico	8,750		2,084		134		0		6,801
Utah	26,901		5,028		140		0		22,012
Rest of U.S.	9,317		1,590		15,623		0		23,350
1972 Glen Canyon									
Arizona	39,119		6,476		164		5,989		38,796
California	2,389		329		2,400		0		4,460
Colorado	24,294		4,089		223		0		20,428
Nevada	10,355		1,607		56		0		8,804
New Mexico	12,778		1,951		120		0		10,948
Utah	22,301		4,145		125		0		18,281
Rest of U.S.	7,008		1,646		13,964		0		19,326

Note: Numbers have been rounded in some cases.

Table 9-3. Composition of Net Direct Expenditures for the Projected Navajo Plant, by State ($1,000)

State	Direct expenditures from additional power	−	Payment to Navajo plant to cover cost	+	Profits returned to states	+	Operation and maintenance	=	Net direct expenditures
Arizona	402,552		123,001		2,176		163,178		444,905
California	120,554		42,934		605		0		78,224
Colorado	0		0		0		0		0
Nevada	65,945		22,885		322		0		43,383
New Mexico	0		0		0		0		0
Utah	0		0		0		0		0
Rest of U.S.	0		0		0		0		0

Note: Numbers have been rounded in some cases.

tributed to all regions proportional to the fraction of total federal purchases made in each region after subtracting operations and maintenance expenditures for Glen Canyon; and (3) operation and maintenance expenditures were returned to Arizona.

Tables 9-1 and 9-2 give results for the Glen Canyon case. Noting from table 9-1 that Arizona received 994,854 megawatt hours of electricity in 1973 from Glen Canyon Dam, and given that this was the largest allocation, it is not surprising to see the largest resultant direct expenditure from the additional power, $40,136,000. From this amount, $6,943,000 was returned to the U.S. Treasury, and $184,000 was allocated back to Arizona as federal expenditures. Because the power plant is located in Arizona, the operations and maintenance expenditures were assumed to remain there. The result is a net direct expenditure of $41,000,000.

The adjustments for the Navajo Generating Station were as follows: (1) payments for power "purchased" by the participants must

Table 9-4. Effect on GNP of Power Production in the Lake Powell Area ($1,000)

Project and state	Net direct expenditures	+	Indirect expenditures	=	Effect on GNP
1973 Glen Canyon					
Arizona	41,000		10,214		51,214
California	7,246		11,223		18,469
Colorado	24,598		9,828		34,426
Nevada	20,748		5,666		26,414
New Mexico	6,801		2,988		9,789
Utah	22,012		11,331		33,343
Rest of U.S.	23,350		64,838		88,188
Total					261,868
1972 Glen Canyon					
Arizona	38,796		9,327		48,123
California	4,460		8,630		13,090
Colorado	20,428		8,221		28,649
Nevada	8,804		4,443		13,247
New Mexico	10,948		2,858		13,806
Utah	18,281		9,378		27,659
Rest of U.S.	19,326		54,882		74,208
Total					218,782
Projected Navajo plant					
Arizona	444,905		86,020		530,925
California	78,224		62,545		140,769
Colorado	0		11,749		11,749
Nevada	43,383		16,641		60,024
New Mexico	0		9,798		9,798
Utah	0		24,815		24,815
Rest of U.S.	0		210,448		210,448
Total					988,528

be subtracted; (2) profits from the power generation must be redistributed back to the regions; and (3) operation and maintenance expenditures are returned to Arizona. In both cases, the result is then net direct expenditures that were multiplied by the Metzler Model into changes in GNP by region.

Even though there are six participants in the Navajo Generating Station when aggregated by region, only three gross allocations were traceable. (Of the six, four market electricity in Arizona, one in California, and one in Nevada.) Thus, for the Navajo Generating Station, net direct expenditures are zero for Colorado, New Mexico, Utah, and the region "rest of the United States". As we will see, this does not necessarily preclude GNP changes effected through the regional multipliers.

These changes are presented in table 9-4 in which direct expenditures have been singled out to give some idea of the magnitude of respending effects for different states and regions. Note that among the individual states, California's indirect expenditures are largest in proportion to direct expenditures, while Nevada's are the smallest. This is because the California economy is better integrated and less dependent on imports than the Nevada economy, and it implies that an increment in power sold to California will have a greater increase in local gross product, and consequently in local employment, than will a similar increment sold to Nevada. The small size of indirect expenditures vis-à-vis direct expenditures in most states is significant and explains, as noted, why the stimulating effect of energy investments on the general economy tends to be modest in the Southwest.

The effect of power production on employment in the various states can be seen in table 9-5. Given that the employment coefficients are quite similar in magnitude, it is not surprising that the states which receive a large proportion of the power also experience large employment changes. Recalling the 1973 Glen Canyon case in table 9-4, note the large indirect expenditure of $64,838,000 for the category "rest of the United States." This results in a relatively large change in employment caused by indirect expenditures for this category. This example illustrates well the interdependence of the regional economies when exogenous effects are traced through the Metzler Model.

The total effect of current energy development in the Lake Powell area (using 1973 Glen Canyon figures and those projected for the Navajo Generating Station) is an increase in GNP of 1.25 billion dollars and an increase in employment of approximately 76,000 people. Of this overall increase in GNP, 47 percent goes to Arizona, reflecting the fact that this region contains the generating stations under analysis and especially that it is allocated the largest share of the power; 24 percent goes to the region listed as "rest of the United States" (exclusive of the Southwest), reflecting the importance of

Table 9-5.   Incremental Change in Employment from Power Production

Project and state	Region employment coefficient (people / $1,000)	×	Change in GNP ($1,000)	=	Increment in employment (no. of people)
1973 Glen Canyon					
Arizona	.0632		51,214		3,237
California	.0562		18,469		1,038
Colorado	.0634		34,426		2,183
Nevada	.0621		26,414		1,640
New Mexico	.0672		9,789		658
Utah	.0590		33,343		1,967
Rest of U.S.	.0581		88,188		5,124
Total					15,847
1972 Glen Canyon					
Arizona	.0632		48,123		3,041
California	.0562		13,090		736
Colorado	.0634		28,649		1,816
Nevada	.0621		13,247		823
New Mexico	.0672		13,806		928
Utah	.0590		27,659		1,632
Rest of U.S.	.0581		74,208		4,311
Total					13,287
Projected Navajo plant					
Arizona	.0632		530,925		33,554
California	.0562		140,769		7,911
Colorado	.0634		11,749		745
Nevada	.0621		60,024		3,727
New Mexico	.0672		9,798		658
Utah	.0590		24,815		1,464
Rest of U.S.	.0581		210,448		12,227
Total					60,286

indirect expenditures resulting from interregional trade; 13 percent goes to California, a relatively closed and highly integrated economy with a large local multiplier; and 16 percent goes to Southwestern states other than California and Arizona (Colorado, Nevada, New Mexico, and Utah), which are regions with large propensities to import.

The second largest increase in GNP (24 percent) occurs completely out of the Southwest and is composed almost entirely of indirect expenditures. This suggests that energy-related development in the Southwest has a broad expansionary influence on the economy at large even when the energy is consumed locally.

Finally a more careful look at Arizona is warranted before we focus on the local Page area economy. For Arizona, the economic and employment effects are substantial. But a look at table 9-2 is revealing. The first column can be taken as indication of sustainable economic stimulus in the areas where power is consumed, mostly Phoenix and Tucson. The column headed "operations and maintenance" is an indicator of the continuing economic stimulus in the producing region, around Lake Powell and Page. The point to note is that *the stimulus is almost all in the consuming region and not in the producing region*. Major stimulative effects on regional economies occur only outside the Poverty Diagonal.

ECONOMIC EFFECTS IN THE IMMEDIATE LAKE POWELL REGION

As one moves closer to the sites of the energy resources, one finds that the phenomenon of "leakiness" of the economy, which was apparent in the macroeconomic studies of the states, is even more strongly in evidence in the local economies of those areas. One finds that there is a relatively enormous effect on the local economy during the transient phase of development, which consists of the opening of mines and the construction of plants. But this is almost entirely the direct result of the payroll from the project itself with little indirect effect on other elements of the local economy. Many permanent residents of the region are in fact severely disadvantaged by the development because of increasing costs and declining amount and quality of services. Others improve their economic position, at least temporarily.

If the Southwest is to be a major exporter of energy and energy resources, it must import most of the capital and labor needed to construct and operate the production and extraction facilities. This is because the needed skills are usually only available to a small extent in the local labor force and the capital available in the region is far too little to finance these giant developments. A single project may employ thousands of workers whose presence, along with their families and an associated service population, would create significant economic and social impacts on all but the larger cities. In most parts of the Southwest, the sites for such projects are dictated by the location of resources and are typically isolated from the larger cities that would be able to provide the necessary services for thousands of new people in a very short time without massive disruption. Of necessity, new towns may spring up almost overnight in rural areas, or small agricultural towns may be adopted by industrial developers and their size increased several fold. The latter become new and different places with the influx of new people and new money looking for a supply of goods and services.

The objective in this section, therefore, is to examine the relationship among new jobs, people, and the local economy of such boomtown communities. For this purpose Page, Arizona, the town associated with Glen Canyon Dam, the Navajo Power Plant, and the Black Mesa Mine, is used as a historical example and case study.

The social situations which tend to occur in boomtowns have been described in an enlightening manner primarily by John Gilmore and his associates at the Denver Research Institute. One example is

Sweetwater County, including the town of Gillette, Wyoming.[3] A brief review of the situation there is useful background for our consideration of the development of Page.

During the period 1970 to 1974, rapid expansion of trona mining and the construction of the Jim Bridger Power Plant (built for the Pacific Power and Light and Idaho Power companies) occurred in the county. Population and employment levels increased from about 19,000 to about 37,000 and about 7,000 to about 15,000 respectively. The quality of municipal and other local services declined markedly. In the state of Wyoming, the average doctor–population ratio is about 1:1,100; in Sweetwater County this ratio increased from 1:1,800 in 1970 to 1:3,700 in 1974. Mental health clinic caseloads increased eightfold. In 1974, there was an estimated deficit of 138 schoolrooms in the county. Capital costs for providing schoolrooms are estimated to be on the order of $5,100 per child; 1970–74 increases in assessed valuation for school districts were but $2,100 per child, however. By 1974, the deficit in municipal facilities for homesites (water, sewage, roads, electricity, and the like) was approximately 1,400 home sites (4,600 mobile home spaces needed). With little expansion in police facilities, crime rates increased by 60 percent between 1972 and 1973 alone.

The statistics quoted above are only the grossest indicators of the morass of social, institutional, and economic conditions that may attend the disruptions brought about by rapid, large-scale economic developments in small communities. Increased rates of alcoholism, broken homes, and suicides were among the many manifestations of breakdowns in social order in Sweetwater County reported in Gilmore and Duff's seminal work concerning the anatomy of a boomtown.

On the other hand, the economics of the boomtown phenomenon are poorly understood for two reasons. First, since boomtowns are characterized by rapid change, their economies are in disequilibrium, yet theoretical economic models almost always treat equilibrium situations. The latter is a situation in which economic variables either are not changing or else are changing uniformly through time. Second, collection of the primary economic data in the private sector, especially from business, is time consuming and difficult because respondents fear that confidentiality will not be maintained and are often unsympathetic to the perceived aims of the researcher. In addition, such data collection is labor intensive and therefore expensive.

---

[3] John S. Gilmore and Mary K. Duff, *The Sweetwater County Boom: A Challenge to Growth Management* (Denver, Colo., University of Denver Research Institute, July 1974).

The next section will describe briefly in nontechnical language some of the theoretical work by the Southwest Project team in boomtown economics. This discussion will help to develop an analytical framework for understanding the boomtown experience in general and the Page experience in particular. Subsequent sections will present a detailed analysis of the Page economy based on primary data collection.

THE BOOMTOWN PHENOMENON

The boomtown experience is generally characterized by external economic pressure for resource development which, as already noted, gives rise to a rapid influx of population. This, in turn produces an immediate shortage of public services and private goods, and a set of social and environmental problems that usually degrade the quality of life for workers and their families. Although these effects reflect a complex reality, the economic explanation centers on the existence of disequilibrium in three critical areas: the labor market, the market for private capital, and the level of public investment in social capital. We begin by examining the factors affecting the external economic forces fostering and driving localized booms.

The initial construction phase of the typical boomtown is associated with a remarkably rapid growth of the labor force and takes place over a three-to-ten year period for major projects such as the construction of power plants or dams. One could hypothesize a construction phase with a more gradual buildup of the necessary labor force spread over a longer interval, which would consequently reduce or eliminate many of the problems associated with boomtowns. The question becomes, then, why does one observe such a hurried buildup in the construction phase?

To answer this question, we need only consider the economic incentives operating over the construction period. Clearly, the objective in any such process is to minimize the cost of construction at the date of completion. Since borrowing must occur as construction progresses to cover current costs (including wages), and because these costs cannot be repaid until operations begin, labor costs incur compound interest over the construction period as part of the total cost of construction. This implies, for instance, that for a five year project with a six percent interest rate, labor that costs $10 in the first year of construction has an actual cost of $13.50 (including compound interest), at the completion date. In contrast, $10 spent on labor during the third year only costs about $11.30 at the completion date. Clearly a strong economic incentive exists to use labor, and for that matter all inputs to the construction process, as late in that process as is consistent without too great a loss of productivity. Furthermore, the higher the interest rate, the greater the incentive both to utilize inputs as late as possible and to shorten the overall construction period. Figure 9-1 illustrates the effect of imposing a positive interest rate (r) on a hypothetical labor-use pattern over time. Note that for the positive interest rate case ($r = 6\%$), the total area under the curve, or the total amount of labor used in the construction process, is larger than that for the zero interest rate case, which indicates a decrease in labor productivity. This occurs because of the necessity to sacrifice

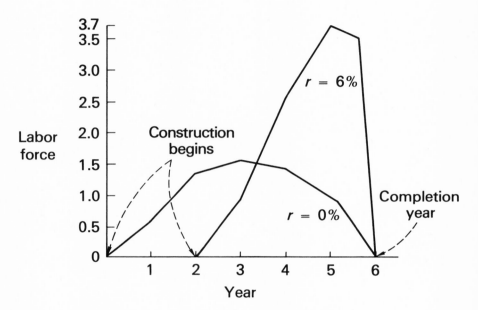

Figure 9-1. Effect of a positive interest rate on a labor-use pattern

some labor productivity to hasten construction in order to reduce the total cost of construction, which now includes interest costs. Accordingly, with positive real interest rates, labor productivity will actually drop over time during the life of the construction project as a result of the economic incentive explained above. Gilmore has suggested that labor productivity drops for sociological reasons as boomtown conditions worsen with the continued influx of new workers and population. Unfortunately, the analysis presented here complicates verification of Gilmore's hypothesis that the quality of life affects productivity, because such a productivity loss also has economic origins and is an inherent feature of the construction process brought about by cumulative interest costs during construction.

Several other factors can be demonstrated to exacerbate the intensity and brevity of the construction phase associated with the boomtown phenomenon. First, the more sensitive (elastic) the labor supply is to increases in wages (in other words, the greater the number of additional workers that can be induced into a region for a given increase in wages), the more rapid the boom will become. Given that there has been substantial unemployment recently and a tradition of regional mobility in the construction trades, it is clear that the elasticity of labor supply is large for most boomtowns. Second, if the production processes for construction exhibit about constant returns to scale (in other words if labor productivity does not drop substantially for faster rates of construction), then, at any given rate, it becomes feasible to shorten the construction period without further loss of productivity while saving on interest costs during construction.

In summary, the forces underlying the boomtown phenomenon are those of natural resource, rather than human resource, development. The pattern of employment is affected by the interest rates on borrowing during construction, the supply of labor to the region (affected by unemployment rates), the returns to scale of the construction process, and the human environmental conditions of the region containing the natural resources under development.

We now turn to a detailed examination of the case of Page, Arizona. The experience there reflects many, but not all, of the facets of the boomtown phenomenon. The specific situation and the primary data collected permit an especially penetrating look at the economic aspects of the phenomenon.

THE CASE OF PAGE, ARIZONA

As noted at the beginning of this chapter, construction of Glen Canyon Dam and companion steel Arch Bridge began in 1957. To provide housing for construction workers, the U.S. Bureau of Reclamation created the community of Page, Arizona, a few miles from the dam site. In only a year the population went from zero to about 3,000; three years later it had doubled to 6,000, half of whom were construction workers. Following the completion of the 700 foot dam in 1964, the population dropped to 2,500, and then to just half of this after the 950 megawatt hydroelectric station was completed in 1966 (figure 9-2).

Through 1970, the population of Page remained under 1,500 even though the new Glen Canyon National Recreation Area was being discovered by hundreds of thousands of recreationists who were attracted to Lake Powell, which was still filling up behind the dam. Page's second phase of development was thus the establishment of water-based recreation, an industry which continues to grow gradually.

The dam's water storage function also led to the third phase of development at Page, production of electricity via huge, coal-fired, steam-electric generating units. Construction activities associated with the Navajo Power Plant doubled the population in the first year, and shot it up to a new peak of over 8,000 in 1973. But with construction nearing completion in 1976, the population of Page fell rapidly and stabilized at about 3,800 during late 1976, thus ending Page's third phase of development. Figure 9-2 also demonstrates the timing pattern of large-scale construction projects discussed in the previous section, characterized by sharp and dramatic peaks as opposed to smoother, more gradual phasing of construction activities.

It is fruitful to examine the relationship between the number of construction workers and the associated population during the two booms. There were about 2.0 persons per worker during construction of the dam, and about 2.7 with the Navajo plant. This supports the argument that the decision of families to accompany construction workers is related to the availability of private and public amenities. Note that no town existed prior to construction activities on the dam, while Page, a small town, was present to help provide public and

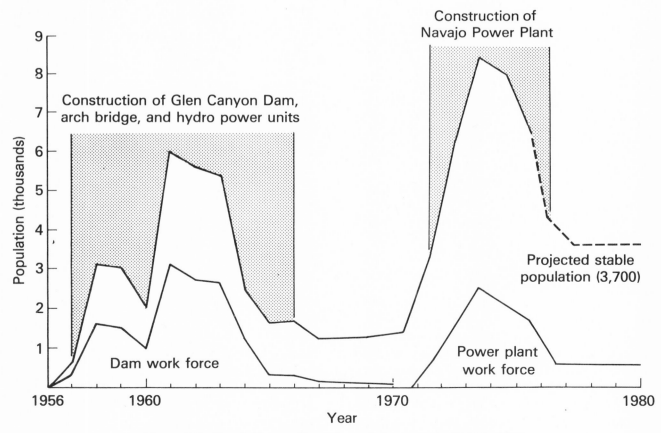

Figure 9-2. Population profile of Page, Arizona, from 1956 to 1980

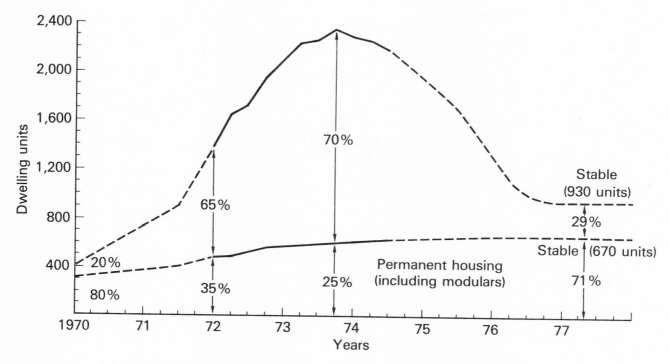

Figure 9-3. Dwelling units by type for Page, Arizona, from 1970 through 1980

private services during construction of the Navajo project. Lake Powell is an amenity which was not available during construction of the dam but was available to power plant workers. Together with higher wages, these factors made Page more attractive during the power plant boom than it was for the families of construction workers in the earlier boom period.

Figure 9-3 presents a graphic view of housing by type of residence over the period of the more recent boom. The influx of mobile homes was so great that the typical ratio of mobile homes to permanent housing was inverted between 1970 and 1973, when permanent housing made up only 25 percent of the total. As the permanent housing trend continued, the ratio reverted back to near the original mix as construction workers left Page.

The most salient characteristic of small regional or community economies is their virtual total dependence on exports from a few sectors for their survival. This applies especially to boomtown economies like Page which have grown up very rapidly in response to an undiversified set of industrial developments. Were Lake Powell to dry up, the industries of electric power, government, and recreation would vanish, and

The Page Area Economy

so would Page. It is essential that this dependence on a few export sectors be mirrored within the framework of the model used to analyze such economies.

The choice and formulation of an economic model depend upon the questions to be answered and the data available for making a model operational. Perhaps the most important question is how personal income varies in response to changes in the levels of activity of the basic industries of the local economy, that is, the export industries. Personal income provides one measure of the effect of local economic activity, namely its monetary contribution to the welfare of the individuals within the community. Each export industry injects money into the local economy by making transactions of three types: payments to local businesses, payments to local households, and payments to local government. But not all of these transaction dollars represent benefits to people in the community. For example, a one dollar transaction between a visiting tourist, representing the recreation (export) industry, and a restaurant operator will result in substantially less than one dollar of personal income for restaurant employees and other Page residents. This results from leakages in this business sector. Much of each business dollar is used to purchase goods and services from outside the local economy, with only a small fraction of each dollar reaching the paychecks of local residents. On the other hand, a one dollar transaction between the Salt River Project and one of its employees at the Navajo Power Plant will result in more than one dollar of personal income to Page residents because the initial dollar of personal income is partially recycled within the local economy for consumer goods and services, and a fraction of that amount makes it into someone else's paycheck the second time around. The sum of the direct and indirect effects of each type of transaction between an export industry and the local sector of an economy is called its multiplier effect. A systematic method of accounting for these effects in one comprehensive set of multipliers is embodied in the technique of input–output analysis.

The export industries in an input–output model of an economy export goods and services out of the local economy and import dollars in return. These dollars are imported through transactions with one or more parts of the internal sector of the local economy. The export sector of the Page area economy has been defined to include the following industries: (1) the U.S. Bureau of Reclamation, which constructed and operates the Glen Canyon Dam, hydroelectric plant, and the city of Page; (2) the U.S. National Park Service, which manages and constructs facilities associated with the Glen Canyon National Recreation Area (GCNRA); (3) federal aid to the local school system; (4) state and county aid to the local school system; (5) the Salt River Project, which constructed and operates the Navajo Power Project near Page; and (6) visiting recreationists drawn to the national recreation area. The internal (or endogenous) sector of the local economy is defined to include three subsectors: (1) all local business, (2) local households, and (3) local government (which consisted only of the Page schools since other local government functions were managed and operated by the Bureau of Reclamation). The input data for the model must thus include three pieces of information for each export industry, representing the level of transactions between that industry and each of the three subsectors of the internal economy.

The heart of the model adopted by the Southwest Project team, as indicated above, is a set of multipliers. In general, each of the export industries can make transactions either directly with a given internal subsector or indirectly with the internal subsector through one of the other internal subsectors. Thus, there are three multipliers for each internal subsector, for a total of nine multipliers, as shown in table 9-6.[4]

Table 9-6.   Community Multipliers (Direct, Indirect, and Induced Effects)

	Business	Household	Local government
Business	1.1696	0.4904	0.3098
Household	0.2237	1.0964	0.6002
Local government	0.0054	0.0071	1.0040

Note: See text for explanation of multipliers.

The input–output model was applied over the entire span of years from the inception of Page until 1975, the last year for which data were available to the research team, and then projected through 1980. Input data representing payments from each of the six industries in the export sector to each of the three subsectors of the internal economy were collected. Where gaps existed in the data set, estimates were made using the best techniques that could be devised in each case. Data on recreational expenditures had to be estimated throughout, using data on recreation visitation in combination with estimates of expenditures from the results of another part of the Lake Powell research. It is believed that the resulting data set has a fairly high degree of reliability.

The analytical results of the model are presented in graphic form. The time profile of personal income is in figure 9-4. All results were

Application of the Model

[4] Berry C. Ives, William Schulze, and David Brookshire, "Boomtown Impacts of Energy Development in the Lake Powell Region," *Lake Powell Research Project Bulletin* no. 28 (September 1976) (Los Angeles Calif., University of California Institute of Geophysics and Planetary Physics).

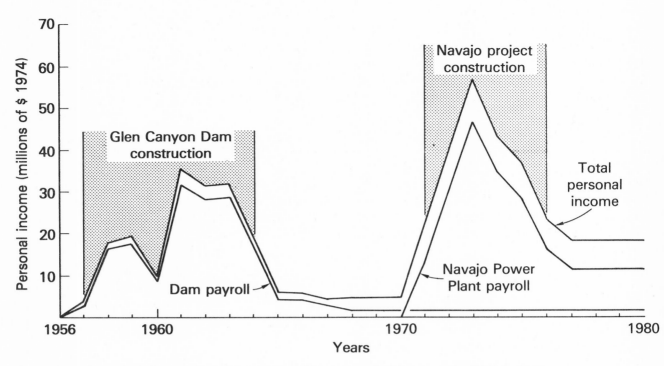

Figure 9-4. Page area economy personal income and major payrolls, 1956 to 1980

normalized to 1974 dollars using the consumer price index. The nearly one-to-one relationship between the major payrolls and total personal income, inclusive of direct and indirect effects, is obvious and dramatic. This is characteristic of boomtowns in the extreme case, where the magnitude of the new payroll is very large relative to the original export base. In addition, the roller coaster impression typifies abrupt booms, which have a temporary construction phase that is large in terms of the required work force relative to the permanent operating work force. The latter is usually beginning to develop about the time construction is peaking.

Direct and indirect personal income for selected years, by export industry of incidence, are shown in table 9-7. The years selected illustrate the changing character of the local economy. During 1961 the dam construction phase was peaking and accounted for virtually all personal income. By 1969, recreation had developed significantly, accounting for 52 percent of personal income including expenditures of the National Park Service. Bureau of Reclamation activities, including operation of the dam facilities and managing Page (still an unincorporated municipality) were down to 37 percent. In 1973, both of these industries were dwarfed by the Salt River Project's construction of the Navajo power project, which was then peaking and responsible for 90 percent of personal income. This new industry

Table 9-7. Personal Income by Export Sector for Selected Years for
the Immediate Page Area Economy
(percentage of total)

Export sector	Year				
	1961	1969	1973	1977	2000
Salt River Project	0	0	90	69	62
Bureau of Reclamation	98	37	3	9	8
Recreation					
Recreationists	0	31	3	10	16
National Park Service	0	21	2	6	9
Other	2	11	2	6	5
Total	100	100	100	100	100
For reference					
Personal income ($)	$35,237,000	$4,120,000	$56,723,000	$17,852,000	$19,242,000

Note: Immediate Page area includes the city of Page plus Wahweep Marina.

should have been in a stable operating phase by 1977 and will have
accounted for two-thirds of total personal income generated in the Page
economy. Recreation and dam operation will account for about one-
sixth and one-tenth of total personal income, respectively. In terms
of personal income, the level of permanent economic activity in the
Page area will have quadrupled since 1969.

Total business receipts are presented in the same fashion in figure
9-5. The pattern here is markedly different, however. This is because

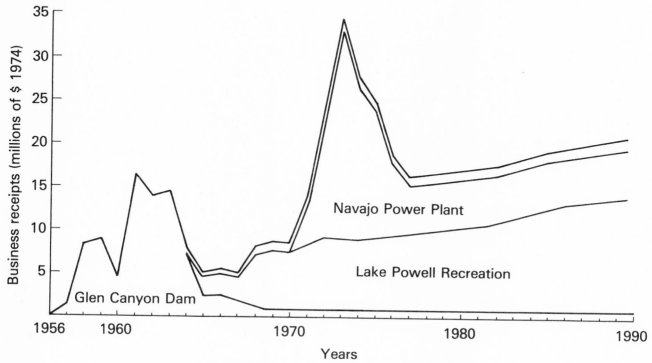

Figure 9-5. Page area economy business receipts by export incidence, 1956 to 1990

of the large effect that imported recreation dollars have on business receipts relative to the personal income generated by these transactions. Thus, although recreation is relatively big business in the Page area, leakages in the industry cause most of these dollars to be exported so that they never reach the household subsector. There appears to be great potential for increasing personal income from recreation business if more support services can become established, thereby retaining and recirculating a larger portion of recreation business receipts within the local economy. This depends to some extent on the administrative policies of the National Park Service, which controls services in the immediate area of Lake Powell. Support services are likely to increase naturally, however, as recreational visitation continues to increase.

Generalities from the Page Experience

The construction of Glen Canyon Dam and related facilities gave rise to a large boom in employment and income in the immediate region. Because of the extremely open nature of the Lake Powell area economy, the payments made to workers leaked out of it quickly and had very little sustaining stimulative effect on the economy. Most of the payments during the boom were made to persons now no longer in the region. The enormous investment laid the economic base, mostly mining activities and recreational usage of the lake (with very little from the power plant), for one modest town in the region.

The history of Page also illustrates that at least some of the adverse effects of a boomtown situation can be mitigated by advance planning and "front end" money. The larger number of persons in Page per employed worker during the second (Navajo Power Plant) boom supports the hypothesis that there will be a greater tendency for families to move to a boom situation if levels of public and private services and amenities are higher. While there is no reason to think that investments in infrastructure were optimally provided, nevertheless, since Page was a "company town" of the Bureau of Reclamation, it was planned along with the other investments.[5] Such coordinated planning does not happen when the town is separate from the investment projects. The undesirable results of the latter have been graphically described by others, as indicated early in the chapter.

[5] Members of the Southwest Project team did extensive theoretical and empirical work on optimum planning under boomtown conditions. This work is quite technical and is not reported here. Interested readers should consult the list of publications at the end of this book.

As we have noted, the Southwest may see the development of many boomtowns as a result of rapid energy and other mineral development. The specific counties where these are likely to be located were simulated by means of the Southwest regional model, with results reported in chapter 8.

Experience and logic tell us that such towns are usually undesirable if not disastrous places in which to live, and their existence is of little or no benefit to the regional community at large. The following paragraphs review the main elements of this situation and some things which could be done about it.

1. The need for such basic public services as sewers, roads, utility lines, and school facilities ordinarily arises before there is anything like adequate public funding available at the local level to provide them. In addition, normally little or no advance planning occurs. Front end money and advance planning are needed to come to grips with this situation. While there is no reason to think that the planning and investment in Page was ideal, the contrast with the disastrous situation in Gillette referred to earlier reinforces this point.

2. What might be called public environmental services are frequently even more neglected. As a result, the usual appearance of the towns is dreadful and urban recreational opportunities outside the home are virtually nonexistent. A suitable urban environment requires landscaping, parks, playgrounds, and community centers. Again, these are matters which require planning and timely money. The greater presence of families in Page during the second boom illustrates the importance of this point for fostering a normal family life.

3. The worst quality of life is frequently experienced by the women in boomtowns. They usually must live in mobile homes in which housekeeping does not occupy much of their time and which are physically very confining. As indicated above, at one point three-quarters of the homes in Page were mobile homes. Women also suffer most from the poor utility and amenity services in such towns. In addition, because they are based on a heavy extractive industry or construction, these towns usually provide very few opportunities for women to work outside the home. They are single industry towns whose economic activity is usually administered from a distant location and so provide few white collar jobs in the town. It is possible to see opportunities for improving this situation. A systematic effort could be mounted to identify employment opportunities in work that can be conducted at home. In addition, use could be made of university

SUMMARY OF BOOMTOWN PROBLEMS AND POLICY IMPLICATIONS

extension services to provide continuing education opportunities. Even something as prosaic as the mandatory provision of cable television could be very useful. But providing such things in a timely manner requires planned collective action.

4. Members of the indigenous labor force in the Southwest, more often than not Indians, Chicanos, and rural Mormons in the Poverty Diagonal, are usually lacking in training that would fit them for the types of jobs which become available. The heavy importation of workers to Page during the boom period illustrates the point. Therefore, the indigenous workers either do not participate in any benefits which the economic development would otherwise offer or are consigned to the most menial types of work. A systematic and timely program of manpower training could therefore accomplish two things: it could make better use of indigenous populations, therefore requiring less movement into the area, and it could help some of the most economically disadvantaged parts of the U.S. population.

5. Heavy capital investments tend to leave little permanent economic base behind, once the construction phase is over. Consequently, as happened in Page, the bust is often as sharp as the boom. In addition, when durable infrastructure, both public and private, has been put in place during the boom, the remaining population may not be sufficient to sustain it and taxes may become burdensome. In cases where there was an existing population, the combination of high prices during the boom and high taxes afterwards may be disastrous for them. To this end, economic methodology for urban infrastructure planning in boomtowns was developed by members of the Southwest Project team.

MITIGATING THE PROBLEMS

Clearly, mitigating the bad effects of boomtown development involves advance planning, proper institutional arrangements for the implementation of plans and, certainly not least, a large amount of front end money. These are the essential ingredients that have been lacking in virtually every boomtown development in the nation's history. The federal government, in cooperation with the states, must take a leading role in coming to grips with this situation. It appears to be beyond the means or at least beyond the will, of most of the states to deal with it by themselves or to successfully impose it on the industries exploiting the resources and therefore causing the problems, although imposing it on the industries, as indicated later, may be the most desirable situation.

Consequently, as part of the nation's resources policy, and particularly as part of its energy policy, the federal government should take the lead in addressing the boomtown problem. It could do this by making available to the states loans at moderate interest rates to provide the front end money required where large natural resources developments giving rise to a boom situation are contemplated. These loans could be used to provide the funding for basic public services, environmental public services, useful and satisfying activities for women and young people, and for manpower training.[6] Such a loan could be repaid in two ways. First, for the basic public services (the schools, the public utilities, the electric lines, and the sewers), the money could be repaid from user charges or normal taxes on the people using these public services. Where a bust as well as a boom situation is expected, facilities could be provided at a level, and using technologies, that will not be unduly burdensome for the remaining population.[7] The low interest charged on the capital would also be helpful in this regard.

The part of such a loan going for environmental services, for setting up activities for women, and for manpower training would be repaid by severance-type levies on the extraction of the minerals (these would be mandated as a condition of the federal loan). This not only would provide a repayment mechanism for the loan but would do so in a manner which causes at least some of the social costs of the minerals extraction to be reflected in the private costs of development companies and in product prices.

Thus, the first element in a strategy to mitigate the ill effects of boomtown development would be the provision of repayable front end money for specified purposes by the federal government. Public officials in the region should use their influence in Washington to make sure that the boomtown problem is addressed as part of the development of a national energy policy.

The second element is the planning and implementation of livable communities. Although a challenging task, the actual process of planning for the basic public services and environmental public services should be quite manageable. Planning capabilities already exist in state planning departments and in the planning department

---

[6] There is precedent for such an approach. In 1975 the U.S. Congress enacted amendments to the Coastal Zone Management Act relating to onshore impacts of outer continental shelf development. Included in the amendments are federal funds to assist with planning and to offset the cost of infrastructure and service investments required by impacted communities (P.L. 92-583, 94th Cong., 1 sess.). A bill was introduced by senators Hart (D. Colorado) and Domenici (R. New Mexico) which would extend this approach to boomtowns.

[7] The most informative discussion of the latter problem is found in R. Cummings, and coauthors, "An Inquiry Regarding Surrogate Measures for Social Benefits Attributable to Municipal Infrastructure in Boomtowns," mimeo (Albuquerque, N.M., University of New Mexico, Department of Economics, 1976).

of the Navajo Nation, and they could probably be augmented rather readily. The economic demographic model described in chapter 2 could play a very useful role in such planning. In making plans, the location of the town as well as its character should be considered. It may be possible to situate a town in such a way that it could serve mining operations at several deposits sequentially and thus extend its life and make capital investments in it more worthwhile. As revealed by the Page experience, construction booms and the presence of heavily capital-intensive industries in remote areas provide but a slender support for a sustained strong local economy. The more sociological aspects of planning, for example, coming to grips with the plight of women in these communities, are more subtle, but as indicated previously, it is not too difficult to think of promising possibilities in this area also. Experience suggests that the most difficult part of this element of the approach will be to see that the plans are actually implemented. Indeed, successful implementation of urban planning in the United States is a rare event. Here again the federal government would be in a position to play a leading role by laying requirements on the states that all public and private development in areas designated to be boomtowns would have to proceed in accordance with the plan or else the state would lose its eligibility for the provision of federal front end money.

A program of the sort sketched here could make the boomtown situation at least a tolerable one. To a large extent it could avoid the unhappiness, alcoholism, high divorce rates, and low productivity characteristic of such situations, to the extent, of course, that they are in fact caused by living conditions. In addition some positive effect, not mere mitigation of adverse effects, could accrue from the program, especially in the areas of education and manpower training.

In those cases where it is extremely difficult and costly to establish a decent community close to the operation, and where the boom and bust situation is likely to take place over a relatively short time, it may be better not to try to establish a community at all. In such cases it would probably be more attractive to provide for barracks-type living for the workmen with long work days while they are on the job but extended periods of time off to be at home. A ferrying service, using buses where distances are not too large and an aircraft shuttle where they are, would be a necessary part of such an approach.

CONCLUDING COMMENT ON THE ROLE OF THE STATES

The need for the federal government to take a lead role in coming to grips with the boomtown problem has been emphasized, reluctantly, in what has been said previously. Despite the difficulty of doing so, the states should also strive to take their own initiatives. That action is possible at the state level is illustrated by events in Wyoming, which while outside the Southwest region has similar problems. This example is well worth a brief review.[8]

The Wyoming Community Development Authority (WCDA) is an organization unprecedented in America. Its mission is comparable to the foreign development banks created subsequent to World War II in an effort to bring prosperity to poor countries. It is designed both to promote economic growth and to manage it. The authority has two divisions: the Civic Project Division and the Housing Division. The latter is analogous to the housing authorities in most states and many cities; the former is the core of the impact management system. Both divisions operate by borrowing funds on the national tax-free securities market and investing them in the utilities, housing, public facilities, and streets of communities affected by the siting of large industrial facilities. A special reserve fund built from coal and mineral severance tax receipts serves to insure the bonds, making them attractive to prospective buyers.

Much of the authority's power lies in its unwritten relationship to the Wyoming Industrial Siting Council (WISC). The council's permits often contain requirements that lend the force of law to the authority's plans. One permit, for example, contained provisions requiring the developer of a $1.5 billion power plant to guarantee the financing of some $25 million in public facilities and housing in a community near the site. The authority offered to finance the required items under the developer's guarantee; the permit in effect will improve the strength of the authority's bonds and will give it substantial influence over the project's design and construction.

Thus two independent agencies in Wyoming, together with certain other elements of state government to which they turn for research support (for example, the state Department of Economic Planning and Development) and policy guidance (the governor's office), effectively control most large private and public investments in the state and enjoy substantial indirect influence over small commercial and residential investments induced by the changing industrial base.

If the states through their planning and permitting procedures could put the burden of infrastructure development on industry, while being helpful in planning and finance, this would ensure planning of communities and public facilities in conjunction with proposed major investments and also place the costs where they belong. Americans have, for good reason, a highly unfavorable image of the "company town." But as the contrast between Page and Gillette shows, the company town situation can be considerably better than the inde-

---

[8] This section is based on an unpublished paper by Edward H. Allen, "Economic Planning Makes a Debut in America," n.p., n.d.

pendent community situation. Furthermore, the planning and permitting processes which are now widely available at the state level
(for example, in the Four Corners region, Arizona, Colorado, and
New Mexico have some form of power plant siting authority) could
help prevent the evils of earlier company towns by setting standards
for their development and operation.

10 THE SPECIAL CASE OF THE NAVAJOS

Some 34 percent of the nation's rural Indian population resided within the Southwest Poverty Diagonal in 1970, with the Navajo Reservation dead center in it. The Southwestern Indians are, as we saw in chapter 2, the poorest segment of the regional population but also the most distinct culturally. Their importance for energy development transcends their numbers—over 200,000 in 1970—and their ethnic characteristics, however. In 1973, the Navajo Reservation alone yielded 11,000,000 barrels of crude oil, 4,500,000 cubic feet of natural gas, and 10,915,300 tons of coal. These resources earned a meager $8,545,250 in royalties and lease revenues, which, in turn, comprise the major portion of the tribe's annual income. Known reserves include 2.5 billion tons of coal, 100 million barrels of crude oil, and 23 billion cubic feet of natural gas. There are, in addition, 80 million pounds of uranium.[1] In effect, a very poor and numerically small segment of the regional population owns a significant portion of the mineral resources essential for future national development. The continued underdevelopment of Indian reservation economies, despite the extraction of these resources, poses a major problem for the future for the Indians themselves and for others concerned about their continuing poverty. In this chapter we will use the case of the Navajo Tribe to illustrate some of the reasons for the continued poverty of reservation populations in an era of rapid development of resources which they own.[2]

[1] The Navajo Tribe, Office of Program Development, *The Navajo Nation Overall Economic Development Program* (Window Rock, Ariz., The Navajo Tribe, 1974) pp. 22, 27, 56, 58.

[2] Work by the Southwest Project research team included an extensive survey of resources on the Navajo Reservation. The interested reader should consult the list of publications at the end of this book.

The extraction of mineral resources in the Southwest has, as we have seen, involved the infusion of large amounts of capital into rural, underdeveloped regions. Although the profits from the ventures return to investors elsewhere and the consumption of the end product most often takes place at some distance from where the resources are located, still local populations expect to benefit in a number of ways. Increased employment is expected to improve the standard of living. Payrolls should create a demand for services which in turn creates more jobs and general business improvement. Finally, the increased cash flow is expected to contribute taxes to local and state governments, thus improving the public sector of the economy.

In the Poverty Diagonal, Indians and non-Indians have similar expectations concerning the benefits to be derived from the coal mining and power production that has started to develop there. Both populations have experienced a decline of the rural economy since the early years of the twentieth century and have seen their children migrate to distant urban centers in search of jobs. The rural Mormons, living to the north of Lake Powell, expect that with new employment opportunities their children will remain at home and so preserve a distinctive Mormon way of life. In a like manner, the Navajos of the western portion of the reservation look forward to enhancing a traditional Navajo life-style. Both groups feel they should experience a better standard of living *in situ,* with better jobs, schools, and services developing in their home communities. Neither group desires, or expects, a further erosion of the family or extended kin group so important to their respective life-styles.

Yet, as discussed in chapter 9, the experience of Page, Arizona, during and after the building of the Glen Canyon Dam indicates that non-Indians are not much more likely to realize their expectations than are the Navajos. Briefly, the new jobs are taken by skilled workers from outside the region, outmigration of local populations is not halted, and, after the construction phase is over, the boom turns to bust. For the Navajos, the situation is made more complex by the special status of Indian reservations and the almost total lack of skilled workers in the area. Local Navajos do not benefit from the new jobs, new businesses are owned by non-Indians in off-reservation towns so that no development of service occupations occurs on the reservation, and, with tribes lacking the ability to tax, revenues go to county and state rather than to tribal government.[3]

It has been estimated that, if the higher rates of resource extraction are realized (see chapter 2), Navajo mineral resources will be

[3] Whether Indian reservation sovereignty includes the power to tax is an unresolved question. We consider some of the implications of inability to tax further on.

exhausted in approximately fifty years. The exceedingly difficult problem facing the Navajo Tribe is that of utilizing revenues from mineral resource development in such a manner that a diverse and dynamic reservation economy is created that will provide the Navajo people with a standard of living comparable to that of other Americans. To accomplish this goal the tribe must (a) receive a larger share of the returns realized from resource extraction; (b) employ a larger proportion of Navajos than has been possible heretofore; (c) find a way to tax new development so that the public sector of the economy can be controlled by the tribe rather than by the federal government. Should the goal of a more prosperous and more self-sufficient reservation economy not be realized, the reservation will be in much the same position when its nonrenewable resources are gone as it is now; that is, dependent upon the federal government for the largest proportion of its payroll and for the funding of most health, education, and welfare programs. In sum, the reservation itself would experience some sort of a "boom" followed by a "bust" in much the same way as the many small towns in the area (see the discussion of Page in chapter 9).

To appreciate the magnitude of the task facing the tribe, it is helpful to remember that although the Navajos are the largest single tribe in the United States, the present (1978) reservation population of approximately 135,000 people is only that of a small city. Yet this population, undereducated and lacking job skills, must somehow manage an area the size of West Virginia, with natural resources at least comparable to those of other areas in the West of the same size. It is clear that for some time to come the tribe must depend upon the federal government to provide expertise and managerial assistance.

The Navajos attract attention because of the vastness of their land holdings and the extent of their natural resources, yet other tribes of the Southwest share the same problems to a greater or lesser degree. The Pimas, Papagos, Maricopas, and Colorado River tribes of southern Arizona seek to defend their water rights during a time of increased demand throughout the region. The relatively small Laguna Tribe seeks to benefit from large uranium deposits within and adjacent to its reservation without losing its ethnic identity and tribal cohesion —and these are but a few of the examples that might be cited.

Chapter 2 reported the stark disparity between the economic status of the Indian peoples of the Southwest and that of the surrounding populations, even their fellow residents in the Poverty Diagonal. The condition is certainly not new, nor is political and public awareness of the problem lacking. As noted in the chapter on water rights, two recent presidents, Richard Nixon and Lyndon Johnson, have made

THE PERSISTENCE OF INDIAN POVERTY AND UNDERDEVELOPMENT

strong statements on the subject. Johnson pronounced, "With rare exceptions, Indian communities are so underdeveloped that there is little, if any opportunity for significant social or economic progress . . . our goal must be: a standard of living for the Indian equal to that of the country as a whole."[4]

Yet the problem remains unsolved. Despite the fact that the relative position of the Navajos moved from 28.6 percent of the median family income in 1959 to 37.5 percent in 1969, the absolute difference was 50 percent greater in 1969 compared with 1959.[5] Since that time, Navajo per capita income has declined: from $686 in 1969 to $567 in 1974 (in 1967 dollars).[6] During the same period, the per capita income of the general U.S. population increased from $2,283 to $2,991. In 1974, the per capita income for Navajos was only about 19 percent of the national figure. There are very few exceptions to this trend among Indians in the Southwest. Among them, the Zunis of New Mexico achieved better incomes from jewelry making because of a recent resurgence of interest in Southwestern Indian arts and crafts, while the Lagunas of New Mexico have benefited from renewed uranium mining in their area.

The reasons for the persistence of Indian poverty have been widely discussed. It is generally recognized that the development of reservation economies is impeded by several factors: (1) the extremely low levels of accumulated capital either in the forms of skills and education or in money—the median years of schooling for Navajos 25 years or older is only 3.4, for example, and there was, until recently, only one bank on the reservation; (2) the geographical isolation and low population densities of many of the Southwestern reservations; (3) the difficult status of the Indians as domestic wards of the federal government; (4) the uncertain status of water resource ownership (this was discussed in chapter 4) and taxing authority; (5) the ambivalent attitudes of the Indians themselves toward economic development. The problems posed by the special status of Indians and their reservations require some elaboration as background for the further consideration of the economic consequences of the Lake Powell developments for the Navajos.

[4] Lyndon Johnson, as reported in U.S. Department of the Interior, *The Westwide Study* (Washington, D.C., April 1974).

[5] Gerald J. Boyle, "Revenue Alternatives for the Navajo Nation," *Working Papers in Economics* (Albuquerque, N.M., The University of New Mexico, 1973).

[6] S. J. Kunitz and J. E. Levy, "Navajos," in Alan Harwood, ed., *Ethnicity and Medical Care* (Cambridge, Mass., Harvard University Press, 1981).

Traditionally, the federal government has discharged its obligations to Indian tribes by supporting services rather than capitalizing the private, or productive, sector of reservation economies. During the nineteenth century it was argued that the cultural level of Indians was such that they were unable to participate successfully in a market economy. There was much truth in this view, and reservations were established in large part to protect tribes from exploitative and unscrupulous non-Indians. Indian resources were to be preserved for use at some future date when Indians would be more competent to handle their own affairs. At the same time, however, it must be recognized that when these resources were discovered, they were exploited for the benefit of non-Indians. W. T. Hagen has outlined the history of this expropriation of Indian land, mineral resources, and water.[7] When gold was discovered in the Black Hills, for example, Indian lands were relocated to a more isolated and less desirable location. Government officials, as on the San Carlos Apache Reservation, would often mine mineral resources for personal profit. In the Apache case, the agent not only escaped prosecution but sold a mine to the inspector sent to check on him. Between 1887 and 1934, the Indians were separated from some 86 million acres, over 62 percent of all Indian lands. Most of the lands remaining were isolated, desert or semidesert, and generally not desired by the white population.

With the advent of the Roosevelt Administration and the "New Deal for American Indians," there was a considerable shift in federal policies and practices. But, by this time, much of the damage had been done. Water was utilized by non-Indian populations, states had extended their authority into many reservations, and isolation and ethnic separatism had become a way of life. At present, to the degree that reservations have natural resources of any value, they have generally been sold in the ground for royalties and a very few jobs. The nonextractive industries that have located on reservations are those attempting to escape high labor cost areas. In effect, it is the lack of skills and education of Indian labor that is attractive. Because there is surplus manpower on reservations and because labor costs are low, there are labor-intensive manufacturers making such things as fish hooks and nets or, more recently, assembling electronics components.[8]

THE ROLE OF THE FEDERAL GOVERNMENT IN DEVELOPING RESERVATION ECONOMIES

---

[7] W. T. Hagen, *American Indians* (Chicago, The University of Chicago Press, 1961).

[8] A. L. Sorkin, *American Indians and Federal Aid* (Washington, D.C., The Brookings Institution, 1971).

Despite the creation of a few tribal enterprises since the New Deal years, government agencies, primarily federal but also state and tribal, continue to be the more important employers, and employment in these agencies is predominantly in the human services sector. This imbalance is well exemplified by the Navajo Reservation where unemployment and underemployment is between 50 and 60 percent and where fully two-thirds of employed Navajos work in service-related occupations. Of those Navajos with wage or salaried employment, 77 percent are employed by federal and local government. In an important sense, the provision of services is also labor intensive and can absorb many people who would otherwise remain unemployed. The Navajo Tribe reports that in 1974, 9,458 Navajos had full-time employment in public services, while only 519 were employed full time in mining activities.[9]

Historically, the principal threats to the preservation of Indian resources have come from non-Indian demands for the land and minerals contained therein, which it was the government's obligation to protect. Currently, except for water, as we saw in chapter 4, Indian ownership of natural resources is no longer in dispute. Rather, the concern expressed by many commentators is that the U.S. Bureau of Indian Affairs has not exercised proper care in approving contracts between the tribes and the various extractive industries, with the result that the economic benefits accruing to the Indians are considerably less than could have been obtained by hard bargaining.

In 1923, the first tribal-wide Navajo council was created by the secretary of the interior specifically for the purpose of approving oil and gas mining leases. At its first meeting this council unanimously voted away its power to control these resources by approving a resolution drawn up in Washington "granting the Commissioner to the Navajo Tribe the authority to sign 'on behalf of the Navajo Indians' all oil and gas leases which might in the future be granted on the treaty portion of the reservation."[10] A form of coercion was used which soon became familiar to Navajo leaders. The council was told that the "Navajos . . . would suffer more than anyone else if they failed to . . . grant consent." And this because the government itself would not consent to add more lands to the reservation if the tribe did not accede to its demands. This acquiescence has all but disappeared in the 1970s. Presently, individual Navajos are bringing suit against various agencies of the federal government claiming that such

9 The Navajo Tribe, *Navajo Nation Development Program,* p. 24.
10 L. C. Kelly, *The Navajo Indians and Federal Indian Policy 1900–1935* (Tucson, Ariz., The University of Arizona Press, 1968) p. 69.

agencies have "made decisions to further production of uranium yellow cake" without preparation of adequate environmental impact statements as called for by the National Environmental Policy Act.[11] At the same time, the Navajo Tribal chairman, Peter MacDonald, has said that "all coal, oil and mineral leases on the . . . reservation will be reviewed and renegotiated—under threat of tribal takeover."[12]

An understanding of the concern Indians feel about current non-Indian development of reservation resources, including water resources, can be gained from a look at events leading up to the construction of the Navajo Generating Station.

THE NAVAJO GENERATING STATION

The plan to produce electrical power for the benefit of several basin states by utilizing coal from the Black Mesa Mine on the Navajo Reservation and Colorado River waters impounded in Lake Powell by the Glen Canyon Dam involved the Navajo Tribe as an active participant in negotiations for water in 1968. The project called for the federal government to construct the dam and subsequently to become a major purchaser of the electricity generated at the site. A consortium of western utility companies led by the Salt River Project was to build the coal-fired generating station on land near Page, Arizona, and thereafter to generate, transmit, and supply electric power to their customers. In effect, the resources of large private power companies were to be pooled with those of the Bureau of Reclamation.

The Navajo Generating Station would need approximately 34,100 acre-feet of water each year and Congress commanded that this amount was to be charged against Arizona's 50,000 acre-foot entitlement. It was clear to all concerned that the Navajo claim had to be quantified so as not to exceed the Arizona entitlement and, in addition, that the needs of the generating station had to be charged against the unquantified Navajo entitlement.

The Navajo Tribe finally agreed to the construction of the power plant as well as to the use of 37,100 acre-feet per year of its entitlement to Colorado River water in Arizona. Specifically, the tribe granted 34,100 acre-feet of its share of the Arizona portion of Upper Basin water for use by the generating station and 3,000 acre-feet by the town of Page. The grant of water for power generation extended for the life of the power plant or for the next fifty years, whichever would occur first.[13]

[11] *Window Rock Navajo Times* (Arizona), January 4, 1979, p. A-1.
[12] *Tucson Arizona Daily Star,* January 10, 1979, p. A-6.
[13] The Navajo Tribe, Navajo Tribal Council, *Navajo Tribal Council Resolution #CD-108-68* (Window Rock, Ariz., December 1, 1969).

Direct benefits to the tribe from the generating station itself were few—$45,000 annually from the plant site lease and some $200,000 in wages of Navajo workers at the plant—and it becomes necessary to discuss briefly just how it was possible for the Navajos to accept this arrangement with any degree of equanimity. Research conducted by investigators of the Lake Powell Research Project indicates that the federal government did not exercise its stewardship functions adequately because of conflicting interests.[14] In consequence, the tribe was not provided with adequate technical advice, with any alternative solutions, or with an accurate estimation of economic benefits.

The federal government was a major capitalizer of the venture and a major purchaser of power to be generated by the Navajo Generating Station. It was natural for the secretary of the interior to press for a successful and speedy conclusion to the negotiations. To this end, the Bureau of Reclamation contributed its considerable technical capacities. The Bureau of Indian Affairs, by contrast, was incapable of providing the tribe with the expertise necessary for it to make informed decisions. The Bureau of Indian Affairs, in fact, had to rely on the Bureau of Reclamation for data and advice. Lacking independent sources of data and advice and, in addition, being pressured by the Department of the Interior and its sister agency, the Bureau of Indian Affairs presented the tribe an either–or option: either the tribe accepted limitations on its water rights or it would not receive any economic benefits from the Black Mesa coal mines.

Throughout the negotiations, the coal mining activities on Black Mesa were presented as being contingent upon the successful completion of the Navajo Generating Station, although no evidence was produced to show that this resource would not be exploited independently. In fact, the tribe was presented with an inflated estimate of the compensation they would receive for waiving their water rights as a result of linking the two developments. That this occurred is not surprising in light of the fact that the tribe received almost all of its information from the non-Indian interests in the negotiating process: the Salt River Project, the Bureau of Reclamation, and the Upper Colorado River Commission.[15]

[14] B. McCain, "Final Report," unpublished report prepared for the Lake Powell Research Project, in the possession of Jerrold Levy, University of Arizona, Tucson, 1974; R. Conn, "Tribal Water Rights and the Navajo Generating Station," report prepared for the Lake Powell Research Project, in the possession of Jerrold Levy, University of Arizona, Tuscon, 1974; Lynn A. Robbins, "Navajo Energy Politics," *Lake Powell Research Bulletin,* no. 54 (1978) (Los Angeles, Calif., University of California Institute of Geophysics and Planetary Physics).

[15] B. McCain, "Final Report," pp. 36–43; *Problems of Electrical and Power Production in the Southwest,* U.S. Senate Report 92-1015, Senate Committee on Interior and Insular Affairs, 92 Cong. (1972), p. 1626; The Navajo Tribe, Navajo Tribal Council, "Record of the Navajo Tribal Council" (Window Rock, Ariz., December 10, 1968) pp. 360–362.

Whatever misgivings individual Navajo leaders may have harbored, they were not expressed during Tribal Council discussions. It is probable that the tribe's overriding desire to increase its revenues and to provide job opportunities for its constituents predisposed it to consider the question of economic benefits to the exclusion of other considerations. It also appears likely that the fear of losing all benefits from the coal mining ventures constrained the tribe from bargaining aggressively for optimal returns from the Navajo Generating Station itself. Tribal politicians interviewed by Robbins maintained that they feared being held politically responsible for any action which would impede economic development.[16] They also felt their lack of knowledge put them in an untenable position. Although they suspected the Bureau of Indian Affairs of keeping them in ignorance of all the facts, they were afraid that admitting ignorance publicly would make them appear foolish and ineffective in the eyes of their constituents.

The Navajos' experience has shown them that if they press for unlimited water rights, they risk jeopardizing economic development, while accepting limitations on their rights does not guarantee equitable economic benefits. During the 1970s, the tribe began to bargain more aggressively in lease negotiations with coal and uranium companies. Whether there is still room for bargaining for expanded water rights in Arizona is an unanswered question.

THE ISSUE OF INDIAN AUTHORITY TO TAX

Tax revenues are a major benefit accruing to regions where extractive industries are located and account for much of the enthusiastic support given to mining companies in many western states. The question posed by large-scale mining operations on Indian lands is whether tribal governments are to be viewed as private owners of resources entitled to lease payments and royalties or whether they are also to be accepted as governments on a par with those of the surrounding states, entitled to collect tax revenues for the public good and responsible for providing public services. As in the case of Indian water rights, the sovereignty of tribal governments has been recognized by the federal government in principle but without clear definition of the extent and limitations of this sovereignty. Historically, specific decisions concerning the extent and nature of Indian sovereignty have been made as the need arose with the result that many areas of current concern, including taxing authority, have yet to be resolved. It is necessary not only to examine some of the legal complexities involved but also to discuss some of the possible political and social consequences of such a development before asking whether it is economically beneficial.

---

[16] Robbins, "Navajo Energy Politics."

Early in the nineteenth century, the U.S. Supreme Court ruled that ". . . Indian tribes possessed all sovereign powers over domestic matters within their territorial boundaries unless the United States decreed to the contrary. This sovereign power has even been declared free of restrictions emanating from the Bill of Rights."[17] The power to tax is an ordinary aspect of sovereignty so that Indians ought to possess this power since Congress has not acted to withdraw it. Historically, however, the federal government's definition of Indian sovereignty has been narrowed as non-Indian populations and economic interests penetrated Indian country. For example, the jurisdiction of Indian courts has been limited to crimes committed by Indians against other Indians, and the federal government has reserved the right to try "major" crimes committed on reservations in federal court. Since 1974, however, the federal government has taken a more positive view concerning tribal authority over non-Indians.

But if the principle of domestic sovereignty is clear, the fact remains that Indian tribes have not often attempted to assert their powers of sovereignty over non-Indians, especially when, by doing so, they would come into direct conflict with the states. There are many reasons for this hesitancy, not the least of which is economics. Most tribes are both small and poor. Engaging in lengthy litigation with a state is beyond the means of most tribes and it is not always clear that the expense would be justified by the gains realized. For example, the Shoshone-Bannock Tribe of Idaho has never moved to stop the state from collecting income taxes on payrolls despite the fact that states are generally prohibited from taxing wealth produced on the reservation. With a total population on the reservation of no more than 2,000, it is unlikely that the revenues to be gained would equal the costs of litigation in the foreseeable future. Instead, many tribes have seen the need to preserve their claims to land as having higher priority. Because, however, the Navajo Tribe is the largest in the nation and because it commands such a wealth of natural resources, it may very well be that it stands to lose a large amount of money by not exerting its right to tax non-Indian enterprises on the reservation.

In 1972 the Navajo Tribal Council adopted a motion to levy taxes on large business operations on the reservation, and in 1974 the Tribal Council created a Navajo Tax Commission charged with the task of preparing measures for taxing non-Indians. Nevertheless it took two years before the membership of the commission was decided upon. There are a number of reasons for the tribe's reluctance to move aggressively in this area. First, there is the fear that taxes should be

[17] C. E. Goldberg, "A Dynamic View of Tribal Jurisdiction to Tax Non-Indians," *Law and Contemporary Problems* vol. 40, no. 1 (1976) p. 169.

imposed upon Navajos as well as non-Indians. Second, there is a reluctance to shoulder the responsibility to provide services to non-Indians, fearing that this would be the first step in making tribal institutions replicas of those found among the general population and thus destroying Navajo distinctiveness. Finally there is the recognition that the tribe does not have the bureaucratic capacity to design and administer an adequate tax program. Currently, the tribe does not even have the manpower necessary to audit and enforce the royalty and lease obligations of the various mining and oil companies.[18]

The Indian Civil Rights Act of 1968 was designed to make Indian governments follow dominant-society values guaranteed by the Bill of Rights and subsequent civil rights legislation in their dealings with Indians and non-Indians. Potentially the act could be used to force the tribe to tax Indians and non-Indians equally under its equal protection clause. The minimal returns to be realized from taxing Navajo payrolls or business enterprises would not justify the expense of establishing a tribal-wide bureaucracy to administer the program. The recognition, by the Supreme Court in 1974 (*Morton* v. *Mancare*), of the legality of the preferential hiring of Indians by the Bureau of Indian Affairs suggests that the difficulty posed may not be insurmountable. However, even if the tribe were permitted to tax non-Indians while exempting Indians, there is real reason to expect the courts to demand that non-Indians be given the right to vote in tribal elections, to serve on tribal juries, and so forth, as the rights due to taxpayers in the general population.

Perhaps even more imminent, however, is the threatened conflict between tribal and state interests. Although Congress has the power to grant states taxing authority over Indians as well as non-Indians on reservations, it has never done so in a general way. Specific states have been granted jurisdiction over reservation Indians with Indian consent. The tax exempt status of Indian lands, however, has remained intact.[19] In general, federal law has been interpreted to allow state taxation of mineral extraction on Indian reservations. Thus, any Indian assertion of the same authority will immediately be contested by the companies and states already exercising this power.

As the Navajos seek to modernize and benefit from resource development, they will be under pressure either to come increasingly under state jurisdiction or to take on the characteristics and responsibilities of non-Indian governments. Both routes threaten cultural distinctiveness and tribal separatism. According to Goldberg: "To avoid such negative consequences, as well as costly litigation, it may

[18] Gerald J. Boyle, "Revenue Alternatives," pp. 17–19.
[19] C. E. Goldberg, "A Dynamic View," p. 183.

be necessary for the tribe to seek a congressionally sanctioned compromise or to negotiate directly with the states for sharing of revenues and responsibilities."[20] But, are the revenues the tribe would collect of such a magnitude that the risks and expenses involved would be worth incurring? Or, conversely, can the tribe afford to continue, as it has, taking the royalties and lease payments while hoping that these and increased job opportunities will be sufficient to create a viable reservation economy? As a first step in answering these questions, we first look at the tax revenues derived from the Navajo Generating Station and the Black Mesa Coal Mine and try to estimate the net profit to the tribe should it collect these revenues at the same time it assumed the responsibility for public services currently provided by the state of Arizona.

Because information on revenues derived from taxes other than that on property is not available, the estimated benefit from tribal taxation is a minimum one at best. The total property tax bill paid annually by private owners of the Black Mesa Coal Mine and the Navajo Generating Station comes to $22,944,444. Thus, one major development complex on the Navajo Reservation yields more in property taxes alone than the tribe realized from royalty and lease payments from all the coal, natural gas, and petroleum production on the reservation in 1974 ($17.84 million). Similar tax revenues, were they to be collected from all present and projected developments on the reservation, would go a long way toward enabling the tribe to reach its goal of achieving a large increase in its standard of living.

It must be recognized that some of these tax revenues are already benefiting the Navajos in the form of various public services. Unfortunately, it has not been possible to determine the actual sums spent by state and local government on the reservation. The state claims to have provided welfare services to the Navajo costing $6.2 million in 1972.[21] Only $984,000 of this amount actually comes from state coffers, the rest being financed by the federal government. A similar problem plagues estimates of the amount actually spent on the reservation by school districts, counties, and cities. In the case of education, for example, the federal government makes an in-lieu-of-tax payment for every reservation Indian child in a public school. There is no doubt but that there is some double payment to state and local government for some of the services rendered. Nevertheless, in the light of the fact that the tribe is actively engaged in revenue-sharing negotiations with the state and federal governments, it is not unrealistic to compute an

---

[20] Ibid., p. 188.

[21] Ernst and Ernst internal audit for the Navajo Tribe for the fiscal year 1972 (unpublished).

amount based upon the Navajos' proportionate representation in the two counties where the generating station and coal mine are located and to assume that these funds are, in fact, being spent on the reservation at present. The estimated Navajo share of state, county, and school district property tax revenues comes to approximately $12.5 million. Assuming a Navajo right to tax property values in full, the net gain to the tribe would come to approximately $10.4 million annually. More detail on these calculations is shown in the appendix 10-A.

It is clear that the state and local governments will object strenuously to any attempt on the part of the Navajo Tribe to exert full taxing authority. Whether the cumulative amounts to be gained by the tribe from taxing all extractive industrial activities will be worth all the effort it would take to do it has not yet been decided. A possible compromise lies in more active participation by the tribe in revenue-sharing negotiations.

EXPECTATIONS AND REALITY: DEVELOPMENT IN THE LAKE POWELL REGION

There has never been any vocal Navajo opposition to persistent tribal efforts to increase employment opportunities on the reservation, and the tribe's economic goals were clearly and comprehensively stated in the Navajo Ten Year Plan of 1972 and in later economic development plans.[22] Whether the development of Navajo natural resources has helped the tribe to realize its goal of a standard of living more nearly equal to the national average began to be questioned by Navajos only in the 1970s. The development of the coal resources of Black Mesa and the construction of the Navajo Generating Station at Page, Arizona, were highly visible and dramatic and played an important role in educating Navajos to the possible damage to the environment and to their life-style that such large-scale operations might entail. Before discussing the tribe's recently awakened concern over these matters, it is important to examine in some detail the economic effects of energy development as exemplified by that undertaken in the Lake Powell region and to see whether tribal or local expectations have been met.

The most immediate goals of the tribe have always been to receive adequate payment in the form of royalties and lease payments from the sale of the resources themselves and to provide jobs for as many Navajos as possible. Though not explicitly stated, there has always been an implicit expectation that Navajos would somehow benefit from the taxes generated by these large-scale developments. In addition to these direct benefits, however, the tribe has also hoped that increased Navajo payrolls would have a multiplier effect; that is, increased

---

[22] The Navajo Tribe, *Navajo Nation Development Program.*

Navajo spending would stimulate business activities on the reservation, which in turn would create more jobs for Navajos. Finally, there is concern about the accelerating rate at which younger, better educated Navajos are leaving the reservation in search of jobs. The tribe hopes to keep more of these skilled Navajos on the reservation by providing better job opportunities.

The expectations of Navajos living in areas immediately adjacent to the strip mines parallel those of the tribe. Their concerns, however, are more oriented to the local situation, as might be expected. While the Navajo Tribe is concerned about creating jobs for Navajos regardless of place of residence, local Navajos have expected to get the new jobs themselves. They do not want Navajos from other parts of the reservation to migrate to the job sites and deny opportunities to the unemployed Navajos already living there. In addition, local populations have come to expect that they would receive water from Lake Powell, electricity from the generating station, and coal from the strip mine.

It is not difficult to understand the expectations of Navajos living in the Lake Powell region—a region which is the least developed of the reservation. Unemployment levels are higher there than in other areas of the reservation. Families are larger and transportation, housing, and access services are poorer. The Lechee Chapter was one of the most sparsely populated areas of the western Navajo Reservation before the construction of the Glen Canyon Dam. Prior to the stock reduction programs of the 1930s, only eight stock owners grazed sheep in the vicinity, and this was only during the winter months.[23] As indicated in chapter 4, in 1956 work began on the Glen Canyon Dam and the town of Page was built on Manson Mesa. With U.S. Highway 89 routed through Page, the Colorado River bridged, and the highway extended another 70 miles to Kanab, Utah, the isolation of the area abruptly came to an end.

The population of Page grew to 6,000 during the construction of the dam (see chapter 9). About 10 percent of the workers employed at the dam site were Navajo and virtually all of these were unskilled. When construction on the dam was completed in 1963, the population of Page decreased to 1,000, of whom fewer than 100 were Indian. The on-reservation Navajo community, which had grown up by the Lechee Chapter House, consisted of only seven households with a population of thirty-eight. By 1970, when construction of the station was begun,

---

[23] D. G. Callaway and coauthors, "The Effects of Power Production and Strip Mining on Local Navajo Populations," *Lake Powell Research Bulletin* no. 5 (1978) (Los Angeles, Calif., University of California Institute of Geophysics and Planetary Physics).

the population of Page had grown to 1,540 and approximately 106 Navajo families were living in the large Page–Lechee area.[24]

Black Mesa, the location of the Peabody coal mining operation, is an isolated highland in the west-central portion of the reservation some 2 million acres in extent. Prior to the development of the coal mine, which opened in 1970, there were no graded roads in the area, and the average family lived 10 to 15 miles from the nearest paved highway. To reach the highway connecting Tuba City and Kayenta, Black Mesa dwellers had to descend from the rim of the plateau on roads that were impassable during much of the winter. In 1973, Black Mesa was more densely populated than was the area around Lechee (6.4 versus 3 persons per square mile) and it was more seriously overgrazed. The area around the coal mines had a larger and poorer resident population than did Lechee. Given these conditions, it is not surprising that many Navajos feel that any development of the area would be beneficial and it is to this question that we now turn our attention.

It is difficult to assess accurately the net dollar amounts realized by the private corporations participating in the Lake Powell developments without access to the sums spent for taxes of all types, operating expenses, and annual proceeds from the sale of electricity. One can, however, make some rough comparisons between what the tribe receives in lease payments and royalties on the one hand and what the Peabody Mine receives from coal sales.[25]

Available estimates of total on-reservation investment by corporations have ranged from $300 to $600 million (about 1970 prices) for the combined mining and power production operation. Included in these sums are: $52.5 million for the railroad transporting coal from the mine to the generating station; $143 million for transmission lines; some $200 million over a 50 year period for environmental protection; between $40 and $45 million for the Black Mesa Mine. Investment in tribal resources includes the land area to be stripped by mining activities (44,000 acres), the generating station site (1,021 acres), and an ash disposal site (765 acres). In addition there is the guarantee of 34,100 acre-feet of Navajo water rights allotment for cooling the generators and 3,000 acre-feet for the town of Page. It has been argued that these resources would not have been utilized by the tribe if the projects under discussion had not been created. It is important to remember, however, that the guarantee of water to the

Royalty and Lease Payments

---

[24] Ibid., p. 9.
[25] Material for this section is primarily from McCain, "Final Report."

generating station effectively prohibits any other major utilization of water by the Navajos for the life of the project.

The Navajo Tribe has contracts to sell approximately 455 million tons of coal at the rate of 13 million annually over a 35 year period and some 37 billion gallons (127,750 acre-feet) of subsurface water over the same period of time to operate the slurry line that transports coal from the Black Mesa Mine to the Mohave Generating Station near Bullhead City, Nevada.

Based on current projected figures the total revenues accruing to the Peabody Coal Company over a 35 year period will be about $750 million. The Navajo Tribe will receive $76 million in royalties while the Hopi Tribe will receive $25 million. The Navajo Tribe will also receive $315,000 as their share of the water revenues.[26]

The Navajo Generating Station, with a net capacity of 2.25 million kilowatts and net output of 750,000 kilowatts, is expected to produce enough electricity to meet the household needs of 1.9 million people. The revenues to be received for electricity have not been estimated but the amount must come to more than the $750 million earned from coal sales, and the difference should be added to the total revenues of the corporations. During the first twenty-five years the Navajo Tribe will receive $169,000 annually for the Navajo Generating Station site, the ash disposal area, a rail loading site, and a pumping station site. The tribe will also receive $125,000 annually for transmission line rights of way and $108,000 annually for the railroad right of way. In addition, $375,000 were donated by the corporations to the Navajo Community College in Tsaile, Arizona (a one-time gift of $250,000 and $25,000 annually between 1969 and 1974 for a professional chair).[27]

Assuming that coal production reaches the estimated 13 million tons each year, the Navajo Tribe can expect to receive some $2.6 million dollars annually from all royalties, leases, and rights of way after 1976. This amount comes to about 12 percent of the estimated amount earned by coal sales alone. Whether the proportion is equitable is a question which cannot be answered by assessing revenues alone. Benefits from taxes, payrolls, and the multiplier effect must be taken into consideration. Equally important, however, is the less tangible question of whether, by striking the bargain in its present form, the Navajo Tribe has (a) furthered its goal of economic self-sufficiency, or (b) sold its resources for far less than would have been possible if it had been in a position to consider alternate development plans.

[26] U.S. Senate, *Problems,* pp. 199–203.
[27] Lynn A. Robbins, "Industry and Income: The Navajo," *Southwest Economy and Society* vol. 2, no. 3 (Spring 1977) p. 64.

One of the selling points made by industry representatives to the tribe *Jobs for Navajos* was that construction of the generating station and the mining activities would provide a substantial number of jobs for Navajos. In 1974, during the construction phase of the project, 495 Navajos were employed at the Navajo Generating Station by the Bechtel Corporation and by the Salt River Project. An additional 179 Navajos were employed by various subcontractors, the railroad, and the pipeline companies. The two operating mines on Black Mesa (Black Mesa #1 and the Kayenta Mine #0252) employed a total of 180 Navajos.[28] The total of 854 jobs was to decline by about 50 percent when the construction phase of the generating station was completed in 1976. It has been estimated that an annual Navajo payroll of about $5.5 million would result over the projected 35 year period of operation if Navajo employment can be maintained at about 500 with an average annual income of $11,000.

It is important to remember that, with the completion of the construction phase, the newly unemployed Navajos had to seek jobs in other parts of the reservation, a circumstance which did little to promote economic or social stability in the area. Whether Navajos were getting an equitable proportion of the total number of jobs available is also an open question. Only 10 percent of the 200 jobs with the Salt River Project went to Navajos while 25 percent of the 1,659 with Bechtel were held by Navajos. Twenty-two percent of the 812 positions with the railroad, pipeline company, and other subcontractors were filled by Navajos. This compares unfavorably with employment at the mines, which was 90 percent Navajo. Even at the Four Corners Power Plant, Navajo employment reached 37 percent while 55 percent of 8,634 positions provided by the Bureau of Indian Affairs, the U.S. Public Health Service, and the public schools on the reservation were filled by Navajos. Industry representatives have argued that there are few Navajos with the requisite skills in the construction trades and that Navajo employment is further hindered by the high turnover rate among Navajo workers generally and especially among Navajos enrolled in the training programs created by the private companies involved in constructing and operating the generating station.

Recognizing that the underdevelopment of the Navajo labor force may be the major factor inhibiting Navajo employment, the fact remains that overall levels of unemployment remain high in the area generally and that Navajos employed in energy projects most often occupy the lowest paid positions.

In 1973, the peak year of hiring for construction, the Bechtel Corporation employed 274 Navajo construction workers. Of these,

---

[28] The Navajo Tribe, *Navajo Nation Development Program*, pp. 24–25.

44 percent were laborers and 29 percent were apprentices in skilled trades. Only 27 percent were journeymen in skilled jobs.[29] A majority of those employed by Peabody Coal Company were laborers. In areas sampled by the Lake Powell Research Project in 1972 and 1973, Navajo unemployment ranged from 3 to 10 percent in the town of Page and in the trailer camp next to the generating station. These settlements were comprised almost entirely of Navajos who had migrated to the area for the express purpose of gaining employment at the generating station. Among the settlements comprised primarily of indigenous Navajos, unemployment stood at 32 percent near the Lechee Chapter House and 21 percent among Navajos settled by the highway just south of Page.[30]

STEMMING THE BRAIN DRAIN

That employment went to migrant Navajos is further shown by the fact that only 22 percent of the skilled workers interviewed had resided within 80 miles of the generating station prior to taking jobs there—moreover, 63 percent had held jobs in off-reservation areas. By contrast, only 6 percent of the unskilled workers interviewed had lived off the reservation prior to taking a job at the generating station and 48 percent were indigenous to the immediate area. Clearly, the expectations of local Navajos were not met, for the best jobs were taken by immigrants.[31]

If the local Navajos felt left out, however, it seemed that the tribal desire to bring skilled young Navajos back to the reservation was being fulfilled. Those skilled workers who had taken up residence in trailer camps in Page and next to the generating station were younger, better educated, and more acculturated than the local unskilled workers. The immigrants sought medical treatment from private physicians rather than from the Indian Health Service. They were unionized, more knowledgeable about state and national politics, and had a positive attitude toward the wage economy and their standard of living. Yet, when asked where they would prefer to live, 48 percent of the skilled workers said they preferred to live away from the reservation. Only 4 percent of the unskilled workers expressed similar desires, while 67 percent wanted to remain on the reservation, and 29 percent expressed no preference. Several skilled workers volunteered the information that they only moved to Page because of the highly paid jobs available at the generating station.

---

[29] Callaway and coauthors, "The Effects of Power Production," p. 11.
[30] Ibid.
[31] E. Henderson, "Skilled and Unskilled Blue Collar Workers: Occupational Diversity in an American Indian Tribe," unpublished paper of the Lake Powell Research Project, in the possession of Jerrold Levy, University of Arizona, Tucson, 1978.

The intrusion of the immigrants, skilled and unskilled alike, was resented by the local population. In addition to the fact that they took jobs some local Navajos felt were rightfully theirs, there were some social and political disruptions. Local Navajos feared that immigrant Navajos would exert their right to vote in the Chapter House organization—the Navajo equivalent of the New England town meeting and the only level of government below that of the Tribal Council itself. There was fear that the newcomers would attempt to graze livestock in an already overgrazed area. Residents of the area had been led to believe electricity and water would be made available to them. When this proved not to be the case they felt cheated and their resentment found expression when the need to provide water, sewage disposal, and electricity for the trailer camp next to the generating station was discussed. It was argued that all the developments in the area had not brought these services to local Navajos, a situation which left the task to the Navajo Tribal Utilities Authority and the Indian Health Service. Because these agencies had not been able to meet the demands of local Navajos, any services they might provide the trailer residents would, in effect, be at the expense of the indigenous population. In the event, these disruptions were short lived, and the local inhabitants' fears failed to materialize to any great extent. Immigrant wage workers were not interested in local politics and did not bring livestock into the area. The construction phase was completed before the newcomers' presence became important.

These local resentments and apprehensions are worth commenting upon because they presage the kinds of complications that will develop whenever new wagework settlements are created. Because the town of Page is not on reservation land, non-Indian workers did not become intrusive. Wherever non-Indian settlements must be created on the reservations, however, problems of law enforcement, interracial relations, and legal status will become salient. And wherever development projects create more permanent settlements, local resentment of immigrant Navajos will be an important factor determining community benefits.

The Multiplier Effect

During discussions with the tribe concerning the merits of the generating station, it was claimed that the Navajo payroll of approximately $5.5 million would generate an additional $8 to $10 million boost to the economy annually although it was never mentioned that this multiplier effect would benefit non-Indian to the almost total exclusion of Navajo owned business.[32] The largest proportion of Navajo personal

[32] McCain, "Final Report."

income—67 percent—is spent off the reservation. Twenty percent goes into savings and taxes (3 and 12 percent respectively) or is unaccounted for (5 percent). Only 13 percent is spent on the reservation.[33] As 62 percent of all businesses on the reservation are owned by non-Indians, it is clear that Navajos do not benefit greatly from this added cash flow.[34] Businesses on the reservation employ Navajos but because most are general merchandise retail outlets, more expensive items like automobiles and appliances must be bought in towns off the reservation.

In the Balance   We have seen that the Navajos have quantified their water rights in the Colorado River for the life of the generating station without receiving payment for the water actually used to cool the plant, or for water used by the town of Page, which houses employees of the plant. Although they received some benefit from the taxes paid by the corporations to the state and local governments, the tribe signed a waiver of all rights to tax the corporations directly for the lifetime of the generating station. The tribe has nevertheless levied taxes on mining and power production on Indian land, but these taxes are being challenged by the companies. We have seen also that, with the exception of the few years of the construction phase, no more than 500 jobs are being provided for Navajos and most of these are provided by the strip mine and not by the generating station. We have seen also that most of the Navajo payroll, multiplier effect, and tax revenues go to non-Indians. The power generated is not used on the reservation nor is any of the water impounded by the Glen Canyon Dam. With the exception of a small amount of coal given free to local Black Mesa families for heating purposes, none of the coal is used by Navajo-owned business for any purpose.

Tribal hopes to stem the brain drain are unlikely to be fulfilled. Local Navajos have not received a large share of the jobs generated by new investment and what jobs they have are primarily unskilled. In 1978, with construction completed, unemployment levels in the area remained high. Aside from the tax monies being spent on the reservation by the public school system, the major benefit realized by the tribe is the money received annually as royalty, right of way, or

---

[33] Lynn A. Robbins, "The Navajo Nation and Industrial Developments," unpublished report of the Lake Powell Research Project, in the possession of Jerrold Levy, University of Arizona, Tucson, n.d.

[34] K. Gilbreath, *Red Capitalism: An Analysis of the Navajo Economy* (Norman, Okla., University of Oklahoma Press, 1973) p. 130.

lease payments—some $402,000 annually from the generating station and the railroad and approximately $2.6 million in royalties from the mine.

Whether the bargain struck by the tribe gives the Navajos an equitable share in the benefits cannot be decided in a definitive way. It does seem that the major goals of Navajo employment and the creation of a more self-sufficient economy are not much furthered by Navajo participation in the Navajo Generating Station. The coal mine not only provides more jobs, it also provides the most revenue. The royalty agreements allow for limited adjustments in royalties as the price of coal goes up and features of the leases can be renegotiated at various intervals. The negotiations for the generating station involved a quantification of Navajo water rights and a possible waiver of their rights under the Winters Doctrine. In addition, the tribe explicitly waived its right to tax for the life of the power plant. One is led to ask how the Navajo Tribe entered into the agreements permitting the construction of the Navajo Generating Station. Did the Navajo Tribe make an informed decision?

We have already mentioned that the information provided the tribe and the Bureau of Indian Affairs came solely from the U.S. Bureau of Reclamation, the Salt River Project, and the Upper Basin River Commission, all with a vested interest in the Navajo project. It was natural for these agencies to present their arguments as persuasively and aggressively as possible. Throughout the negotiations three points were stressed: (1) the coal mine and the power plant were intimately connected. The tribe would not realize the benefit from coal royalties unless the power plant was built; (2) the benefits to the tribe were substantial and could not be realized by any alternate course of action; (3) time was of the essence: if the agreements were not signed immediately there would be no project at all.[35] The tribe simply had no independent information which would permit it to question any of these assertions.[36]

Strip mining is a highly visible activity. The unexpected size of the excavation equipment and the desolateness of the denuded landscape are shocking to many Navajos. Equally dramatic is the emission plume produced by a coal-fired generating station seen stretched across an otherwise crystal clear Southwestern sky. Once the Navajo develop-

CHANGING NAVAJO AWARENESS: FACING THE FUTURE

[35] B. McCain, "Final Report."
[36] Ibid., p. 75.

ments were underway, environmentalists brought the "rape of Black Mesa" to the attention of a nation already concerned about pollution. If Navajos were uninformed during the 1960s when the contracts were negotiated, they experienced an information explosion after 1970. Not surprisingly, the Navajo Tribe adopted a more aggressive stance when presented with new proposals to develop the uranium resources of the eastern reservation, and Navajos generally began to voice doubts about the wisdom of pursuing a policy of unrestrained resource exploitation.

The news media tend to represent the Navajo position as a battle to preserve a traditional culture threatened by the forces of modernization. Indeed, Navajo rhetoric itself often supports such an interpretation. The repeatedly expressed desire to preserve the livestock economy, for example, gives the impression that the vast majority of Navajos wish to preserve a pastoralism characteristic of nineteenth century reservation life. To so define the issue is, in our opinion, both incorrect and potentially damaging to Navajo interests. Navajo goals as expressed in interviews and action are more sophisticated and pragmatic and it is to a consideration of what these are that we now turn.

Interviews administered in the Lake Powell region, around Burnham in the eastern reservation, and to members of the Tribal Council reveal that Navajo politicians reflect popular opinion when they support economic development in order to increase job opportunities.[37] Considerable resentment of environmentalists was expressed for two reasons; they were outsiders who wished to impose their views and solutions on the Navajos; and they gave environmental concerns a higher priority than economic opportunity. Residents of Burnham Chapter felt that neither the tribe nor the energy companies allowed them to make informed decisions as a community. Their point was that they were not allowed to participate as equals in the decision-making process. They emphasized that they were not against modernization, but felt that they could better understand the developments in their area if they could have the time to reach decisions in their own way. This, they explained, meant taking adequate time to discuss alternatives to company proposals and to reach community consensus.

In no area studied by the Lake Powell Research Project did the annual per capita cash income from livestock exceed $30.[38] Pastoralism was simply not a viable alternative to wagework in any of the areas studied. Moreover, despite the important position accorded

---

[37] Robbins, "Navajo Energy Politics"; G. M. Schoepfle and coauthors, "A Study of Navajo Perception of the Impact of Environmental Changes Relating to Energy Resource Development," mimeo., third quarterly report (Shiprock, N.M., Navajo Community College, 1978).

[38] Callaway and coauthors, "The Effects of Power Production."

sheep raising in Navajo culture, considerably more income was earned from cattle than from sheep sales although few households are engaged in cattle raising. In the aggregate, welfare payments were more important for an unemployed family than was income from all livestock operations, and no households were able to rely entirely on livestock. Yet the Navajos' insistence on protecting their pastoral activities is not only an expression of cultural conservatism. Home consumption of livestock is an important contribution to the diet of those rural families who are unable to obtain steady employment. Especially interesting is the fact that 73 percent of all Navajo households living in Page owned some livestock. In a job-scarce environment, employed Navajos retain their livestock as a hedge against unemployment, and wage earners in Page and the settlement near the power plant will not relinquish their stock permits as long as they live in a boom-and-bust economy.

Even when we look at some of the more highly publicized instances of Navajo protest, we do not find local inhabitants rejecting modernization while favoring an older way of life. In 1974, the American Indian Movement (AIM) initiated a protest against the Peabody Coal Company that was supported by local residents and Navajo tribal chairman, Peter MacDonald. The major grievances centered on the compensation received by families forced to relocate because of mining activities—relocation itself was not opposed—and the alleged desecration of Navajo burial sites by the coal company.[39] In December 1978, Navajos in the Crownpoint area of the eastern reservation joined with Friends of the Earth, an environmentalist organization, to bring suit against six major federal agencies to stop uranium development until environmental impact statements (EIS) were prepared.[40] Local residents were concerned about pollution, threats to health from radiation, and the flooding of grazing land. However, according to the director of the Navajo legal aid program (DNA), "the aim of the suit is not to stop uranium development but to provide people with more information."[41] The preparation of impact statements will, it is hoped, guarantee public discussion and will "better prepare people to deal with their fate."[42]

During the 1970s, the Navajo Tribe has also moved to strengthen its bargaining position. In 1975, Chairman MacDonald helped form an Indian-style OPEC known as the Council of Energy Resource Tribes (CERT). The organization now includes twenty-two western

[39] Robbins, "Navajo Energy Politics."

[40] *Window Rock Navajo Times* (Arizona), January 4, 1979, p. A-1; January 18, 1979, p. B-15.

[41] *Window Rock Navajo Times* (Arizona), January 4, 1979, p. A-3.

[42] Ibid.

Indian tribes and serves as an advisory and coordinating council on matters pertaining to the utilization and conservation of the energy resources possessed by its members. In 1972, the chairman signed a uranium exploration lease with the Exxon Corporation which, among other things, gave the tribe a 59 percent share of the gross income from all future sales of uranium. It is important to note, the chairman signed this lease without the prior approval of the Bureau of Indian Affairs.

In 1975, the Tribal Council exerted its right to be a full participant in lease negotiations by vetoing a lease renewal that had been signed unilaterally by the chairman with the El Paso Natural Gas and Consolidated Coal Companies.[43]

After many years of resistance to the unionization of Navajo workers, the Tribal Council took a major step toward modernization when it signed an agreement with the Building and Construction Trades Unions of the AFL-CIO, in July 1974, which provided for the recruitment, training, and placement of Navajo workers in the construction trades.[44] At present, the following major industrial projects employ unionized Navajo labor: the Navajo Generating Station, the Black Mesa Mine (United Mine Workers), the Utah International Mine (Operating Engineers), the Four Corners Power Plant, the McKinley Mine (Operating Engineers), and the Page-Black Mesa Railway. Unionized workers, in the 1970s, accounted for a significant proportion of Navajos employed in the private sector of the economy.

Finally, the tribe has moved to exert its sovereignty by announcing its intent to enact two taxes and a penalty fee on the reservation: a business activity tax; a possessory interest tax; and a sulfur emissions penalty. All have been challenged in federal courts by the large energy and utilities companies doing business on the reservation.[45] In July 1978, a federal judge in Phoenix, Arizona, ruled that the power to tax is an inherent part of tribal sovereignty. Company appeals will probably reach the U.S. Supreme Court. Nevertheless, the Navajo Tax Commission plans to start the collection process and estimates that the first-year revenue from the two taxes would bring about $28 million into the tribal treasury. If no sulfur cleanup takes place the first year, the emission fee would be about $34 million.

As the Navajos face the future, two goals are salient: (1) greater economic self-sufficiency; (2) tribal sovereignty and self-determination. Although neither will be realized easily, the second poses a serious problem for a technically advanced nation, which, while it becomes

[43] Robbins, "Navajo Energy Politics."
[44] Ibid.
[45] *Window Rock Navajo Times* (Arizona), January 25, 1979, p. A-16.

increasingly centralized, espouses the values of cultural pluralism. To what extent can the nation tolerate a regional and ethnic separatism when the Indian tribes in question control resources important for the resolution of the current energy crisis? On this topic, the Carter Administration announced that the federal government will not pressure tribes to develop their energy resources or "countenance attempts to force unwanted energy development."[46] But if public pronouncements are clear, advice provided the Navajo Tribe by officials of the Bureau of Indian Affairs is reminiscent of that given in the 1960s. At a public hearing conducted in January 1979 by the Department of the Interior concerning uranium development in the Eastern Navajo Agency, a series of problems was discussed—a population explosion, water shortages, the threat of radiation, land deterioration, livestock reduction, and interracial friction. Despite the serious consequences of uranium extraction, however, Richard Wilson, a Bureau of Indian Affairs energy and minerals officer, is quoted as saying that the onslaught of uranium mining cannot be stopped. "What you can try to do is to try and get out of the way."[47]

APPENDIX 10-A. CALCULATION OF POSSIBLE GAINS TO THE NAVAJO TRIBE FROM HYPOTHETICAL TAXATION OF THE NAVAJO POWER PLANT, BLACK MESA COAL MINE, AND RELATED FACILITIES

The objective of this appendix is to show how we determined the net gains to the Navajo Tribe if it were to act as a sovereign authority with the power to tax the Navajo Power Plant and the Black Mesa Coal Mine. The analysis, which at first glance appeared to be straightforward, actually required considerable economic detective work—gathering fragments of data, making deductions and assumptions, and presenting evidence. This was necessary because of the lack of available data from both state and tribal sources. The causes of this unavailability are the confidentiality of records in the state of Arizona, and the lack of a consolidated accounting system in the Navajo Tribe. This appendix outlines the assumptions and procedures used to deal with these problems.

The Objective

[46] Anne Wexler, Assistant to President Carter, speaking before the executive council of the National Congress of American Indians (NCAI), January 16, 1979, quoted in the *Window Rock Navajo Times* (Arizona), January 18, 1979, p. A-13.
[47] Ibid., p. B-15.

Ownership of the Navajo Power Plant and Present Returns to the Navajo Tribe

The Navajo Power Plant and its related facilities are owned by four utility companies in addition to the U.S. Bureau of Reclamation and the Salt River Project (a quasipublic water and power project); such ownership includes percentage interests in the value of the power plant, interests in the Black Mesa and Lake Powell Railroad (which supplies coal to the power plant), and varying interests in the network of transmission lines that deliver the power generated at the plant. Total value of the facility, including railroad and transmission lines is approximately $760,000,000.[1] The ownership, by percentage interest, is broken down as follows:[2]

U.S. Bureau of Reclamation	24.3
Salt River Project	21.7
Los Angeles Department of Water & Power	21.2
Arizona Public Service	14.0
Nevada Power Company	11.3
Tucson Gas and Electric	7.5

Royalties and other payments received by the Navajo Tribe from operation of the Navajo Power Plant under existing contracts are as follows:[3]

one-time payment on the Black Mesa and Lake Powell Railroad	$108,000
annual lease payment on property to continue indefinitely	$169,000
contractual payment to terminate in 1979	$140,000

From 1976 to 1979 the Navajo Tribe received $309,000 annually. Thereafter the tribe receives only the annual lease payment of $169,000.

Ownership of The Black Mesa Coal Mine and Present Returns to The Navajo Tribe

The Black Mesa Coal Mine is owned by the Peabody Coal Company and supplies coal to both the Navajo and Mohave power plants. Located on the Navajo and Hopi Indian reservations, the mine is scheduled to produce at an estimated capacity of 13,000,000 tons of coal per year, 8,000,000 of which will be used to supply the Navajo Power Plant. Full cash value of the mine is estimated by the Arizona Department of Property Valuation at $22,700,000.[4]

At the present time, the royalty per ton of coal mined at Black Mesa accruing to the Navajo Tribe is $0.30. We are, however, only interested in the proportion of royalties accruing from operation of the Navajo Power Plant. Therefore, the amount of coal destined for the Navajo Power Plant (8,000,000 tons per year) multiplied by $0.30 per ton yields the royalty payment we are concerned with. This is approximately $2,400,000.

---

[1] William Gauglon, Salt River Project, Phoenix, Arizona, to John Tregear, June 1976.

[2] Ibid.

[3] Ron Faich, Navajo Tribal Office of Planning and Development, Window Rock, Arizona, to John Tregear, June 1976.

[4] Larry Shaw, Arizona Department of Revenue, Phoenix, Arizona, to John Tregear, June 1976.

There are two specific reasons to include a breakdown of specific property tax levies by the state of Arizona: (1) Such levies are necessary to determine the property tax resources that the Navajo Tribe presently receives; and (2) the structure of a tax levied by the Navajo Tribe will be modeled after the Arizona property tax system.

In Arizona, mines and utilities are assessed respectively at 60 and 50 percent of full cash value. Therefore, the full cash value of the Black Mesa Coal Mine, $22,700,000, multiplied by the assessment rate of 60 percent yields an assessed value for property tax purposes of $13,620,000.

Although the Navajo Power Plant is valued at $760,000,000, the effective full cash value is much less than this amount because both the Bureau of Reclamation and the Salt River Project are exempted from taxation, and while the Salt River Project makes payments in lieu of property taxes to state, county, and local governments, the Bureau of Reclamation makes no payment whatsoever. We will turn later to estimation of these lieu payments by the Salt River Project. Nonetheless, the full cash value subject to ordinary property taxation is the percentage of the Navajo Power Plant privately owned multiplied by the estimated value of the complex. This amount is $760,000,000 (value of power plant) $\times$ 54.0 percent (portion privately owned), which equals $410,400,000. The assessed value is 50 percent of this (assessment rate for utilities), or $205,200,000.

The relevant property tax rates for the state of Arizona (in 1975) are as follows:[5]

Levy by:	Per assessed $100.00
State	$1.60
School District	$4.91
City	$0.80
County	$2.75
Total	$10.06

Arizona Property Tax Structure

Methodology

To determine the net benefits from a transfer of taxing authority from the state of Arizona to the Navajo Tribe first requires the calculation of presently received revenues from the state of Arizona. This was accomplished in the following manner. With regard to the Navajo Power Plant two types of payments are made to cities, counties, school districts, and the state of Arizona. These are property taxes paid by the private owners of the plant and payments made by the Salt River Project in lieu of property taxes. Since the Black Mesa Coal Mine is privately owned, we needed only to determine the property taxes paid by the Peabody Coal Company.

[5] William Nowlin, Arizona Department of Revenue, Phoenix, Arizona, to John Tregear, June 1976.

We first estimated payments made to governments in Arizona by the Salt River Project.

Payments Made by the Salt River Project to City, County, School Districts, and the State of Arizona

Although not required to pay property tax on its interest in the Navajo Power Plant, the Salt River Project makes payments estimated at approximately 70 percent of actual private property tax liability to the state of Arizona and those counties, school districts, and cities in which Salt River Project interests are located. Even though the Navajo Power Plant is located in Coconino County and 95 percent of total payments are made to cities, school districts, and county government in Coconino County, a 5 percent interest lies within Navajo County, representing ownership of the Black Mesa and Lake Powell Railroad in addition to various transmission lines that traverse Navajo County.

As estimated by Salt River Project personnel, payments made by the Salt River Project, specified by level of government receiving revenues are given in table 10-A-1.[6]

Table 10-A-1.   Payments Made by the Salt River Project on
Investments in Coconino and Navajo Counties

(dollars)

Level of government receiving revenue	Payments
In Coconino County	
State of Arizona	625,500.00
School districts	990,400.00
Coconino County	315,700.00
Tuba City	229,000.00
In Navajo County	
State of Arizona	11,353.00
School districts	109,442.00
Navajo County	9,314.00

It should be recognized that benefits do not mean direct transfers of money to the Navajo Tribe but that benefits are services which are available and provided for all citizens of these counties; therefore, we have assumed that benefits to Navajos are proportional to the percentage of the Navajo population of the total population within these counties. From revised 1970 census data, these percentages are 32 percent and 49 percent respectively for Coconino and Navajo counties. Allocating school district and county monies in this manner yields the adjustment given in table 10-A-2.

[6] Don Jones, Salt River Project, Phoenix, Arizona, to John Tregear, June 1976.

Table 10-A-2.   Adjusted Payments Made by the Salt River Project on
                Investments in Coconino and Navajo Counties

(dollars)

Level of government receiving revenue	Payment
In Coconino County [a]	
State of Arizona	625,500.00
Apportioned benefits to Navajos of county and school district payments in Coconino County	417,952.00 [b]
Tuba City	229,000.00
In Navajo County [c]	
State of Arizona	11,353.00
Apportioned benefits to Navajos of county and school district payments in Navajo County	58,190.00 [b]

[a] Assuming that 95 percent of privately owned investment lies within the county.
[b] Summing county and school district money for Coconino and Navajo counties and multiplication by the appropriate percentage of Navajo population yields the following calculations: Coconino County—$1,306,100.00 × 32% = $417,952.00; Navajo County—$118,756.00 × 49% = $58,190.00.
[c] Assuming that 5 percent of privately owned investment lies within the county.

Property Taxes Paid by Private Owners of the Navajo Power Plant to City, County, School Districts, and the State of Arizona

The total assessed value of that portion of the Navajo Power Plant and the facilities owned privately is $205,200,000. Assuming that 95 percent of privately owned investment lies within Coconino County and 5 percent within Navajo County, the portions of assessed value within Coconino and Navajo counties are:

Coconino County	$194,940,000
Navajo County	$ 10,260,000

Using the Arizona property tax levy rates, the calculations in table 10-A-3 were made of property taxes paid by the private owners of the Navajo Power Plant to school districts and local, county, and state governments on investments in Coconino and Navajo counties.

Allocating county and school district monies in the same manner as was used previously when determining benefits accruing to Navajos of Salt River Project payments yields the adjusted property tax payments in table 10-A-4.

Property Taxes Paid by the Peabody Coal Company on the Black Mesa Coal Mine to County, School Districts, and the State of Arizona

The Black Mesa Coal Mine is located entirely in Navajo County and therefore the following analysis deals only with property tax payments made to the state of Arizona, Navajo County, and associated school districts.

The full cash value of the Black Mesa Coal Mine is $22,700,000. Assessed at 60 percent of full cash value, the assessed value of the mine is then $13,620,000. Table 10-A-5 contains estimates of property tax revenues from the Black Mesa Coal Mine.

Table 10-A-3.   Property Taxes Paid by Private Owners on Investments
in Coconino and Navajo Counties

(absolute figures in dollars)

Level of government receiving revenue	Tax levy rate on assessed value of $194,940,000 (percent)	Property tax estimate
In Coconino County [a]		
State of Arizona	1.60	3,119,040.00
School District	4.91	9,571,554.00
Coconino County	2.75	5,360,850.00
Tuba City	.80	1,559,520.00

Level of government receiving revenue	Tax levy rate on assessed value of $10,260,000 (percent)	Property tax estimate
In Navajo County [b]		
State of Arizona	1.60	164,160.00
School District	4.91	503,766.00
Navajo County	2.75	282,150.00

[a] Assuming that 95 percent of privately owned investment lies within the county.
[b] Assuming that 5 percent of privately owned investment lies within the county.

Table 10-A-4.   Adjusted Property Tax Payments Made by Private
Owners on Investments in Coconino and Navajo Counties

(dollars)

Level of government receiving revenue	Payment
In Coconino County	
State of Arizona	3,119,040.00
Apportioned benefits to Navajos of county and school district payments in Coconino County	4,778,369.30
Tuba City	1,559,520.00
In Navajo County	
State of Arizona	164,160.00
Apportioned benefits to Navajos of county and school district payments in Navajo County	385,098.84

Table 10-A-5.   Property Taxes Paid by the Peabody Coal Company
on Investments in Navajo County

Level of government receiving revenue	Tax levy rate on assessed value of $13,620,000 (60%) (percent)	Property tax estimates (dollars)
State of Arizona	1.60	217,920.00
School District	4.91	668,742.00
Navajo County	2.75	374,550.00

Again, allocating county and school district monies proportionally to the percentage of the Navajo population residing within Navajo County, yields the adjustments shown in table 10-A-6.

Table 10-A-6.   Adjusted Property Tax Payments of the Peabody Coal
Company on Investments in Navajo County

(dollars)

Level of government receiving revenue	Payment
State of Arizona	217,920.00
Apportioned benefits accruing to Navajos of county and school district payments in Navajo County	511,213.08

Summary of Property Tax Revenues Accruing to the State of Arizona and State Disbursements to the Navajo Tribe

With the appropriate figures from this analysis we compiled the following table 10-A-7, which shows the property tax revenues the state of Arizona receives from the operation of the Navajo Power Plant and the Black Mesa Coal Mine.

Table 10-A-7.   Property Tax Revenues to the State of Arizona from the
Navajo Power Plant and the Black Mesa Coal Mine

(dollars)

Plant and mine	State property tax revenue
Navajo Power Plant	
Salt River Project	636,853.00
Private interests	3,283,200.00
Black Mesa Coal Mine	
Peabody Coal Company	217,920.00
Total	4,137,973.00

According to the summary of an unpublished audit performed by the accounting firm of Ernst and Ernst for the fiscal year 1972 and assuming revenues have remained relatively unchanged, the state of Arizona through its Department of Public Welfare provided the following programs to the Navajo Tribe:

Old Age Assistance	$1,234,000.00
Assistance to the Blind	$82,000.00
Aid to Dependent Children	$3,438,000.00
Aid to the Permanently Disabled	$790,000.00
Foster Boarding and Medical Care	$98,000.00

It must be kept in mind, however, that all of these programs with the exception of Aid to Dependent Children are funded entirely by the federal government. Aid to Dependent Children is financed by the federal and state governments in a 75:25 ratio; therefore, of the $3,438,000 disbursed, only 25 percent of this, or $859,500, is actually provided by the state of Arizona.

Although we recognize that the state of Arizona does provide other services such as highways, we have concluded that inclusion of these data, if they were available, would not alter substantially the validity of the conclusions we are attempting to derive.[7]

Analysis of Net Benefits to the Navajo Tribe If It Were a Sovereign Taxing Authority

There are now sufficient data to determine the benefits that would accrue to the Navajo Tribe from taxation and from the Navajo Power Plant and the Black Mesa Coal Mine. Assuming it adopts a tax structure comparable to the Arizona state tax, the tribe would receive not only its percentage of school district, county, and city monies but also that amount the state collects as its share of the property tax. It should be noted that the state of Arizona arrives at its computed share of revenues by first estimating the budget required to operate the state government, then collecting a sufficient amount to cover this budget. Whether this same percentage would be required to finance Navajo government is questionable, and the justification for use of this figure should be taken as somewhat arbitrary.

The level of benefits which the Navajo Tribe now receives from property tax revenues for county, school district, and cities is shown in table 10-A-8.

Table 10-A-8.   Total Monies Received by the Navajo Tribe from City and Apportioned County and School District Property Tax Revenues

(dollars)

County and project	Amount
Coconino County	
Salt River Project	
Apportioned county and school district	417,952
Cities	229,000
Private owners	
Apportioned county and school district	4,778,369
Cities	1,559,520
Navajo County	
Salt River Project	
Apportioned county and school district	58,190
Private Owners	
Apportioned county and school district	385,099
Peabody Coal	
Apportioned county and school district	511,213
Total	7,939,343

As calculated previously, the total amount the state now collects as its share of the property tax is $4,137,973.00. If the Navajo Tribe by taxing autonomously, and solely, received not only its share of the benefits accruing from county, school district, and city property tax revenues, but

[7] From available information, we estimate that total funding from various other state sources is approximately $500,000. These revenues in most cases originate as funds necessary to maintain public records, libraries, commissions and boards, and inspection services.

also the state's share of property tax revenues, it would have a combined tax revenue of:

total city, county, and school district property tax revenue accruing to the Navajo Tribe at present	$ 7,939,343
total state revenue	$4,137,973
total combined revenue	$12,077,316

Assuming that the federal government would continue to fund those programs it presently funds in the same proportions, the Navajo Tribe would stand to lose only the state's share of Aid to Dependent Children of $859,500. Therefore, the net benefit to such a taxing scenario is the difference between the state's share of property tax revenues and the state's contribution of $859,500. This net benefit is $3,278,473.

Under this arrangement and if lease terms were left unchanged, total revenues to the tribe on investment from the following sources would be:

taxes	$12,077,316
royalties from:	
Navajo Power Plant (until 1979)	$309,000
Black Mesa Coal Mine	$2,400,000
total annual income	$14,786,316

The above discussion assumes that the tribe has complete autonomous taxing authority. But in order to avoid problems of jurisdiction and double taxation, the tribe might tax only the actual property on which the facilities are located. Note, however, that both leases prohibit this for at least thirty years.

Property Taxation of Land Values by the Navajo Tribe

But for the sake of hypothesis, if the land were valued at one-fifth of the complex then for the Navajo plant:

total value would equal	$760,000,000
taxable value would equal	$410,400,000 (excluding the Bureau of Reclamation and Salt River Project holdings)
land value would equal (20% of $410,400,000)	$82,080,000
assessed land value would equal	$41,040,000 (assessed at 50% full cash value)

If the Navajo Tribe then taxed at the rate of $10.06 per $100 of assessed value, the tribe could gain approximately:

$41,040,000/100 × $10.06 = $4,128,624 annually for a

total value of	$22,700,000
land value of	$4,540,000
assessed land value of	$2,724,000 (assessed at 60% full cash value)

Taxed at the going rate of $10.06 per assessed $100.00:

$$\$2,724,000/100 \times \$10.06 = \$274,034$$

Then assuming no legal restraints and assuming the ability to tax the property upon which these complexes exist, the Navajo Tribe could gain over $4,402,658 annually. Where the tribe would then stand on balance would depend upon what benefits from existing state sources it could retain.

Two Final Comments

The property tax was chosen for analysis simply because it was the only tax about which any sort of analysis was feasible. Other taxes such as the corporate income tax, severance tax, sales tax, or payroll taxes were not feasible for reasons concerning the privacy of tax records and the unwillingness of those companies involved to release the information. And finally, aside from contractual obligations and jurisdictional obstacles, a major problem in implementation of any taxing scheme by the Navajo Tribe is the general disorganization of tribal financial and accounting structures. The Ernst and Ernst study, cited earlier, undertaken at the request of the Navajo Tribe, states the following (and things have not improved substantially since its completion): "If the Navajo Tribe is to consider any type of taxing mechanism, until the system of accounting and program coordination is developed and *implemented* (since the necessary resolutions already exist), such a mechanism will continue to be an impossibility."

11 A PERSPECTIVE

In the preceding chapters we have ranged widely across the landscape of Southwestern resource and environmental issues and at times delved deeply into a number of those issues. In the belief that there is much to be learned by considering the regional context in which national policies are implemented, we begin this concluding chapter by stepping back to take a brief look at the broad national and international context against which the events unfolding in the Southwest can be understood.

A GLOBAL PERSPECTIVE

In the past twenty-five years in the United States, as well as in other nations, there has emerged an increasing public consciousness of the finiteness of the world and its resources—minerals, energy, water, environment, and the various life forms themselves. This consciousness has been intellectually crystallized into the notions of "spaceship earth," and the "limits to growth." It has found active and fervent expression in the environmental movement, recycling drives, wilderness preservation, and pressures for conservation of materials and energy. It has led nationally to the clean air and clean water acts, mandated controls on auto emissions and gasoline consumption, and many other measures. It has been reinforced by international events such as the oil embargo of 1973 and the sharply higher prices of energy that have persisted since that time. Its global dimension has been emphasized by the threatened deterioration of the ozone layer and a possible "greenhouse" effect of carbon dioxide buildup in the global atmosphere.

Many of these developments have created strong conflicts which even after heated debate, remain unsettled. Even now it still is possible to dispute on either side the seriousness, for example, of the "energy crisis." But regardless of whether it is "the moral equivalent of war" or only a painful economic adjustment to increasing scarcity of particular energy fuels, the conclusion is really only a question of degree. For there can be little doubt that the historical human practice of solving societal problems by expanding geographical frontiers and thereby enlarging the pie that can be divided will no longer work its magic, at least for a humanity that remains almost exclusively earthbound. To be successful, future courses of action must accept the existing and developing environmental and resource constraints on human activity and work within them to find solutions that are compatible with the existing circumstances.

At the same time, however, that awareness of the constraints upon human actions has increased, the world's population has continued to expand greatly. One result has been the abject poverty in which much of the world still lives. In a world or regional society that possesses such extremes of affluence and poverty, the seeds of conflict will not permit this disparity to be ignored on pragmatic grounds, even apart from the ethical norms that compel the search for solutions. Yet, just as it has in the past, humanity resists any Malthusian perspective in which a bleak future is seen as inevitable. Instead, strong impulses seek to "unleash the productive forces" in society and create a future in which improvement, both material and spiritual, is the expected condition. It is these impulses that provide the motive force for finding and implementing solutions, and in the final analysis it is the vitality of this force that will determine the future.

The task itself is well defined. Solutions must be found which will substantially improve the lot of the world, national, and regional populations. But the work must accept certain strong restrictions which constrain those solutions that are acceptable and feasible. First, human beings must find a solution which is environmentally benign in that it relies upon forms of productive activity compatible with the basic environmental character of the locality, region, or nation with which they are concerned. Second, human beings must seek long-term solutions that rely on sustainable productive activity and explicitly recognize the limited and temporary nature of the benefits that can be extracted from nonrenewable resources. Third, they must seek to fashion solutions that are robust in their ability to handle different populational patterns and levels. Finally, the solution must meet some implicit, though unmeasured, criterion of equitable distribution of income and wealth. Without the latter, the solution may succeed on environmental grounds, but fail to win societal or ethical acceptance.

The observations above are certainly not new and have been stated in many different ways by many persons. They are useful, however, as an illuminating backdrop against which to summarize the experience of the Southwest as it faces these same issues and tasks in the regional context.

In the early chapters we described the principal features of the region which form the natural and human heritage of the modern Southwest. These features include its aridity, its delicate environment, its large stock of natural resources, especially energy resources, the aesthetic character of its natural environment, and the three distinct cultures that have created its modern society. In our judgment the juxtaposition of these factors suggests a role for the Southwest, in some respects, as precursor to the nation in confronting the issues summarized in the preceding section and in crafting ways of solving them.[1] Let us elaborate on this theme.

Beginning in chapter 3, we examined in some detail three major problems for the region: water, environment, and economic development. Each of these is a facet of the societal task outlined above. Water, in its global dimension, is a problem commonly described under the term "desertification." Its Southwestern aspect is reflected in the approaching condition of full appropriation in virtually all basins, in the increasing cost of water particularly in urban areas, and in the growing use of water right transfers in meeting new uses. Environmental preservation, particularly of air quality, is a long-recognized international problem whether it be acid rains or ozone deterioration. Its Southwestern aspect is reflected chiefly in the problem of maintaining the visibility conditions for which the region is well known and which full appreciation of the region's aesthetic character requires. The problem of economic development, particularly elimination of the disparities among different peoples, has always been one of humanity's most persistent and intractable global problems. It has increased in complexity in the modern era when environmental concerns have arisen as further constraints on paths that economically poor populations can successfully follow. In our examination of this problem in the context of the Southwest we concentrated on (1) the fluctuations in local economies in the region as they experience the boom and decline associated with large energy development activities and (2) the economic condition of the Indian tribes, most particularly the Navajos. There remain other important economic development problems which

---

[1] We recognize, of course, that the various regions in the United States differ greatly in character and in the problems they confront. But the problem of achieving economic development within the constraints of limited natural resources is, or promises to become, a problem everywhere.

have only been highlighted in this book. Chief among them are the particulars of a sustainable economic base for the region that does not depend heavily on nonrenewable resources. These omissions simply point to the need for a continuing research effort to understand the Southwest's problems and develop solutions for them.

Returning to the theme with which the book began, events in each of the areas that have been examined are being largely propelled by external national and international forces acting upon the region. The momentous one is the increasing pace of resource extraction, but the migrational flow of population into the region and, more recently, the proposed MX missile system also add substantially to the pressures on water, environment, and local economic conditions.

These stresses created by the conjunction of regional constraints and external forces can be viewed as opportunities for innovative solutions to problems faced by the nation as a whole. Within this context we present the broad conclusions reached as a result of this investigation into the experience of the Southwest and its prospects for meeting the societal task described earlier in the chapter.

SPECIFIC CONCLUSIONS

We can offer no categorical statements about the region's success in meeting the task before it. There are simply too many important contingencies as yet undetermined to allow statements to be made unconditionally. Of particular importance is the time period within which the regional institutions must evolve. Under any of the scenarios that resemble crash programs, it is unlikely that adaptation can occur quickly enough to avoid serious social or environmental damage. Yet, despite the frequency with which they are proposed, crash programs may not be the future course upon which the nation embarks. Certainly, recent history in the Southwest suggests the possibility that development may proceed in a more measured fashion for the region as a whole even though individual communities have already seen boom-and-bust conditions. Acknowledging uncertainties about the future, it is certainly possible to provide a broad assessment of the direction in which events are moving in each of the subject areas investigated.

Water

Although there is a popular conception that water will be a severe limitation to resource development in the Southwest, our assessment reaches a somewhat different conclusion. The water institutions in the region *are* adapting to a condition of full appropriation and the increasing importance of water transfers. The process of institutional change is slow as should be expected given the century-old objective of developing new water sources in contrast to the modern demand for transfer. Traditions change slowly, and it is certainly arguable that they should. Nevertheless, in most basins new uses are being accommodated even though at steadily increasing prices for water rights.

This relatively optimistic conclusion must be tempered with a few qualifications, however. First in importance is the unresolved equity issue itself, particularly with regard to Indian rights. A concluding discussion of this unresolved question appears later in this chapter. A second qualification concerns the need to allow environmental or instream water uses equal footing with other uses within the water laws of the region. Of the western states, only Colorado has such a law currently. Third, the blanket assessment given for the region as a whole should not cover up the water difficulties of particular basins in which rights may have been consolidated in the hands of one user with little flexibility left for new uses.

Environment

There is more difficulty with the environment in general than with the water area, principally for two reasons. First there is as yet no settled opinion about the degree of environmental preservation desired by society, regional or national, beyond that level necessary to avoid demonstrable calamities. The Southwest, as a principal battleground for preservation of aesthetic amenities, suffers from the collective indecision. Secondly, as a matter of policy, we are still experimenting with different means of achieving whatever level of preservation is judged satisfactory. Existing approaches embodied in national and state legislation tend to be complex and cumbersome and provide little flexibility in accommodating new uses. Greater use of economic incentives in environmental policy seems desirable at both the national and regional level.

With regard to the Southwest environment, it is possible to paint optimistic scenarios in which a consensus is reached on the two issues just stated and the costs of environmental preservation become an accepted part of decision making. In this instance, environmental protection would be possible even in the face of large-scale resource development. It is equally possible to project a scenario in which serious environmental damage is done to the region, some of it irreversible.

Economic Development

As measured in terms of eliminating the economic disparities that exist within the region, the problem of economic development is proving to be the most intractable. Although some improvement can be seen, particularly in reference to those Indian tribes that possess valuable deposits of energy resources, the immediate outlook remains poor.

Referring back to the equity issue surrounding water rights, the prospect seems to be one of increasing tension before all sides in the issue seek accommodation. To a large degree the same atmosphere pervades the division of economic benefits in other resource areas.

To a certain extent consolidation and sharpening of the distinct interests is a necessary prelude to any settlement of equity questions, and that perspective may provide the hopeful cast to this issue. More fundamentally, however, the problem is complicated greatly by the cultural differences that predate the current situation. Policy solutions to this problem must recognize this broader aspect to be successful.

GENERAL CONCLUSION

We began this chapter with a description of a task facing the Southwest, as well as the society itself, as the development of a sustainable economy, compatible with the environmental and cultural character of the individual region or locality. Viewed through a conventional paradigm of economic development by means of industrialization and population growth, many of the Southwest's features stand out as strong disadvantages to sustained economic improvement. In particular, the arid and environmentally pristine character of the region— or at least the spirited defense of these regional attributes—is seen by some as a large obstacle to the introduction of manufacturing facilities, energy facilities, and the like, which historically have been large water consumers and environmentally disruptive. In this view, the road to economic improvement is blocked as long as these obstacles persist. By perceiving the principal regional characteristics as liabilities to be overcome, proponents of this paradigm, instead of hastening regional economic improvement as they desire, may actually be laying the seeds for regional economic poverty by destroying or subverting exactly those regional characteristics which are sustainable indefinitely. An alternative paradigm would convert these same regional characteristics, which the conventional view labels as liabilities, into regional assets. Instead of the arid character of the region being an obstacle to the introduction of large water-using industries, it becomes an asset in the health services it can provide and the solar energy possibilities it has, as well as in other positive properties that come with aridity. Instead of being an obstacle to industrial development, environmental non-degradation becomes the base for sustainable tourist industries, art colonies, and the general psychological benefits that go with seeing spectacular sunsets and majestic mountains. Similar statements can be made about most of the other features of the region.

In this light, the relevance of the Southwest to the nation as a whole lies beyond its role as a domestic repository for energy fuels and a prime recreation area. We have argued that the Southwest may be a precursor to the nation in approaching the finite boundaries of its physical environment (while at the same time still containing some of the poorest subsocieties within the nation who strongly desire economic improvement). If the Southwest does play this role, then its future is of particular importance to the nation in determining whether solutions that live within constraints and turn liabilities into assets can be found and, if found, implemented. Although the characteristics of other regions will differ from those of the Southwest, the lessons that can be learned in the Southwest by way of policy formation and management should be of value in approaching similar problems in other regions. Moreover, it is not being too optimistic to assert that the Southwest has not yet reached "a point of no return" in which the region has charted an irreversible course antagonistic to environmental and resource compatibility. In fact, for some factors in its future we have assessed the prospect in relatively optimistic terms. Others are more troublesome but still remain solvable. So, not only is there a valuable opportunity to learn from the experience in the Southwest, but the nation still retains the possibility of success in this region itself, *if* enough time is given to the region to allow adaptation to occur and *if* the regional society is able and willing to view its future comprehensively and take action on that basis.

PUBLICATIONS RESULTING FROM THE SOUTHWEST UNDER STRESS PROJECT

(Most of the unpublished reports in this list can be obtained from the Department of Economics at the University of New Mexico, Albuquerque.)

Anderson, Frederick, Allen V. Kneese, Philip Reed, Serge Taylor, and Russell Stevenson
    1978   *Environmental Improvement Through Economic Incentives* (Baltimore, Johns Hopkins University Press for Resources for the Future).

Anderson, Orson L.
    1975   "Utah Coal for Southern California Power: The General Issues," *Lake Powell Research Project Bulletin* no. 13 (November) (Los Angeles, University of California, Institute of Geophysics and Planetary Physics).
    1977   "The Competitive Position of Navajo Coal for the California Electricity Market," *Proceedings of the Navajo Nation Energy Conference, Tsaile, Arizona* (Los Alamos, N.M., Los Alamos National Laboratory) (LA-6927-C).

Anderson, Orson L., D. L. Carey, R. Purtich, and M. Rogozen
    1977   "Colorado River Basin Coal for Electrical Power Generation in Southwestern California," *Lake Powell Research Project Bulletin* no. 58 (September) (Los Angeles, University of California Institute of Geophysics and Planetary Physics).

Anderson, Orson L., and M. Rogozen
    1977   "The Role of Transportation of Energy in the Development of the Southwest," *Lake Powell Research Project Bulletin* no. 50 (August) (Los Angeles, University of California, Institute of Geophysics and Planetary Physics).

Baker, Bertram D., Robert L. Elderkin, and Donald R. Dietz
    1980   "The Impacts of Energy Development on Big Game in North-

western Colorado," in Walter O. Spofford, Jr., Alfred L. Parker, and Allen V. Kneese, eds., *Energy Development in the Southwest: Problems of Water, Fish and Wildlife in the Upper Colorado River Basin,* Volume II (Washington, D.C., Resources for the Future).

Baxter, Jeffrey D.
    1976   "An Investigation into the Explanatory Capability of Forecasting Models of Recreational Demand" (Ph.D. dissertation, Department of Economics, University of New Mexico, Albuquerque).

Baxter, Jeffrey D., and Mark Evans
    1980   "Potential Impacts of Energy Development on Population Growth and the Economy of the Four Corners States," in Walter O. Spofford, Jr., Alfred L. Parker, and Allen V. Kneese, eds., *Energy in the Southwest: Problems of Water, Fish and Wildlife in the Upper Colorado River Basin,* Volume I (Washington, D.C., Resources for the Future).

Behenke, Robert H.
    1980   "The Impacts of Habitat Alterations on the Endangered and Threatened Fishes of the Upper Colorado River Basin," in Walter O. Spofford, Jr., Alfred L. Parker, and Allen V. Kneese, eds., *Energy Development in the Southwest: Problems of Water, Fish and Wildlife in the Upper Colorado River Basin,* Volume II (Washington, D.C., Resources for the Future).

Ben-David, Shaul, Robert Lansford, Fredric Roach, B. Creel, and B. Beattie
    1977   *Regional Water Management with Full Consumptive Use* (Las Cruces, N.M., New Mexico Water Resources Research Institute).

Ben-David, Shaul, Robert Lansford, Fred Roach, B. J. Creel, Thomas H. Stevens, Raymond J. Supalla, Lynn Gelhar, William D. Gorman, Richard W. Mead, and Donald B. Wilson
    1979   "The Economic Feasibility of Dual Purpose Nuclear Desalination of Groundwater," *Water Resources Bulletin* (December).

Ben-David, Shaul, Scott A. Noll, and Fredric Roach
    1979   "Trombe Walls and Direct Gain: Patterns of Nationwide Applicability," *Proceedings of the Third National Passive Solar Energy Conference* (Los Alamos, N.M., Los Alamos National Laboratory) (Report #LA-UR79-239).

Ben-David, Shaul, Fredric Roach, and Scott Noll
    1978   "The Comparative Economics of Selective Passive Solar Designs in Residential Space Heating Applications," *Proceedings of The Workshop for Systems Simulation and Economic Analysis for Solar Heating and Cooling,* San Diego, California, June 27–29.

Ben-David Shaul, and Fredric Roach
    1978   "Nuclear Desalination in New Mexico: A Preliminary Analysis of Economic Feasibility," *Proceedings of the Western Economic Association 1978 Annual Conference* (Los Alamos, N.M., Los Alamos National Laboratory) (Report #LA-UR078-1376).

Ben-David, Shaul, Fredric Roach, Scott Noll, and William D. Schulze
    1978   "Impact of the National Energy Plan on Solar Economics," in

T. N. Veziroglu, ed., *Alternative Energy Sources: An Interrelated Comparison,* Volume 3 (Washington, D.C., Hemisphere Publishing Company).

1978   "Impacts of the National Energy Plan on Solar Economics," in Francis de Winter and Michael Cox, eds., *Sun, Mankind's Future Source of Energy, Proceedings of the International Solar Energy Society Congress, New Delhi, India, January 1978,* Volume I (New York, Pergamon).

Ben-David, Shaul, and William D. Schulze

1976   "Economic Impact of Climate Change on World Agriculture," in U.S. Department of Transportation, *Economic and Social Measures of Biologic and Climatic Change,* CIAP, vol. 6 (Washington, D.C., GPO).

Ben-David, Shaul, William D. Schulze, J. Douglas Balcomb, Roberta Katson, Scott Noll, Fredric Roach, and Mark Thayer

1977   "Near Term Prospects for Solar Energy: An Economic Analysis," *Natural Resources Journal* vol. 17, no. 2 (April).

Bishop, A. Bruce, and Donald B. Procella

1980   "Physical and Ecological Aspects of the Upper Colorado River Basin," in Walter O. Spofford, Jr., Alfred L. Parker, and Allen V. Kneese, eds., *Energy Development in the Southwest: Problems of Water, Fish and Wildlife in the Upper Colorado River Basin,* Volume I (Washington, D.C., Resources for the Future).

Bonem, Gilbert, and Richard Mead

1979   "Copper Smelting in the Southwest U.S.," *New Mexico Business* vol. 32, no. 3 (April).

Boyle, Gerald J.

1977   "Taxation of Uranium and Steam Coal in the Western States," *Proceedings of the Non-Renewable Resource Taxation in the Western States Conference,* Tucson, Arizona, February 1977.

Brookshire, David

1976   "Macroeconomic Approach to Regional Environmental Modelling and Planning" (Ph.D. dissertation, Department of Economics, University of New Mexico, Albuquerque).

1980   "Adjustment Issues of Impacted Communities or Are Boomtowns Bad?" *Natural Resources Journal* vol. 20.

Brookshire, David, Berry Ives, and William D. Schulze

1977   "The Impact of Energy Development on Recreation Use and Value in the Glen Canyon National Recreation Area," *Lake Powell Research Bulletin* no. 33 (Los Angeles, University of California, Institute of Geophysics and Planetary Physics).

Brookshire, David, William D. Schulze, and Berry Ives

1976   "The Valuation of Aesthetic Preferences," *Journal of Environmental Economics and Management* vol. 3, no. 4 (December).

Brown, F. Lee, Rahman Khoshakhlagh, and Charles DuMars

1977   *Forecasting Future Market Values of Water Rights in New Mexico* (Las Cruces, N.M., New Mexico Water Resources Research Institute and the Bureau of Business and Economic Research)

Brown, F. Lee, and Allen V. Kneese
    1978   "The Southwest—A Region Under Stress," *American Economic Review* vol. 68, no. 2 (May).

Brown, F. Lee, and A. O. Lebeck
    1976   *Cars, Cans, and Dumps: Solutions for Rural Residuals* (Baltimore, Johns Hopkins University Press for Resources for the Future).

Brown, F. Lee, James W. Sawyer, and Rahman Khoshakhlagh
    1977   "Some Remarks on Energy Related Water Issues in the Upper Colorado River Basin," *Natural Resources Journal* vol. 17, no. 4 (October).

Casey, Ellen G.
    1978   "Energy Development Scenarios for the Four Corners States and the Upper Colorado River Basin," in Walter O. Spofford, Jr., Alfred L. Parker, and Allen V. Kneese, eds., *Energy Development in the Southwest: Problems of Water, Fish and Wildlife in the Upper Colorado River Basin,* Volume I (Washington, D.C., Resources for the Future).

Church, Albert M.
    1977   "Market and Non-Market Evaluation of the Mining Firm," *Proceedings of the Non-Renewable Resources Taxation in the Western States Conference,* Tucson, Arizona, February 1977.
    1978   "Conflicting Federal, State and Local Interest—Trends in State and Local Energy Taxation—Coal and Copper—A Case in Point," *National Tax Journal* vol. 31, no. 3 (September).
    1981   "Land Use and Air Quality in Albuquerque, New Mexico," *The Southwestern Review,* in press.

Church, Albert M., Patrick Burnham, Diana Jones, Gary Peterson, Barbara Sanders, and Allen Kneese
    1976   "The Effect of Local Government Policy Tools on Land Use and Environmental Quality—A Case Study of Albuquerque, New Mexico," revised final report (Washington, D.C., U.S. Environmental Protection Agency).

Crocker, Thomas
    1977   "Economic Implications of Alternative Property Rights Systems for the Geothermal Resources," in J. D. Morgan and C. Barbacz, eds., *Proceedings of the Third Annual University of Missouri-Missouri Energy Council Conference on Energy* (Rolla, Mo., University of Missouri).
    1978   "Benefits of Air Pollution Control," in A. Hershaft, ed., *Critical Review of Estimating Benefits of Air and Water Pollution Control* (Washington, D.C., U.S. Environmental Protection Agency) (Socio-economic Studies Series, EPA-600/5-78-014).
    1978   "In the Midst of the Energy–Environment Tangle: Resource and Environmental Economics at the University of Wyoming," in J. E. Disinger and C. Schoenfeld, eds., *Environmental Education in Action, II* (Columbus, Ohio, Ohio State University Press).

Crocker, Thomas, Richard Adams, and Narongsakdi Thanavibulchai

1979   *A Preliminary Assessment of Air Pollution Damages for Selected Crops within Southern California* (Washington, D.C., U.S. Environmental Protection Agency) (EPA 600/4-79-001c).

Crocker, Thomas, Shaul Ben-David, Allen Kneese, and William Schulze

1979   "Epidemiology and Economics: An Example Application to Cancer," in S. J. Mushkin and D. W. Dunlop, eds., *Health: What Is It Worth?* (Elmsford, N.Y., Pergamon Press).

1979   *Experiments in the Economics of Air Pollution Epidemiology* (Washington, D.C., U.S. Environmental Protection Agency) (EPA 600/5-79-001a).

Crocker, Thomas, and David Brookshire

1979   "The Use of Survey Instruments in the Economic Valuation of Environmental Goods," in E. Zube and T. Daniel, eds., *Assessment of Amenity Resource Values* (Fort Collins, Colo., Rocky Mountain Forest and Range Experiment Station).

Crocker, Thomas, and Robert L. Horst, Jr.

1977   *Oxidant Air Pollution and Work Performance of Citrus Harvest Labor* (Research Triangle Park, N.C., U.S. Environmental Protection Agency) (EPA-600/5-77-013).

Crocker, Thomas, Robert L. Horst, Jr., and William D. Schulze

1978   "Multidisciplinary Research in Environmental Economics: Two Examples," in M. Glantz, ed., *Multidisciplinary Research Related to the Atmospheric Sciences* (Boulder, Colo., National Center for Atmospheric Research) (NCAR/3141-78/1).

Crocker, Thomas, and S. Sato

1977   "Property Rights to Geothermal Resources: Part I," *Ecology Law Quarterly* vol. 6 (March).

1977   "Property Rights to Geothermal Resources: Part II," *Ecology Law Quarterly* vol. 6 (June).

Cummings, Ronald G.

1977   "An Evaluation of the FEA 'PIES' Model," Proceedings of a National Science Foundation and Resources for the Future-sponsored National Energy Outlook Conference, Reston, Virginia (Washington, D.C., Resources for the Future).

Cummings, Ronald G., H. S. Burness, W. D. Gorman, and R. R. Lansford

1980   "U.S. Reclamation Policy and Indian Water Rights," *Natural Resources Journal* vol. 20, no. 4 (October).

Cummings, Ronald G., and Oscar Burt

1977   "Natural Resources Management, the Steady-State and Approximately Optimal Decision Rules," *Land Economics* vol. 53, no. 1 (February).

Cummings, Ronald G., Oscar Burt, and James McFarland

1977   "Defining Upper Limits to Groundwater Development in the Arid West," *American Journal of Agricultural Economics* vol. 59, no. 5 (December).

Cummings, Ronald G., and Micha Gisser

1976   "Reductions of Water Allocations to Irrigated Agriculture in

New Mexico: Impacts and Technological Change" (Santa Fe, N.M., New Mexico Energy Resources Board).

Cummings, Ronald G., Ronda Hageman, and James McFarland
1976   "Prices, Costs and Taxes in the Petroleum Industry" (Los Alamos, N.M., Los Alamos National Laboratory).

Cummings, Ronald G., D. Hueth, and H. Lampe
1978   "Managing Water Resources for Irrigation and Lagoon Control in Northwest Mexico," in Pierre Crosson, Ronald G. Cummings, and Kenneth Frederick, eds., *Water Resources Management in Latin America* (Baltimore, Johns Hopkins University Press for Resources for the Future).

Cummings, Ronald G., H. Lampe, and James McFarland
1981   "Joint Management of Water Resources in Irrigation and Lagoon Environments," in L. M. Bassoco, Roger Norton, José Silos, and Leopoldo Solis, eds., *Programming Studies for Agricultural Sector Policies* (Oxford, Oxford University Press).

Cummings, Ronald G., and James McFarland
1977   "Reservoir Management and the Water Scarcity Issue in the Upper Colorado River Basin," *Natural Resources Journal* vol. 17, no. 1 (January).

Cummings, Ronald G., James McFarland, T. Springer, and E. Monash
1977   "Longterm Alternatives Between Production Rate and Supply of Oil and Gas," *Proceedings of the Pacific Area Chemical Engineering Conference,* Denver, Colorado, 29–30, August 1977.

Cummings, Ronald G., and Arthur F. Mehr
1977   "Investments for Urban Infrastructure in Boomtowns," *Natural Resources Journal* vol. 17, no. 2 (April).
1977   "A Time Series Profile of Urban Infrastructure Stocks in Selected Boomtowns in the Rocky Mountain States" (Los Alamos, N.M., Los Alamos National Laboratory) (LA-6687-MS).

Cummings, Ronald G., Arthur F. Mehr, Shaul Ben-David, Ronda Hageman, James McFarland, and William D. Schulze
1979   "Wage-infrastructure Trade-offs in Boomtowns: Implications for Investment Planning" (Los Alamos, N.M., Los Alamos National Laboratory).

Cummings, Ronald G., G. Morris, J. W. Tester, and R. L. Bivins
1979   "Mining Earth's Heat: Hot Dry Rock Geothermal Energy," *Technology Review* vol. 81, no. 4 (February).

Cummings, Ronald G., and William D. Schulze
1978   "Optimal Investment Strategies for Boomtowns: A Theoretical Analysis," *American Economic Review* vol. 68, no. 3 (June).
1981   "Does Conservation of Mass-Energy Matter for Economic Growth?" *Journal of Environmental Economics and Management*, in press.
1981   "Ramsey, Resources and the Conservation of Mass-Energy," *Journal of Environmental Economics and Management,* in press.

Cummings, Ronald G., William D. Schulze, and Arthur F. Mehr
1978   "Optimal Municipal Investments in Boomtowns: An Empirical Analysis," *Journal of Environmental Economics and Management* vol. 5, no. 3 (September).

Dean, Norman L., and Alan S. Miller
1977   "Utilities at the Dawn of a Solar Age," *North Dakota Law Review*
        vol. 53.

Evans, Mark O.
1977   "Evaluating the Implications of Structural Change: A Multi-
        regional Input–Output Model of the Four Corners States" (Ph.D.
        dissertation, Department of Economics, University of New
        Mexico, Albuquerque).

Gosz, James R.
1980   "The Influence of Reduced Streamflows on Water Quality," in
        Walter O. Spofford, Jr., Alfred L. Parker, and Allen V. Kneese,
        eds., *Energy Development in the Southwest: Problems of Water,*
        Fish and Wildlife in the Upper Colorado River Basin, Volume II
        (Washington, D.C., Resources for the Future).

Hayes, Gail Boyer
1977   "Please Don't Take My Sunshine Away," *Environmental Action*
        (March 26).
Hillhouse, Karin H., Ellen E. Kohler, Richard A. Liroff, and Alan S. Miller
1977   *Legal and Institutional Perspectives on Solar Energy in Colorado*
        —A Case Study of Land Use and Energy Decision-Making
        (Washington, D.C., National Science Foundation) (available
        from the National Technical Information Service, PB 279-994).

Ingram, Helen, and Nancy Laney
1981   "The Disincentive for Policy Leadership in Energy and the Envi-
        ronment: The Structure of Water Opinion," in Regina Axelrod,
        ed., *Energy and the Urban Environment: Conflict and Resolution*
        (Lexington, Mass., Lexington Books).
Ingram, Helen, and John R. McCain
1977   "Federal Resource Management: The Administrative Setting,"
        Public Administration Review vol. 37, no. 5.
1978   "Distributive Politics Reconsidered: The Wisdom of the Western
        Water Ethic," *Policy Studies Journal* vol. 7, no. 1 (Autumn).
Ingram, Helen, Nancy Laney, and John R. McCain
1979   "Managing a Limited Resource: The Political Constraint on
        Water Policy in the Four Corners States," *Utah Law Review*
        vol. 4.
1979   "Responsiveness of Four Corners State Legislators on Energy
        and Environment Issues," in Michael Steinman, ed., *Energy and*
        Environmental Issues: Making and Implementation of Public
        Policy (Lexington, Mass., Lexington Press).
1979   "Water Scarcity and the Politics of Plenty in the Four Corners
        States," *Western Political Quarterly* (Fall).
1980   *A Policy Approach to Political Representation: Lessons from*
        the Four Corners States (Baltimore, Johns Hopkins University
        Press for Resources for the Future).

Ingram, Helen, and Jerrold Rusk
    1976   *Arizona Speaks* (Tucson, Ariz., Institute of Government Re-
            search, University of Arizona).
Ingram, Helen, and J. S. Ullery
    1977   "Toward a Framework for Evaluating the Impact of Procedural
            Change Upon Policy: The Case of the Kaiparowits Environmental
            Impact Statement," *Lake Powell Research Project Bulletin* no. 58
            (August) (Los Angeles, University of California, Institute of
            Geophysics and Planetary Physics).
Ives, Berry C., William D. Schulze, and David Brookshire
    1976   "Boomtown Impacts of Energy Development in the Lake Powell
            Region," *Lake Powell Research Project Bulletin* no. 28 (Septem-
            ber) (Los Angeles, University of California, Institute of Geo-
            physics and Planetary Physics).

Khoshakhlagh, Rhaman
    1977   "Forecasting the Value of Water Rights: A Case Study of New
            Mexico" (Ph.D. dissertation, Department of Economics, Uni-
            versity of New Mexico, Albuquerque).
Kneese, Allen V.
    1975   *The Case for Effluent Charges as Part of a National Environ-
            mental Program* (Washington, D.C., National Commission on
            Water Quality).
    1975   "Mitigating the Bad Effects of Boomtown Development," *Energy
            Development in the Rocky Mountain Region* (Denver, Col.,
            Federation of Rocky Mountain States).
    1975   "A Theoretical Analysis of Minute 242," *Natural Resources
            Journal* vol. 15, no. 1 (January).
    1976   "Consultants' Reports on Israel's Water Policy," report to the
            World Health Organization, Geneva.
    1976   "Economic and Demographic Modeling Related to Environmental
            Management," *Proceedings of the EPA Conference on Environ-
            mental Modeling and Simulation, Cincinnati, Ohio, April 1976*
            (Washington, D.C., U.S. Environmental Protection Agency).
    1976   *Economics and the Environment* (London, Penguin Books).
    1976   "Evaluating Intangible Damages of Electric Power Development,"
            *Proceedings of a Workshop on the Measure of Intangible Envi-
            ronmental Impacts, Asilomar, Pacific Grove, California* (Palo
            Alto, Calif., Electric Power Research Institute).
    1976   "Implementation of Alternatives," *Simposio Sobre Ambiente
            Salud y Dessarrollo En Las Americas* (Symposium on a Clean
            Environment and Development in the Americas) (Washington,
            D.C., Pan American Health Organization).
    1976   "Natural Resources Policy 1975–1985," *Journal of Environ-
            mental Economics and Management* vol. 3, no. 4 (December).
    1977   "Benefit–Cost Analysis and the Atom," in Rolf Steppacher, Brig-
            gitte Zogg-Walz, and Herman Hatsfeldt, eds., *Economics in
            Institutional Perspective: Essays in Honor of Professor K. William
            Kapp* (Lexington, Mass., Lexington Books and D. C. Heath).

1977   "Quantitative Comparison of Policy Instruments for Environmental Improvement," *Decision Making in the Environmental Protection Agency,* selected working papers, vol. 11b (Washington, D.C., National Academy of Sciences).

1978   "A Commentary on Needed Changes in the 1970 Air Quality Act Amendments," in Ann F. Friedlaender, ed., *Approaches to Controlling Air Pollution* (Cambridge, Mass., MIT Press).

1978   "The Economic and Economically Related Aspects of New Towns in Arid Areas," in Gideon Golany, ed., *Urban Planning for Arid Zones: American Experiences and Directions* (New York, Wiley).

1978   "Energy Conservation Policies," *Natural Resources Journal* vol. 18, no. 4 (October).

1978   "Status Report, Southwest Region Under Stress Project," *New Mexico Business* (June).

1980   "Environmental Policy," in Peter Dingman and Alvin Rabuska, eds., *The United States in the 1980's* (Stanford, Calif., Hoover Institution).

Kneese, Allen V., and Robert U. Ayres
1976   "The Sustainable Economy," in Martin Pfaff, ed., *Frontiers in Social Thought—Essays in Honor of Kenneth E. Boulding* (The Hague, North-Holland Publishing Company, distributed in the United States by American Elsevier Publishing Company, New York).

Kneese, Allen V., and Blair T. Bower
1977   "Issues Surrounding Regional Residuals-Environmental Quality Management Modelling," in Blair T. Bower, ed., *Regional Residuals-Environmental Quality Management Modelling* (Washington, D.C., Resources for the Future).

Kneese, Allen V., Blair T. Bower, and Charles Ehler
1977   "Incentives for Managing the Environment," *Environmental Science and Technology* vol. 11, no. 3 (March).

Kneese, Allen V., and F. Lee Brown
1975   "Water Demands for Energy," *Natural Resources Lawyer* vol. 8, no. 2.

Kneese, Allen V., F. Lee Brown, Michael Williams, Philip Reno, and Jennifer Zamora
1978   "A Policy Study of the Southwestern Region of the United States," a report of the Southwest Region Under Stress Project (Albuquerque, N.M., Department of Economics, University of New Mexico).

Kneese, Allen V., and Charles L. Schultze
1977   "Pollution, Prices and Public Policy," in Stuart S. Nagel, ed., *Policy Studies Review Annual* (Beverly Hills, Calif., Sage Publications).

Kneese, Allen V., and William D. Schulze
1977   "Environment, Health and Economics—The Case of Cancer," *American Economic Review* vol. 67, no. 1 (February).

Kneese, Allen V., and Michael Williams
　　1979　"Air Quality Issues and Approaches in the Southwest," *Natural Resources Journal* vol. 19, no. 3 (July).
　　1979　"Environmental Aspects of Resources Policy in a Regional Setting," in Horst Siebert and coauthors, *Regional Environmental Policy: The Economic Issue* (New York, New York University Press).

Kneese, Allen V., and Jennifer Zamora
　　1980　"The Future of Arid Lands," in Daniel Yaron, ed., *Salinity, Irrigation and Water Resources* (New York, Marcel Dekker).

Kolstad, C. D., D. P. Grimmer, Philip Reno, and J. M. Tutt
　　1976　*Appropriate Technology and Navajo Economic Development* (Los Alamos, N.M., Los Alamos National Laboratory) (LA-6489).

Lansford, Robert, Shaul Ben-David, Thomas G. Gebhard, William Brutsaert, and B. Creel
　　1975　"A Socio-Economic Evaluation of Alternative Water Management Policies on the Rio Grande in New Mexico," *Natural Resources Journal* vol. 15, no. 2 (April).

Levy, Jerrold E.
　　1980　"Who Benefits from Energy Development: The Social Case of the Navajo Indian," *Social Science Journal* vol. 17, pp. 1–19.

Levy, Jerrold E., D. G. Callaway, and E. G. Henderson
　　1976　"The Effects of Power Production and Strip Mining on Local Navajo Populations," *Lake Powell Research Project Bulletin* no. 22 (June) (Los Angeles, University of California, Institute of Geophysics and Planetary Physics).

Levy, Jerrold E., and E. B. Henderson
　　1975　"Survey of Navajo Community Studies, 1936–1974," *Lake Powell Research Project Bulletin* no. 6 (March) (Los Angeles, University of California, Institute of Geophysics and Planetary Physics).

Lord, William B.
　　1980　"Institutional Aspects of Water Allocation in the Upper Colorado River Basin: Implications for Fish and Wildlife," in Walter O. Spofford, Jr., Alfred L. Parker, and Allen V. Kneese, eds., *Energy Development in the Southwest: Problems of Water, Fish and Wildlife in the Upper Colorado River Basin,* Volume II (Washington, D.C., Resources for the Future).

Lutey, James M.
　　1980　"Habitat Evaluation Procedures (HEP)," in Walter O. Spofford, Jr., Alfred L. Parker, and Allen V. Kneese, eds., *Energy Development in the Southwest: Problems of Water, Fish and Wildlife in the Upper Colorado River Basin,* Volume II (Washington, D.C., Resources for the Future).

Maddock, Thomas III, and N. C. Matalas
　　1980　"The Potential Impacts of Energy Development on Water Resources in the Yampa River Basin," in Walter O. Spofford, Jr.,

Alfred L. Parker, and Allen V. Kneese, eds., *Energy Development in the Southwest: Problems of Water, Fish and Wildlife in the Upper Colorado River Basin,* Volume II (Washington, D.C., Resources for the Future).

Mäler, Karl-Göran
1977   "A Note on the Use of Property Values in Estimating Marginal Willingness to Pay for Environmental Quality," *Journal of Environmental Economics and Management* vol. 4, no. 4 (December).

Mehr, Arthur F.
1976   "Measuring Social Benefits Attributable to Social Infrastructure in Boomtowns" (Thesis, Los Alamos National Laboratory, Los Alamos, N.M.) (No. LS-6559-T).

Miller, Alan S., Gail Boyer Hayes, and Grant P. Thompson
1977   "Solar Access and Land Use: State of the Law, 1977," in *Legal Barriers to Solar Heating and Cooling of Buildings* (March) (available from the National Technical Information Service, HCP-M2528-01).

Miller, Alan S., Grant P. Thompson, and the Environmental Law Institute Staff
1977   *Legal Barriers to Solar Heating and Cooling of Buildings* (Washington, D.C., Energy Research and Development Administration) (available from the National Technical Information Service, DSE/2528-1).

Molles, Manuel
1978   "The Impacts of Habitat Alterations and Introduced Species on the Native Fishes of the Upper Colorado River Basin," in Walter O. Spofford, Jr., Alfred L. Parker, and Allen V. Kneese, eds., *Energy Development in the Southwest: Problems of Water, Fish and Wildlife in the Upper Colorado River Basin,* Volume II (Washington, D.C., Resources for the Future).

Parker, Alfred L.
1980   "Potential Impacts of Energy Development on Land Use and Recreation in the Upper Colorado River Basin," in Walter O. Spofford, Jr., Alfred L. Parker, and Allen V. Kneese, eds., *Energy Development in the Southwest: Problems of Water, Fish and Wildlife in the Upper Colorado River Basin,* Volume I (Washington, D.C., Resources for the Future).

Parker, Alfred L., and Allen V. Kneese
1975   "Environmental Consequences of Dispersed and Concentrated Development with Emphasis on Opportunities for Mitigation," *Man, Leisure, and Wildlands: A Complex Interaction* (Eisenhower Consortium, Bulletin 1).

Pazand, Reza
1976   "Environmental Carcinogenesis—An Economic Analysis of Risk" (Ph.D. dissertation, Department of Economics, University of New Mexico, Albuquerque).

Potter, Loren D.
1980   "The Ecology of Colorado River Reservoir Shorelines," in Walter

O. Spofford, Jr., Alfred L. Parker, and Allen V. Kneese, eds., *Energy Development in the Southwest: Problems of Water, Fish and Wildlife in the Upper Colorado River Basin,* Volume II (Washington, D.C., Resources for the Future).

Reno, Philip
1975   "The Navajo: High, Dry and Penniless," *Nation* (March 29).
1976   "The Developing Navajo Nation: Optimizing Resource Use," *New Mexico Business* vol 28, no. 8 (August).
1979   "Planning Indian Economic Development, *Economic Development in American Indian Reservations* (Albuquerque, N.M., University of New Mexico Press).
1981   *Mother Earth, Father Sky, and Economic Development: Navajo Resources and Their Use* (Albuquerque, N.M., University of New Mexico Press).

Roach, Fredric
1976   "An Economic Model for the Rio Grande Basin in New Mexico" (Ph.D. dissertation, Department of Economics, University of New Mexico, Albuquerque).

Rowe, Robert D., Ralph C. d'Arge, and David Brookshire
1980   "Experience on Economic Value of Visibility," *Journal of Environmental Economics and Management* vol. 7, no. 1 (March).

Sawyer, James W., Jr.
1977   "Environmental Quality and the Extractive Industries: The Sulfate Issue," *Proceedings of the 106th Annual Meeting of the American Institute of Mining Engineers* (New York, American Institute of Mining, Metallurgical, and Petroleum Engineers).
1977   "A Skeptical Evaluation of the Sulfate Problem," *Journal of Metals* vol. 25, no. 5 (May).

Sawyer, James W., Jr., F. Lee Brown, and David Abbey
1980   "Energy Development Scenarios for the Four Corners States and the Upper Colorado River Basin," in Walter O. Spofford, Jr., Alfred L. Parker, and Allen V. Kneese, eds., *Energy Development in the Southwest: Problems of Water, Fish and Wildlife in the Upper Colorado River Basin,* Volume I (Washington, D.C., Resources for the Future).

Sawyer, James W., Jr., and Liane B. Russell
1977   "Coal," *Implications of Environmental Regulations for Energy Production and Consumption,* Working Paper No. 5 (Washington, D.C., National Academy of Sciences).

Schulze, William D., Shaul Ben-David, J. Douglas Balcomb, Roberta Katson, Scott Noll, Fredric Roach, and Mark Thayer
1977   *The Economics of Solar Home Heating,* Joint Economic Committee of the U.S. Congress, 95 Cong. 1 sess.

Schulze, William D., Shaul Ben-David, David Brookshire, and Regan Whitworth
1975   "The Macroeconomic Impact of Energy Development in the Lake Powell Area," *Lake Powell Research Project Bulletin* no.

11 (August) (Los Angeles, Calif., University of California, Institute of Geophysics and Planetary Physics).

Schulze, William D., Shaul Ben-David, and Ronald G. Cummings

1977 "The Transition to Alternative Energy Sources," *Proceedings of the American Society of Mechanical Engineers Symposium on the Impact of Energy Development in the Southwest, Albuquerque, New Mexico* (New York, American Society of Mechanical Engineers).

Smith, Richard A.

1980 "Predicting the Impacts of Surface Coal Mining on Trout Populations in the Yampa River Basin," in Walter O. Spofford, Jr., Alfred L. Parker, and Allen V. Kneese, eds., *Energy Development in the Southwest: Problems of Water, Fish and Wildlife in the Upper Colorado Basin,* Volume II (Washington, D.C., Resources for the Future).

Smith, V. Kerry

1979 "Uncertainty and Allocation Decisions Involving Unique Environmental Resources," *Journal of Environmental Economics and Management* vol. 6, no. 4.

Spofford, Walter O., Jr.

1980 "Potential Impacts of Energy Development on Streamflows in the Upper Colorado River Basin," in Walter O. Spofford, Jr., Alfred L. Parker, and Allen V. Kneese, eds., *Energy Development in the Southwest: Problems of Water, Fish and Wildlife in the Upper Colorado River Basin, Volume I* (Washington, D.C., Resources for the Future).

Spofford, Walter O., Jr., Alfred L. Parker, and Allen V. Kneese

1980 "Introduction: An Overview of the Book," in Walter O. Spofford, Jr., Alfred L. Parker, and Allen V. Kneese, eds., *Energy Development in the Southwest: Problems of Water, Fish and Wildlife in the Upper Colorado River Basin,* Volume I (Washington, D.C., Resources for the Future).

Whitworth, Regan

1976 "Structural Change in Interregional Trade," (Ph.D. dissertation, Department of Economics, University of New Mexico, Albuquerque).

Williams, Michael

1977 "Effects of Air Pollution on the Navajo Country," *Proceedings of the Navajo Nation Energy Conference, Tsaile, Arizona* (Los Alamos, N.M., Los Alamos National Laboratory) (LA-6927-C).

1977 "Modeling of Visibility Reductions and Extreme Pollutant Concentrations Associated with Southwestern Coal-fired Power Plants," *Lake Powell Research Project Bulletin* no. 46 (June) (Los Angeles, University of California, Institute of Geophysics and Planetary Physics).

Williams, Michael, and E. G. Walther

1975 "Theoretical Analysis of Air Quality Impacts on the Lake Powell

Region," *Lake Powell Research Bulletin* no. 8 (May) (Los Angeles, University of California, Institute of Geophysics and Planetary Physics).

Wydoski, Richard S.
    1980   "Potential Impacts of Alterations in Streamflow and Water Quality on Fish and Macroinvertebrates in the Upper Colorado River Basin," in Walter O. Spofford, Jr., Alfred L. Parker, and Allen V. Kneese, eds., *Energy Development in the Southwest: Problems of Water, Fish and Wildlife in the Upper Colorado River Basin,* Volume II (Washington, D.C., Resources for the Future).

INDEX

The book was set in Trump display type and Times Roman text type by Hendricks-Miller Typographic Company, Washington, D.C. It was printed on 60 lb. Booktext Natural by BookCrafters, Inc., Chelsea, Michigan.